Underwriting

The Poetics of Insurance in America,
1722-1872

Eric Wertheimer

UNDERWRITING

The Poetics of Insurance in America, 1722-1872

STANFORD UNIVERSITY PRESS 2006

Stanford, California

Stanford University Press
Stanford, California
© 2006 by the Board of Trustees of the
Leland Stanford Junior University

Chapter 4 appeared as an article published under the title "Jupiter
Underwritten: Melville's Unsafe Home," *Nineteenth-Century Literature* Volume 28, Number 2 (September 2003), pp. 176-201. ©2003 by
the University of California Press.

Library of Congress Cataloging-in-Publication Data

Wertheimer, Eric
    Underwriting : The Poetics of Insurance in America, 1722–1872 /
Eric Wertheimer.
        p. cm.
    Includes bibliographical references and index.
    ISBN 0-8047-5089-0 (cloth : alk. paper)
        1. American literature—Colonial period, ca. 1600–1775—History
and criticism. 2. Insurance and literature—United States—History—18th century. 3. Insurance and literature—United States—
History—19th century. 4. American literature—Revolutionary
period, 1775–1783—History and criticism. 5. American literature—19th century—History and criticism. 6. Value in literature.
7. Values in literature. I. Title.
PS195.I56W47 2006
810.9'355609034—dc22

                                                            2005036648

Printed in the United States of America
Original Printing 2006
Last figure below indicates year of this printing:
15   14   13   12   11   10   09   08   07   06

Typeset at Stanford University Press in 10/12.5 Minion

TO MY PARENTS

Contents

Acknowledgments

This book was incited by worry and need—the alarm I felt after the birth of my first child, with no reliable source of income, a temporary worker in corporate America. Somehow I ended up at CIGNA's Philadelphia headquarters, noticing in its library a weird Charles Washington Wright portrait of Benjamin Franklin in a fire hat. For me, this book began then. I acknowledge first the amusing biography of academic projects—products of love and luck, necessity and compromise.

I owe much of my intellectual encouragement to Jennifer Baker, George Justice, Ian Moulton, and Michael Stancliff. I also pay tribute to Dan Bivona, who has become an accidental mentor, and to Betsy Erkkila and David Shields for their constant support. I am grateful as well for the following colleagues and friends: Liz Marini, Teresa Goddu, Darryl Hattenhauer, Devoney Looser, Elizabeth Horan, Duku Anokye, Elvin Padilla, Dottie Broaddus, Max Cavitch, Eric Slauter, Catherine Kaplan, Ormond Seavey, Arthur Sabatini, Allan Gelber, Michael Bérubé, Eduardo Pagán, Houston Baker, Ramsey Eric Ramsey, Ron Glass, Tom Cutrer, Steve Kane, Jon Wells, Bill Warner, Neal Lester, Emily Cutrer, Bert Bender, Dave Golumbia, Angie Michaelis, Meredith McGill, Andrew Parker, Elsa Silva, Bryan Waterman, Ed Russo, Chris Looby, Vince Carretta, Jay Grossman, Frank Shuffelton, John Feffer, Joanna Brooks, Keith Gaby, Ed Gray, Judith Wertheimer, Tom Wortham, Lisa Wells, Mary Davidson, Paul Korshin, Osha Gray Davidson, Hank Ridley, David Lawrence, and Dennis Isbell. Tim Sweet gave the manuscript thorough and constructive editorial input. My research assistant, Stephanie Maroney, has been enormously helpful. An honors seminar, consisting of some of Arizona State University's best and brightest—Vanessa Alvarez, Olivia Amos, Beverly Ashcroft, Casey Lynch, and Betty Wright—contributed insights and questions. John Feneron was an invaluable production editor. I thank Norris Pope for the vast amounts of patience and advocacy he has given this book.

The images in this text are here because of the following people's assistance: Jennifer Macellaro (the Franklin Papers, Yale University Library), Marnie Goodman (the Hartford Insurance Company), Melanie Tossel (Essex Institute/Phillips Library), Alan N. Degutis (American Antiquarian Society), Carol Smith (the Philadelphia Contributionship archives), Carlos Cortinez, and Joan Lowe and Ellen Morfei (ACE archives). I thank as well the staffs at Van Pelt Library at the University of Pennsylvania, the CIGNA Library (Philadelphia), Hayden Library (ASU at the Tempe campus), Fletcher Library (ASU at the West campus), the Ross-Blakely Law Library at ASU, the New York Public Library, and the Library Company of Philadelphia (particularly Connie King). Dara Kane lent her considerable talents to the cover design.

I have received numerous grants from Arizona State University, as well as a sabbatical in 2001–2. My ideas benefited from the opportunity to give talks at the University of Missouri–Columbia, Arizona State University, the University of Pennsylvania, and various conferences under the aegis of the Society of Early Americanists and the Omohundro Institute. Chapter 4 first appeared as an article in *Nineteenth-Century Literature*.

My beloved father, Stephen Wertheimer, was the first writer and thinker I admired. I am grateful for his teaching and our many collaborations.

I remember in this underwriting those who have been lost to me through the preceding seven years. The tender of this book is also the gift of what has been received. My family—each person, young and old—has underwritten me in the fullest sense of the word. Mili, Dani, and Aya: I'm here.

Phoenix, Arizona   E.W.

Preface: Claims

Thus in the beginning all the world was America and more than that is now; for no such thing as money was anywhere known. Find out something that has the use and value of money amongst his neighbors, you shall see the same man will begin presently to enlarge his possessions.

—John Locke, "Of Property,"
The Second Treatise of Government (1690)

The significance of a business is not wholly an affair of its statistics. This note is written lightly and is intended to touch the imagination, because that seems to be the best way to come quickly to the point. The objective of all of us is to live in a world in which nothing unpleasant can happen. Our prime instinct is to go on indefinitely like the wax flowers on the mantelpiece. Insurance is the most easily understood geometry for calculating how to bring the thing about. . . . It helps us to see the actual world to visualize a fantastic world.

—Wallace Stevens, "Insurance and Social Change"

To have [. . .] this pleasure, I suppose one must, at a given moment, stand at the limit of catastrophe or of the risk of loss. Otherwise, one is only applying a surefire program. So, one must take risks. That's what experience is. I use this word in a very grave sense. There would be no experience otherwise, without risk. But for the risk to be worth the trouble . . . and for it to be really risked or risking, one must take this risk with all the insurance possible. That is, one must multiply the assurances, have the most lucid possible consciousness of all the systems of insurance, all the norms, all that can limit the risks, one must explore the terrain of these assurances: their history, their code, their norms in order to bring them to the edge of the risk in the surest way possible. One has to be sure that the risk is taken. And to be sure that the risk is taken, one has to negotiate with the assurances. . . . What I am calling here assurance or insurance are all the codes, the values, the norms we were just talking about and that regulate philosophical discourse: the philosophical institution, the values of coherence, truth, demonstration, etc.

—Jacques Derrida, "There Is No 'One' Narcissism"

First, the proposition that epigraphs may underwrite new claims: John Locke, philosophical underwriter of a large share of Enlightenment thought about property, and Wallace Stevens, poetic underwriter of a latter-day imaginative philosophy, place us in a network of imagination, money, and American legacies—the same concerns I pursue in this book. Stevens's wry insight into "prime instincts" suggests his belief in the power of the imagination to do work upon the material world. This doctrine is perhaps not surprising, since his work, his "actual" work, was with the Hartford Accident and Indemnity Company; the essay I quote from, "Insurance and Social Change," was written for the company magazine, the *Hartford Agent*.[1] Stevens was a booster and defender of the enterprise of insurance, but not uncritically so.

For Stevens, the business of insurance tantalizes us with a "primal" and final promise: that insurance can help to realize perfection. But it is a particular kind of perfection, based in representational stasis (poised ironically and necessarily against the idea of "social change"). The insuring guarantee constitutes a "waxing" preservation, a valuable arrest of the changing unfenceable world that may grow larger still but never die or contract. Insurance offers Locke's "America" perpetually remade by new species of irreversible value and possession, fostering fantasies of an accretive world of abundance. Nurtured by envious neighbors—the very engine of middle-class property acquisition—such hopes grow in places where no thing is ever lost.[2] In the insured fantasy of everyday policyholders, perfection resides within the promise of a replaceable totality. The underwritten property (which may include life itself), with its profoundly inclusive and quantum logic, implies even more—the possibility of an underwritten world at large. Underwritten property is, in concept and deed, the perfect colonizing instrument.[3]

And though a completed world may be summoned by insurance's effective geometry, Stevens understands the absurd lack of dimension and perspective involved in the underwriting method. The grandiosity of such mundane and belittled pursuits as insurance underwriting provokes the embarrassed caution of announcing the "lightness" of his "note." In an embalmed world, made still and symmetrical by drab business-gray procedures, insurance successfully calculates the necessary connection between utopian figures and all material satisfactions. Whether that now-valued entity is human life, house, ship, nation, community, or corporation, insurance is truly hopeful, imaginative, and (as sometimes advertised) comprehensive.

Yet there is an even more disturbing element to Stevens's still life. What kind of "hope" is this? In typically oblique and quietly comic ways, Stevens implies nature's resistance to the imposing demands of capital's relentlessly "pleasant" economies. The poetics of an insured world is regrettable but strangely attractive, subtly designed yet insidiously forceful. How fixed do we really want this world, how resistant to negative change? What is really "lost" in a world where nothing, by a stroke of artifice, is ever lost?[4] Witness the distant pun on "objective"—critiquing perhaps the fetish, even as he exalts the universal commodifying logic of bonded values. Stevens's insured world suggests a Faustian divided mind.

⤶

Why do I begin here, over fifty years after the scope of my study ends? Because Stevens's usefully divided mind—no doubt closely correlated to his dual expertise as poet and insurance executive—performs a critical service. It tenders the strange possibility of a meaningful cultural history of the relationship between insurance and literature. Stevens's musings on insurance and social change intimate knowledge of the problematic artificiality of signified value, both monetary and literary. For my purposes, his insight into how insurance pursues a world of stable and lasting value helps explain why insurance became increasingly important and profitable in eighteenth-century America. In addition, the passage begins to make conceptual and historical linkages to America's other major writing business: literature. Unlikely as it may sound, the problems and hopes of insurance are no less those of the literary imagination.

Obviously, this book's topic has an audacious starting claim: the four main divisions of the insurance business—marine, fire, life, and accident—may be viewed as essential to a material, ideological, and aesthetic reckoning with the emergence of American literature.[5] This assertion may seem more or less plausible depending on the depth of meaning and influence one grants a single form of business enterprise. Spencer Kimball, a scholar of insurance law, uncannily echoes Stevens in lending exponential powers of representation to the practice of insurance underwriting: "Insurance is a small world that reflects the purposes of the larger world outside it."[6] I hope to persuade those who choose not to invest this set of concerns with that importance by opening with an axiom Stevens would probably find banal but very familiar: insurance is a writing business, one of the first. It articulates a seemingly indissoluble representational nexus between property and text, attempting to mark and reconcile these two cornerstones of capitalist logic.[7] This enunciation can be viewed, in turn, as crucial to the development of certain kinds of social and cultural value, aesthetic or monetary, in colonial, early national, and antebellum America.

Because it is a "writing business," insurance also invites comparisons and critical connections with the cultures of writing, whether dictionaries or grammars or poetic elegies, whether autobiography or advertisements for public financing or fictional responses to accidents. This book will sketch out the relationship between insurance and literature by seeking to understand both as material and conceptual artifacts. With respect to commercial underwriting, I want to understand how property and text were linked and thereby inscribed with monetary values that would endure through contracted guarantees against loss. In the literature of Phillis Wheatley, Ralph Waldo Emerson, and Herman Melville, the echoes of commercial life are found in tropes of loss and possession, themes of anxiety and risk, and the evolving and intricately cross-calibrated mechanics of self-mastery and genius. For the authors in this study who are not strictly bellelettristic—Benjamin Franklin and Noah Webster—the overlap between commercial and rhetorical discourses is sometimes more obvious.

In America, the poetics of underwriting fostered an understanding of creative originality and authority that had property ownership as its primary ground, and the loss of property as a constant source of anxiety. Perhaps more so than in other national literary cultures, writers in the United States have been asked to worry about the political economy of the imagination, about what they own and how they own it. The authors who are part of this study are but strong cases in a wider cultural logic in which business discourses persistently challenge and assist literary conventions. As writing that successfully translates material commodities, as well as the precisely narrativized eventualities of their fates, into real value, insurance underwriting asks us to grasp what literary and personal ownership might mean for American writers.

This book's introductory chapter presents a theoretical and historical overview, describing the critical term "underwriting" while tracing its historical emergence as both idea and practice within the sociocultural past. The introduction is followed by five chapters organized around four major commercial centers in eighteenth- and early nineteenth-century America: Philadelphia (Franklin), Boston (twice—once for Wheatley and again, in an admittedly more regionalized sense, for Emerson), Hartford (Webster), and New York (Melville). Each city has a quietly powerful commercial history of localized partnerships that drew on the social energies of the clubbable, pre-corporate, and then corporate republic of letters and news. I hope to reposition the authors as significant participants in a distillation of urbanized texts, read through time, from place to place.

The stories I develop depict a struggle that appears on a larger scale as part of a classic commercial rise to dominance, and on another as the less visible spread of a cultural sublogic of capitalism. Each author and city demonstrates how that struggle takes place and to what extent the logic of underwriting is furthered. Again, the narrative is an uncelebratory success story, since this book concerns the rise of what has become an undeniably powerful business enterprise. Insurance underwriting, as both idea and practice, makes its claim on American culture historically, and today it is very nearly ubiquitous. The broader meaning of underwriting—as a system that helped enable the economic circulation of literary property, that developed the poetics of loss as literary preoccupation and structure, and that secured some of the modern terms of authorship—is told by readings of particular local and personal capacities.

Underwriting also contains intense contradictions, areas of ongoing uncertainty, and a quality of loss that its representational methods cannot ultimately secure. A critical narrative that ignored this would risk accepting success on its own terms, thereby denying a historical unevenness that is hard to see, much less script. This is where literary and commercial underwritings noticeably diverge, for I think literary discourses have tracked and portrayed quite nicely what commercial underwriting has left to courts and statutes. Indeed, what we have come to see as "literature" (the set of texts we have declared, on reaching back, to be more valuable) makes loss its business, and no less than insurance does. Therein lies the greatest thematic connection between literature and insurance, and also their most differentially empowered textual claim. While I do not want to imply in this book that five authors constitute the absolute beginning and end of a broader New History, I maintain that this methodology corresponds to and clarifies the rough irregularity of economic and legal contexts. Using a literary critical scope is one way to undo the pleasant narratives of capital.

Perhaps the best proof that the economic frame I'm using cannot deliver smooth uncontested history is that the story of underwriting—as I have constructed it out of authors, texts, and events—is also one of failure. Such might be expected of any regime of thought that drafts, incorporates, and sells utopian promises. Franklin's representative poetics of self-protective identity is, to be blunt, impossible as anything other than the cultivation of a mystique—women are widowed, buildings burn, a son still dies. Webster's attempts to foundationalize identity, language, and money were and are continuously thwarted by statute, commercial practice, and linguistic flux. Wheatley's nominal and even legal freedom and self-possession can be cleverly obtained or signified through writing, but she cannot manage the broader terms of freedom in a racist society for all the lyrics in her catalog. The designs and promises of Franklin's and Webster's age fail Melville in his attempt to find safety as a writer with less and less market confidence. Emerson's loss of a son can, to some extent, be healed, and he can eventually find words for profound irrevocable loss; but the son can never be truly underwritten. Out of loss, it is hard to make promises. Representation and experience are never as complete and reliable as money and writing aspire to be.

⤙

In the first chapter, I begin recovering a relatively obscure part of Franklin's undertakings, namely, his writing on fire and widows' insurance. I use these projects as a basis for examining how Franklin copes with loss-derived anxiety. In its focus on the peculiarly general absence of fear in Franklin's writing (and especially *The Autobiography*), the chapter sets the analytic terms—risk, loss, and publicity—for issues that govern the poetics of underwriting through the mid-nineteenth century. It also begins to show the communitarian dimensions of the poetics of underwriting, locating Franklin's thinking about such projects in a specifically urban (not yet national) context.

Robert Jerry has described the essence of insurance underwriting as "the primary mechanism by which economic actors in our society transfer risk and distribute loss"(2).[8] Franklin's various endeavors may be viewed as an array of tactics to achieve similar ends. Franklin is essential to any discussion of the power of commerce and print textuality in America, as much for his vaunted optimism in the face of uncertainty as for his practical innovations in business and science. Franklin's social world has voided the notion of trauma—for him, almost everything is readable and printable because traumatic loss, that sinkhole of fear and illegibility, has been successfully removed or mastered.

The second chapter leads from this discussion of Franklin as representative underwriter into the disruptions that occur in 1770's Boston amid the problematic mix of political economy, Christianity, and race. I am particularly interested in how these disturbances serve Phillis Wheatley, a poet who manipulated the changing discourses afforded her by both the commercial and lyric figures of property and loss. This chapter reads both Wheatley's elegiac verse and the authenticity controversy of her 1773 London edition of poetry within the context of her status as a slave, understanding race as a category that began to reverse the bonds of economic determinations because underwriting transformed the meaning of property itself. I contend that Wheatley performed the strange task of property (that is, Wheatley as chattel) underwriting itself, as well as the lives of property owners.

In this part of the study, I trace the racial distortions of white notions of authenticity, originality, poetic genius, and life itself (as a commodity to be possessed and redeemed). I also show how Wheatley's poetics make apparent a material world of inevitable loss that may be successfully offset by the verbalizations of one whose dispossession allows her a different kind of knowledge about property. Wheatley's trauma of loss is not only readable and ongoing, but that very trauma manages to underwrite the distances between material property and imaginative free spaces. This poetics of repossession is unique to someone who, over and over, had to script her own sovereignty. Nonetheless the poetics is not so exceptional as to disqualify other "real world" applications; Wheatley's case offers a new perspective on how insurance underwriting contributed to new economic arguments for abolitionism.

In the chapter on Hartford and Noah Webster, I make connections between Webster's linguistic nationalism (represented by his best-selling American grammars and dictionaries, his advocacy of national copyright law, and his commentary on monetary and credit policies) and the establishment of Hartford as the capital of the American insurance industry. Webster's obsession with the structural foundations of language and national identity augments the poetics of underwriting by a rather transparent analogy that depends on a broad reading of the term "social contract." In contrast to Franklin, Webster's underwriting projects assume deliberately national and individualist dimensions, reflecting the more openly ideological nature of his textual theories. His work on the dictionary, and in favor of U.S. copyright law, argues for a view of language and commerce that was coextensive with an idea of the new American nation as fundamentally ordered by cultural and financial conservatism. The political economy of the book was rooted in the economy of insured words and values answering above all to the possessive individual. Webster's notion of lexical representation derives from the idea of insurance insofar as its efficacy arises from the underwritten link between property and text, a radical contractualism that binds thinking about language's propriety and the value of real property.

With Franklin and Webster, we see incipient moves to appropriate the socializing tendencies of capital accumulation and put them to the uses of individual ownership. Such civic-minded libertarianism amounts to the Adam Smith of the *Wealth of Nations* alone, without the tempering ethics of the *Theory of Moral Sentiments*. The sympathies of Franklin and Webster are driven by abstractions derived from self-interest and incisive understandings of the structures of public outcomes, both men's impulses being inseparable from their own ongoing self-mythologies.

The chapter set in New York returns to the themes set out in the Franklin chapter. I portray Herman Melville in "The Lightning-Rod Man" (1854), as well as "Bartleby the Scrivener" (1853) and *The Confidence Man* (1857), placing scientific and legal discourses of safety and risk against the often comically absurd risks of ownership. These stories are read alongside the Harper Brothers fire of 1853, which caused Melville to rethink the stability of his career, not to mention the endurance of writing and authorship as market phenomena. As a result of the fire, Melville becomes much less complacent than Franklin or Webster about how writing secures either safety or property; indeed, he is radically skeptical. His pessimism stems not from scientific rationality or religious belief but from a kind of nihilistic humanism.

The chapter is also about the managing of probable loss, in contrast to the reckoning with actual loss. How, in short, does one prevent accidental loss, and can this prevention be effected by language at all? This part of my argument elaborates probability's effects on the terms of knowledge in the nineteenth century. How does the new "predictability" return Melville to a brand of humanism paradoxically following from a commercialized mood of antisocial pessimism? Melville's resulting humanism was a lonely thing, ultimately silenced by the discourse of insurance, unable to find an American audience ready to meet tragedy in all its uncalculated complexity.

The final chapter, on Emerson, places us squarely in the moment when corporate culture began to place its final imprint on the culture of underwriting that I trace from Franklin. I read several important essays ("Self-Reliance," 1841, "Experience," 1844), poems ("Threnody," 1846), and books (*The Conduct of Life*, 1860) in the context of Emerson's personal instances of loss, especially the death of his son Waldo, in 1842, and the burning of his house, in 1872. During his life, Emerson moves from the notion that loss is fundamentally unrepresentable to the stolid idea that it can be represented in texts that might redeem the loss. Like Wheatley, Emerson is keen to underwrite the painful distance between representation and the thing itself. This successful struggle places Emerson at the threshold of corporate, non-self-reliant power—socialized individualism— whereas it left Wheatley manumitted but alone and still serving. Emerson's evolving thinking on the meaning of loss becomes an analog of how Americans begin to accept the concept of insurance as a financial necessity in all aspects of middle-class life.

Again, it should be apparent from the outline of the underwriting narrative that this may be read as a social history told as a sequence of situated problems. This manifold view of insurance offers a theoretical key to inquiry, denoted in my study by the term "underwriting."[9] In keeping with the speculative nature of the questions behind this work, the book comprises a web of various critical designs. It is a meditation on theories of writing, illuminating the structures of print and manuscript discourses, exploring a fertile and persuasive feature of American capitalism that came to determine the protocols by which texts enforce meanings with specific values. At the level of cultural and social history, this book examines the practices that made mutually defining modes of loss and reparation profitable and, occasionally, pleasurable. I hope that this book will reverse the skepticism engendered by its unlikely dispositions, and that the terms associated with the conceptual foundations of insurance—loss, risk, publicity—point to the social texts that exist above, beneath, and through American literature.

Underwriting

The Poetics of Insurance in America,

1722-1872

Introduction

Underwriting and Literature

A Value struggle—it exist—
A Power—will proclaim
Although Annihilation pile
Whole Chaoses on Him—
—Emily Dickinson, J806

History

In early June 1721, near Penn's Landing, in Philadelphia, John Copson became the first American to open an insurance office. Strictly speaking, Copson was a broker, decreasing the cost of bringing buyers and sellers together. But brokering meant he was responsible for a more complex array of services and symbols than one might suppose. Such an intermediary function is in the nature of selling financial instruments—the commodity offered is largely symbolic, and the convenience of the offering is part of the service.[1] Like other perceptive businessmen of his time, Copson was adept at capitalizing on many of the innovative practices of the nascent public sphere, particularly tavern sociability and newspaper reading.[2] Part of Copson's job was to be a clearinghouse of social assurances, representing, as he says, the "integrity" and "reputation" of the underwriters "in this city and province" to prospective policyholders.

In so doing, he advanced a product that helped to define and broaden what it meant to be both a man of public virtue and an individual with private interests. This was because Copson's market can be viewed either as a function of the republican world of civic virtue or as a product of the growing world of marketable commodities. And it can be viewed that way because of the conceptual peculiarities of insurance itself. As we see played out in ongoing healthcare debates (as well as in post-9/11 and post-hurricane debates) about public responsibilities versus private capabilities, insurance has always resisted limiting formulations about who "deserves" its security and about who is obligated to provide it. This conceptual and historical flexibility only seems to intensify the stakes in a political determination of the "true" nature of insurance. The question of whether it is, in essence, a private or public method of security continues to roil political discourse and determine the fate of countless lives. To discern this aspect of insurance's ambiguous origins is to begin to understand the earliest sources of the moral problems within America's discourses of commerce and common welfare.

Insurance was both public and private because it placed the individual's fortunes within a network of wealth that was held collectively (though, at times, impersonally). Copson's insurance underwriting sought common exchangeable interests within a community of similarly vested individuals who relied upon one other for an assurance of solvency and payment. In the process of discovering his life and property assured via the emerging science of probability, Copson's customer could begin to understand and manage his numerical place in a broader public. By the same token, the underwriters clarified the relationship between private investment and the kinds of risks that governed everyday life. But those networked numerical assurances alone would not be enough to make a private act fully public, any more than an individual's participation in a joint stock company could be simply considered a public act. Private underwriting became a public affair to the degree that the two became mutually necessary and sustaining. In helping to develop the needs of private interests in a necessarily public context, insurance underwriting[3] grew astride an important boundary of early modern American life.

Insurance underwriting heralded other important changes in the social and cultural practices of colonial America. The discourse of safety pioneered by the insurance industry brought about important transformations in urban design, architecture, and public health.[4] Thus did private interest—measured and assured by texts that did the work of "political arithmetic"—serve and promote public welfare.[5] The assurances of underwriting derived from forms of public knowledge (actuarial statistics to commercial news) and law (contract theory to municipal fire codes), which contributed in turn to the conservation of private property. With the impetus of insurance and its private methods of managing property, government saw fit to promote public infrastructure projects that provided shipping and trade amenities—roads, harbors, and wharves—all of which made cargo and equipment safer and more efficient.

Given the widening significance of "assurance" as a social and cultural practice that merged the interests of the private imagination with the needs and discursive trends of the public, we begin to see Copson as an underrated figure in the evolution of colonial life. His advertisement of May 25, 1721, appearing in the *American Weekly Merchant*, bears this out:

Assurances from Losses happening at Sea ect. [sic] being found to be very much for the Ease and benefit of the Merchants and Traders in general, and whereas the merchants of this city of Philadelphia and other parts, have been obliged to send to London for such Assurance, which has not only been tedious and troublesome, but even very precarious. For remedying of which, An Office of Publick Insurance on Vessels, Goods and Merchandizes, will, on Monday next, be Opened, and Books kept by John Copson of this City, at this House in the High Street, where all Persons willing to be Insured may apply: And Care shall be taken by the said J. Copson That the Assurors or Underwriters be Persons of undoubted Worth and reputation and of considerable Interest in this City and Province.[6]

There is something distinctly transatlantic and genuinely "New World" about this, and the combination seems to augur economic transformations that would lead to political differentiations. In keeping with mercantilist custom, the colonies were exporting marine shipping economies tied to Britain; but they were also bound for economic and cultural reasons to set themselves apart, given the opportunity.[7] One is struck, as well, by the term "public insurance" which seems almost contradictory or quaintly outmoded to the modern ear, but which does that quite logical work of forging urbanized colonial affiliations. Accordingly, Copson seems to be making a plea for independence that drew public allegiance from circuits of economic viability, financial stability, and civic pride. Financial independence for colonial underwriters would obviate the need for the clumsy method of capital formation that was the transatlantic underwriting business with Lloyd's of London (among other brokerages and firms). The incipient insurance business led the way in what would be critical to establishing the contours of the national imaginary—namely, the formation of local (urban, colonial, and national) financial markets.

⌐

Insurance underwriting began its colonywide rise in the northeast, as a result of the burgeoning of transatlantic shipping. According to Mary Ruwell's account of the formation of American marine insurance companies, several other merchant underwriting brokers soon followed Copson into the business—Francis Rawle, Joseph Saunders, and John Kidd.[8] Edwin J. Perkins cites John Kidd as one of six signators to the partnership agreement of the first American marine insurance company with "surviving bylaws," drawn up in Philadelphia toward the end of the 1750's. That company, as Perkins notes, included in its list of partners Thomas Willing, who would go on to be president of the Bank of North America and the First Bank of the United States, and Robert Morris, the superintendent of finance during the Articles of Confederation. At mid-century, Ruwell observes that the hub of underwriting in Philadelphia had become the London Coffee House, on the banks of the Delaware River, close to Penn's Landing: "By 1758, the Insurance Office at the Coffee House had two clerks on duty every day from noon to one and from six to eight at night to take care of writing out policies of insurance and securing underwriting signatures. . . . [B]y the end of the eighteenth century, Philadelphia merchants had used the services of at least 150 private underwriters subscribing in about 15 insurance brokerage offices" (38–39).[9]

Boston's marine insurance scene began not long after Philadelphia's. Joseph Marion, a notary, opened an agency in 1724, thereby breaking free of the coffeehouse "office." Fowler describes his method this way:

> Marion's style of business was in keeping with the tradition of Lloyd's. He drew up policies noting vessel, master, intended voyage, and the premium rate. He then left the document on a table, inviting those who would to sign the policy and note the amount they wished to subscribe. When the full amount was underwritten, the policy was sealed. Marion's notarial office was not as busy as Lloyd's Coffee House, nor did it offer refreshment, it was nonetheless a public rendezvous where men of business were accustomed to visit. For these gentlemen, Marion was simply expanding his line of services [156–57].

Marion was still in business as late as 1745, though Perkins points out that there is scant evidence to establish just how substantial his business was. Benjamin Pollard opened an office in Boston in 1739 with the innovative practice of procuring the underwriters and their capital in advance, rather than waiting for casual connections to materialize. Pollard's unique service was to forge commercially branded intellectual and civic connections, demonstrating just how powerfully knowledge and social capital became the foundation of underwriting.

Perhaps the most successful Boston underwriter in the pre-Revolutionary period was Ezekiel Price. A notary like Pollard and Marion, Price is described by Fowler as "the archetypal insurance man—he knew everyone and everything" (159). In colonial New York City, the Beekman family established marine insurance. Already important merchants, the Beekmans saw marine underwriting as a profitable and somewhat commonsense diversification of their otherwise successful business. Perkins points out that they were not only able to perform all aspects of the insurance business, acting as brokers and underwriters, they also bought a fair number of policies of their own.

Colonial American fire insurance is a newer phenomenon than marine insurance, beginning its emergence in the mid-eighteenth century. Perkins notes perceptively that part of the reason for this had to do with the longevity requirements of a credible fire insurance business.[10] Ship underwriting was sustained by a loose network of backers who could complete the term of almost any policy, since the underwriters were insuring ships that completed their voyages in weeks or months. Fire insurers, by contrast, underwrote houses and buildings, and thus needed to bear the terms of a policy over the course of decades. Firms needed to be well capitalized and less partner-driven, which is why mutuals were often the best form for fire insurance concerns. The first mutual society in the colonies, established in 1735 in Charleston, South Carolina, was The Friendly Society. A large fire wiped out the firm in 1741. The first truly successful fire insurance company was Ben Franklin's Philadelphia Contributionship, which began in 1751 and by 1781 was writing about two thousand policies worth almost $2 million.[11] Fire insurance companies were more likely than banks to have substantial cash reserves, allowing them to play a vital role in the lending activities of banks and in the funding of public works projects. Perkins points out that, aside from the postal system, Franklin's fire insurance company holds the "distinction of being the first large privately managed business enterprise in North America"(293), a historical detail that suggests just how closely related text and money were in their early development into more comprehensive social systems.

By the middle of the eighteenth century, American insurance underwriting began to be a relatively prosperous industry.[12] But London still held sway in contracting the majority of business. During most of the eighteenth century, despite the growth of the underwriting business in Philadelphia and, indeed, in the colonies at large, the bulk of the underwriting business continued to go to London's better-financed companies. Monetary capital, in the form of the numerous individual underwriters to be found in a place like Lloyd's, was just too scarce in the colonies.[13]

This changed by the 1790's, for a number of macro- and microeconomic reasons, not the least of which was the general political economy of nationhood. The essential components of thriving underwriting communities, what Fowler refers to as "information, capital, and men willing to act as underwriters" (157), reached critical mass in the 1790's. This development was of a piece with Alexander Hamilton's successful efforts at establishing national capital markets through the Bank of the United States, the extension of new forms of credit, and the first steps in centralizing the national monetary system. According to Ruwell, insurance companies were no less important than banks in this nationalizing of capital markets and in the building up of a healthy belief in solid credit instruments.

In their effect on capital formation, the early banks and insurance companies were quite similar. Their business effect was monetary: transforming credit into money by accepting bills of exchange or promissory notes from individuals. The banks charged interest or exacted a discount for this service, whereas the insurance companies charged a premium for the risk undertaken. The banks concentrated on short-term commercial loans like the Bank of the United States which made 60-day loans. The insurance company risks usually lasted a couple of months, although 12 month policies were not unusual. Long-term capital formation was a function of their stock capital investment and dividends [15].

In essence, insurance underwriting gained influence in the political and cultural development of the new nation because it became a primary source of finance capital.[14] Once that indispensability to capital markets became well established, insurance companies began to expand the realm of exploitable markets. By the end of the eighteenth century, the British had cleared the moral cloud over life insurance by making a strict legal differentiation between gambling and insurance (outlawing, for instance, the buying of life insurance by individuals on other individuals).[15] Thus the nineteenth century saw the rise of life insurance in America. State governments recognized the potential for growth—those companies chartered after 1790 were vested with the ability to write life insurance policies. But there was a lag between product availability and major consumer demand. The demand for life policies was low until the 1840's when sales increased noticeably.[16]

The emergence of marine, fire, and life insurance, taken together, is the story of a massive but intricately articulated industry. Insurance came to dominate not only the planning and decisions made by cities, towns, and individuals but also the deeper structural fates of various components of the American economy—from slavery to pension funds to public welfare. What that meant as a social phenomenon is manifest for an alert pedestrian looking upward in any major American city—insurance company buildings are among a modern city's tallest, signifying in their opaque reflections a monumental bureaucratic success.

But what underwriting meant in other ways, as both artifact and method, is not so obvious. How did business and literature both benefit from Copson's new marketplace of individual authority, granting value scientifically and textually, and investing faithfully in the fruitful concept of loss? Can underwriting tell us something about the political exclusions of modern America? How and why did we become an underwriting society, if not culture? Why did Copson spawn such successful corporate Goliaths—what cultural patterns and logics were at work? And what does it mean to say we are an "underwriting society"? Beginning to answer these questions is the aim of this book.

A Business Term of Art

To gain a purchase on my framing questions, another question is necessary: What concepts might be said to underwrite the underwriters, first commercial and then literary? To answer this question, it seems vital to go to the very beginnings of money as a practical symbol in the transatlantic sphere. Indeed, one must look to the emergence of not only new forms of money and new methods of accounting but also the concepts that made possible these monetary instruments and commercial practices. Perhaps no point of departure is more crucial than the evolution of modern forms of money—paper, coin, credit, and related instruments of value.

Few critics of the American literary scene have ventured into the symbolic battleground of money, a terrain that has, interestingly, been extremely alluring for literary authors. This has started to change.[17] Marc Shell, in *Money, Language, and Thought,* has noted that the uniform use of paper money as national currency began in the United States, and from this fact he launches a discussion of the critical symbolic functions of coinage and printed money.[18] He goes on to show how historical conceptualizations of literature and money have been remarkably coterminous.

I want to make Shell's point resonate further by shifting and narrowing the focus. A cultural history of property, text, and value cannot be complete without accounting for the rise of eighteenth-century American underwriting businesses. To describe both the emergence of paper currency and the growth of insurance underwriting in America is to delineate in all its tenacity the determination of monetary capital to harness the unreliable phenomenal world, to channel risk, instability, and disappearance into material (or at least textual) certainties.[19] A major part of that description involves the very notion of the imaginative text, literary and commercial. Shell posits (and, indeed, it is a major premise not only of Marxist and classical economic thinking about specie, commodities, and paper money but also of much older theological conceptions of money) that the history of language and money revolves around a common problem: the creation of symbolic value (what we've come to call "meaning") out of an irreducible absence.[20]

Insurance and money bear structural similarities when brought into relation with the philosophically tricky idea of the void. In *Signifying Nothing* Brian Rotman makes semiotic claims similar to Shell's, about money's basis in the supplemental dialectic between substance and void, commodity and representation. Rotman shows how modern forms of money have been primed in crucial ways by the arithmetic evolution of the symbol for nothing. As a concept that can be deconstructed back to an absence in the signifying chain, money (whether coin or paper) bases its power on a bold connection made with—or from—the signified void, asserting in the process the very possibility of creative artifice out of some nihilistically productive, elementally symbolized idea of zero.

Rotman's history of zero in European thought carries through to the notion that contemporary financial markets represent the transformation of money into a metasign not unlike zero, accomplishing what various forms of paper money had teleologically sought for two hundred years: the extension and stabilizing of money's referential meaning (its value) through time. Contemporary capital markets, with their intricate methods of deriving and underwriting, thereby indemnify monetary value into the future, in spite of the lack of any anterior meaning. For Rotman, money has achieved its point of logical rest in the insured realm of purely self-referential significance, where nothing ultimately means *everything*.

But Rotman's basic point centers on zero as a necessary and assuring factor in economic life. Money, in whatever form, presupposes a creative/conservationist dynamic that promises some sort of assurance of value.[21] Economic actors, those who are counters, form relationships with numerical hypotheses. The counting subject must be comfortable with the idea of both wealth and debt, but, in a critical development, he does not have to accept the inevitability of loss and absence. Insurance, then, can be viewed as an important episode in the story of money's conceptual relation to the manufacture of value from nothing.

Printed money extracts, by force of artifice, worth from the generative idea of nothing. Underwritten property (a form of fiduciary or entrusted money) represents, however, the obverse of this creative circuit. Insurance underwriting seeks to efface zero from the realm of property. Thus it places an artificial stabilizer on property's seemingly natural relationship to an unfetishized exchange value (zero). Rather than creating value out of nothing, it keeps value (or meaning or property) from slipping to nothing. Insurance underwriting is that form of monetary value which preserves the notion of material anteriority to what Rotman calls "the counting subject"; it is a crucial means of assuring that money's numbers refer to countable values that will not, indeed cannot, disappear.[22]

Underwriting has stood in opposition to the idea of zero and its negative numerical consequences. Such writing signifies unambiguously the power of language and numbers to match, and vouch for in case of doubt, the worth of a world anterior to the subjective counting mind.[23] What both hard currency and fiduciary forms of money entail is the binding, metonymic presentation of signatures or official inscriptions as the basis of exchange. Monetary capitalization implants itself as a "real" countable entity through both kinds of signed inscriptions, those associated with circulating and fiduciary wealth. As an original and symbolically self-sustaining social foundation, underwriting is far-reaching; and, as Locke points out, it is forever plotting the need for "more." Insurance presumes as its domain everything that may be called property, placing within its conserving matrix of textual warranty all the rights and privileges that property law involves.[24] An insurance contract may be viewed in this light as an extension of the conventional deed, which functioned to transfer title, rights, and obligations contingent to a piece of real property.[25]

Obviously, I take some freedom in using "underwriting" as an analogical term that can claim a kind of poetics or operate as a thoroughgoing semiotic instrument. In my reading, underwriting is essential to the primary act of capitalization, insofar as capitalization makes a claim on the authenticity of its referents and thereby attempts to establish worth (price, value) and financial credibility. In both literary and monetary cases, investments of worth and "authenticity" are predicated on an individually assigned truth-claim, usually the ultimate symbol of thrift—the authorial name and signature (Lloyd's underwriters are still known somewhat poetically as "Names"). Granted through texts that attach a symbolic investment, authenticity also imparts to certain imagining individuals a self-identifying license.[26] That license allows the writer's text to mediate between present and future, predicating a particular kind of self-driven narrative in the literary sphere and enabling contractual obligation in the commercial realm.

In the context of eighteenth- and early-nineteenth-century America, I ask how underwritten authenticity conditioned literary and commercial notions of originality, exposure, possession, and loss. This focus allows for new descriptions of the spaces between self-identity, imaginative possibility, and public expression. How might these descriptions help us to understand the relationship between a writing occupation (that of the professional literary author, the slave poet, or the free "man of letters") and ownership (of literary property/copyright, of a house, of a slave, of one's labor)? In its questions and answers, this book urges critical incongruities, placing great confidence in the idea that monetary and literary representations—underwritten as they are by a grounding textual logic that they may share in different measures—can signify mutually defining actual and fictional worlds.[27]

⌢

The writers in this study are of the corporate age.[28] This statement is true in at least two senses—one recalling the corporate history of Alan Trachtenberg, the other the biopolitics of Michel Foucault.[29] First, it was during the eighteenth century that insurance firms began to sell stock (indeed, they more often than not took the form of joint stock companies); in addition, underwriting moved beyond ad hoc partnerships forged by coffeehouse sociability and into more legally articulated, and thus less personal, more corporate associations.[30] And this study is of the corporate age in the sense that during this period the physical body (both free and slave) began to assume unprecedented commercial and legal importance. Interestingly (and somewhat ironically), it was also the colonial period in America that guaranteed and elevated corporeal satisfactions to objects of economically rationalized desire.[31]

Larzer Ziff has described the shift from "immanence to representation in both literature and society" as part of the rise of print culture and its technologies of appearance. Such a shift transferred materiality as an inherent value from the conflicts of spiritual immanence to the legal and commercial disputes of print representation.[32] One could add to the possible causes of this shift the economic discourses behind the new underwriting mode of signification. The material phenomenal world and its narratives of loss and gain supplanted the destiny of the soul as the beneficiary of organized social energies. Such transformations are of a piece with what Foucault cites as "techniques for rationalizing and strictly economizing on a power that had to be used in the least costly way possible"; such powers were given force by "a whole system of surveillance, hierarchies, inspections, bookkeeping, and reports—all the technology that can be described as the disciplinary technology of labor" (*"Society Must Be Defended,"* 242). In this way human lives, habitations, and cargo became economically rationalized, and thereby fit subjects and objects for the monetary accounting and contractual assurance proffered by appropriately corporate entities.[33]

That procedure evolved, over the course of the eighteenth century, into an enterprise best suited to the legal structure of the public company. The incorporation of America can be traced, at least in part, to insurance as a business organization. Underwriting companies in England evolved out of a complex interplay of financial necessities that spun off their own notions of where the private interest ended and a more corporate or even "public" one began. Many of England's seventeenth-century underwriters were also bankers, a fact that reflects public finance as a critical instrument of statecraft, one whose rise was concomitant with that of insurance underwriting.[34] British underwriters were stimulated by innovations in public finance, capitalizing on the new laws enabling the formation of joint stock companies.[35] Insurance companies were extremely skillful and innovative at bridging the public-private connection that legal and social rules made available. That British innovation was purified and made commonplace in America, where corporate insurance was seen as a public-minded way to develop commerce. State charters granting new corporations were a way for the public to endorse the workings of a company and thereby underwrite politically the money they risked in buying shares.[36] The fluctuation between publicity and privacy that occurs in the realm of corporate responsibilities began during the late eighteenth century, and it took many of its problems, in turn, from the slippages inherent in the legal conceptualization of insurance.

One final observation on the relationship between public and private aspects of insurance, and I make it in the spirit of speculation: as a cultural and social phenomenon, and even more so as a theoretical event in the economic history of the West, insurance may be viewed as a significant vulnerability to capital and money. One suspects that this might be the reason for the paucity of critical thinking on the topic. Indeed, legal historians have obliquely suggested this idea. Banks McDowell notes that critical thinking about insurance as a social and economic phenomenon has been deliberately "under-emphasized" by the insurance industry itself, mostly to avoid the regulation that might come with such close analysis.[37]

His point is well taken. But in several respects, insurance may be viewed as an indication of capital's own distrust and fear of the very idea of the market. Indeed, insurance underwriters' attempt to socialize capital—and, along with it, the risks of an increasingly commodified society—does not so much suggest the triumph of capital's ability to regulate experience and stabilize property as it does a possible inadequacy or instability at the heart of capital's founding logic. For insurance carries within it the seeds of the market's alternative, a rationalization of social welfare through nonmarket redistributive means and a reliance on an idea of the public that suggests the public as a legitimate economic counterweight to private interests. It was that very possibility which got Stevens to think about what insurance really meant, as a shared governmental option for both rich and poor.

Insurance offers, moreover, a glaring example of the wider dangers of the market's inevitable casualties. When insurance companies become insolvent, the consequences can be severe, even socially and politically destabilizing, given the vast exposure many companies have through pension plans.[38] Insurance is its own emblem of both that which is not for sale and that which cannot be assured, inviting us to view documents of doubt about the logic of the capitalist market as an efficient and satisfying social structure.

⤸

From its beginnings at Lloyd's Coffee House in London, the underwriting of property has required signatures. And at least since Kenneth Lockridge, in *Literacy in Colonial New England* (1974), used signatures affixed to wills as an index of male literacy, signatures have been key indicators of reading and writing practices in American cultural and social history. Lockridge's markers are essential to my analysis of the emergence of underwriting as a social and financial practice. For the endorsement of wills through personal signatures is surely a precursor of the commodified conservationist product of insurance policies. By the endorsement of wills, literate men could legally insure the conservation of their property through familial descent.

Underwriting has an iconic importance that arises from the historical semiotics of handwriting, since the idea of underwriting contains within it the material authentication of personal signatures. In *Handwriting in America*, Tamara Plakins Thornton charts the historical implications of nonprint writing in

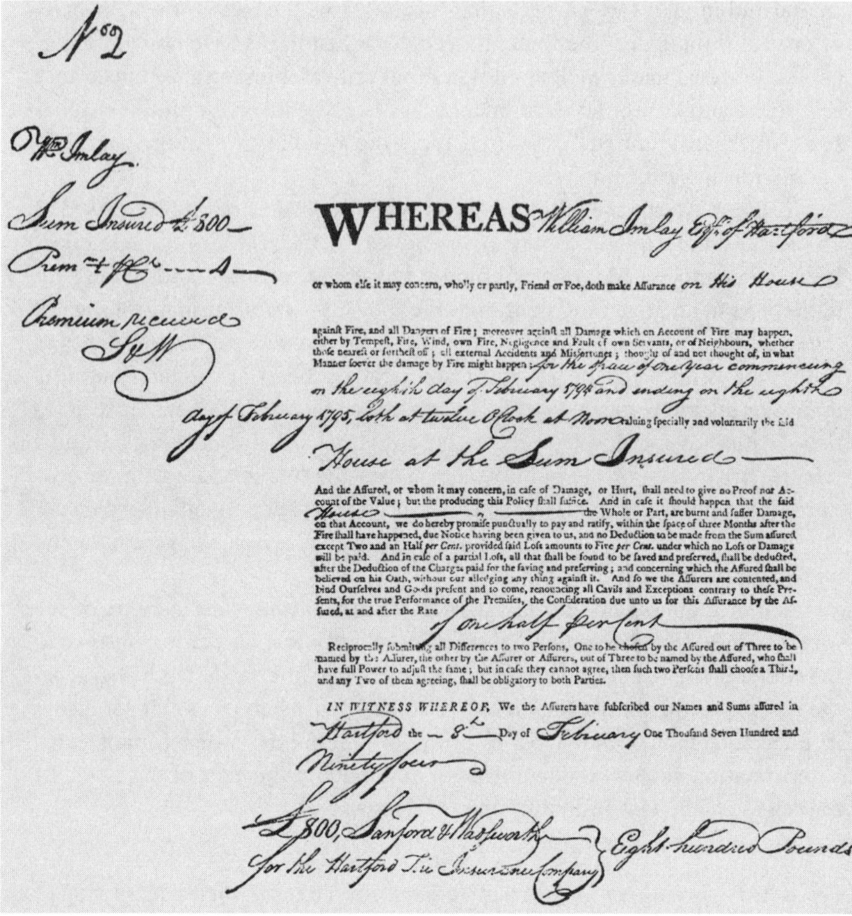

No 2

Wm Imlay

Sum Insured £800

Prem £4 ...

Premium received

S&W

WHEREAS William Imlay Esqr. of Hartford

or whom elſe it may concern, wholly or partly, Friend or Foe, doth make Aſſurance on His House

againſt Fire, and all Dangers of Fire; moreover againſt all Damage which on Account of Fire may happen, either by Tempeſt, Fire, Wind, own Fire, Negligence and Fault of own Servants, or of Neighbours, whether thoſe neareſt or furtheſt off; all external Accidents and Misfortunes; thought of and not thought of, in what Manner ſoever the damage by Fire might happen; for the space of one year commencing on the eighth day of February 1794 and ending on the eighth day of February 1795, both at twelve O'Clock at Noon valuing ſpecially and voluntarily the ſaid House at the Sum Insured

And the Aſſured, or whom it may concern, in caſe of Damage, or Hurt, ſhall need to give no Proof nor Account of the Value; but the producing this Policy ſhall ſuffice. And in caſe it ſhould happen that the ſaid House the Whole or Part, are burnt and ſuffer Damage, on that Account, we do hereby promiſe punctually to pay and ratify, within the ſpace of three Months after the Fire ſhall have happened, due Notice having been given to us, and no Deduction to be made from the Sum aſſured except Two and an Half *per Cent.* provided ſaid Loſs amounts to Five *per Cent.* under which no Loſs or Damage will be paid. And in caſe of a partial Loſs, all that ſhall be found to be ſaved and preſerved, ſhall be deducted, after the Deduction of the Charges paid for the ſaving and preſerving; and concerning which the Aſſured ſhall be believed on his Oath, without our alledging any thing againſt it. And ſo we the Aſſurers are contented, and bind Ourſelves and Goods preſent and to come, renouncing all Cavils and Exceptions contrary to theſe Preſents, for the true Performance of the Premiſes, the Conſideration due unto us for this Aſſurance by the Aſſured, at and after the Rate of one half per Cent

Reciprocally ſubmitting all Differences to two Perſons, One to be choſen by the Aſſured out of Three to be named by the Aſſurer, the other by the Aſſurer or Aſſurers, out of Three to be named by the Aſſured, who ſhall have full Power to adjuſt the ſame; but in caſe they cannot agree, then ſuch two Perſons ſhall chooſe a Third, and any Two of them agreeing, ſhall be obligatory to both Parties.

IN WITNESS WHEREOF, We the Aſſurers have ſubſcribed our Names and Sums aſſured in Hartford the 8th Day of February One Thouſand Seven Hundred and Ninety four

£800, Sanford & Wadsworth for the Hartford Fire Insurance Company — Eight hundred Pounds

FIG. 1. Hartford Insurance Policy for William Imlay, 1794. Courtesy of the Hartford Financial Services Group.

American culture since the colonial period. She distinguishes between the practices of writing and reading and shows how, as the eighteenth century progressed, handwriting increasingly became the province of business (as opposed to that of the clergy). Clerking and bookkeeping required penmanship as well as arithmetic. The reasons she supplies for this development—authenticity, convenience, and portability—play a part in my own understanding of the methods of underwriting as a representational innovation. Enacting all aspects of the innovation, handwriting as a corollary of business practice was an effective way to code gender and class.[39]

Thornton also discusses how such coded notions of script coalesced into associations within mercantile public culture. Insurance policies, such as that of the Hartford Fire Insurance Company of 1794, merged script and print in precise ways, individualizing and standardizing in ways meant to preserve and solidify property values. In the language of the policy: "And the assured, or whom it may concern, in case of damage or hurt, shall need to give no proof nor account of the value; but the producing of this policy shall suffice" (see fig. 1).[40] Through scripted signatures, underwriters would circulate among a select crowd of peers who could supply the money necessary to validate their signatures; at the same time, one could argue that it was the signatures themselves that betokened and kept the value of their personages within mercantile circles.

Literary culture made similar kinds of social associations.[41] It was, at least in the eighteenth century, a form of scribal and print culture that thrived on the middle spaces between the public and the private. Authors would choose script for a more moderate kind of publication that accommodated politically controversial material or, as in the case of female authors, that kept them from the moral compromises which came with the simplistic commercial nature of print culture's marketable pleasures. One suspects that a parallel logic is what granted underwriting signatures their ascriptive power. That is, underwriting signatures promised the ability to assign integrity without the connotation of marketable pleasure; instead, signatures connoted a kind of material and objective gravity, with the florid and mutually reinforcing iconicity of fear, uncertain legibility, and the echoes of a kind of blood coercion.[42]

Signatures are part of the founding logic of underwriting because they are final displays of individual power. They are final because they invoke obligation, identity, and potential blame, without the moral compromises that come with the discourse of debate and pseudonymity in print culture. The signature evokes an authority that does not require any more in the way of rhetorical or monetary persuasion. While Larzer Ziff may be right that, for the purposes of political representation, the "Declaration of Independence . . . signaled the end of personally embodied government" (*Writing in the New Nation*, 114) guaranteed by signature authority, in the commercial realm that personalized authority actually grew in significance and took on distinctly modern characteristics. Just as authors became the notional aspect of Foucault's "principle of thrift" in the economy of aesthetic meaning, signatures evolved to enact that principle in the commercial domain, where free actors required a measure of embodied stability to blend with the externalized ambiguities of republican print culture. Signatures within the practice of underwriting became complete arguments in and of themselves, emblazoning responsibility without the need for discursive elaboration.

〜

I have been silent thus far about the third epigraph underwriting my preface, that of Jacques Derrida. Derrida may be said to underwrite this study insofar as deconstruction, with its paradox-embracing descriptive powers, suggests itself so capably in the theorizing of insurance.[43] A reason for this might be that insurance represents one of the most important moments of capitalist transformation as an explicitly textual phenomenon. As my discussion of Rotman suggests, insurance underwriting gathers around it a network of legitimating practices that invoke textual authority to conserve an original anteriority that deconstruction calls into question.[44]

One might suppose that such instabilities would be silently grafted onto legal attempts to make insurance answer to certain definitions. And, indeed, insurance law, in its attempt to specify axiomatically the bounds of what insurance is, presents a model deconstructive cultural site. John Lowery and Phillip Rawlings, in *Insurance Law: Doctrines and Principles*, claim that defining an insurance contract is an impossible task because the concept itself distorts the set of practices it seeks to explicitly mark with inclusivity. While insurance contracts are clearly a subspecies of contracts under the general law of contract, they contain essential conditions that make final definition impossible:

> Insurance contracts are subject to the general law of contract, but special rules also apply to them which do not apply to most other contracts: for instance, both parties are under a duty of disclosure and, in relation to some policies, the insured is allowed to withdraw unilaterally from an agreement.... For these reasons it is important to define an insurance contract. Unfortunately, legislation has provided little assistance in this task, and, while the courts have made several attempts to supply a definition, these tend to sacrifice clarity for inclusiveness and end up achieving neither. Megarry [...] thought it "a matter of considerable difficulty," and declined the task: "it is a concept which it is better to describe than attempt to define." Similarly, Templeman [...], having noted that there was no statutory definition, though it is "undesirable that there should be, because definitions tend sometimes to obscure and occasionally to exclude that which ought to be included" [3].

A similar problem has plagued the precision of American insurance law. Jerry describes the basic principles of insurance law, but notice his difficulty in discussing the incipient problem of delimiting the peculiar nature of insurance:

> It can be said, then, that a contract of insurance is an agreement in which one party (the insurer), in exchange for a consideration provided by the other party (the insured), assumes the other party's risk and distributes it across a group of similarly situated persons, each of whose risk has been assumed in a similar transaction.
>
> Like any attempted definition of insurance, the foregoing definition does not always yield a clear answer to the question of whether a particular contract is a contract of insurance [17].

That last impasse, the inability to distinguish particular kinds of contracts involving risk distribution, is presumably what has historically caused so much legal ambiguity.

American legal history amply bears this out. Friedman writes that American insurance law saw a sea change in the degree of regulatory control by federal and state governments in the nineteenth century: "Insurance claims were a friction point, where aggregated capital met the ordinary . . . person on the plane of inequality. . . . Insurance litigation, then, was relatively frequent. And hardly any subject was more often the subject of statute than insurance" (443). Statutory law attempted to compensate for the theoretical gaps in contract law. The situation at the state level quickly became almost absurdly complex in the attempt to account for what insurance underwriting meant in theory and practice:

The states passed laws that outlawed discrimination in rates, curbed "unfair" marketing practices, tried to safeguard the solvency of the companies, harnessed foreign insurance companies, and insisted on financial reserves. The volume and scope of this legislation grew to fantastic proportions. The Massachusetts law to "Amend and Codify the Statutes Relating to Insurance," passed in 1887, contained 112 closely packed sections of text. Rococo excess in the size of a statute does not mean that the statute is successful in controlling its subject. Bulk may mean almost the opposite: a frantic and hopeless attempt to control, after prior laws had repeatedly failed [444].

Why might the laws have failed? Perhaps this situation of precluding any satisfactory definition is attributable to the same problematic features that underwriting contracts share with money (as theorized by Rotman). Both species of promise—money as redeemable value, and insurance as redeemable guarantee of value in the event of loss—contend with the artificiality of the divisions between presence and absence, between value and nothingness, between "hard" specie and solely representational currency. Both money and insurance contracts entail slippage between identifiably valuable and utterly worthless entities, since both depend so heavily on the investment one makes in the ability of texts to stabilize the line that partitions what is valuable from what is empty of worth. Insurance, as a contract, invokes the boundary between property and loss, presence and absence, as no other nonreligious practice can claim to do in the social world. And because that demarcation is so deeply axiomatic—a fiction held as certainly (and yet questionably) as Derrida's famous example of the definition of the circle—it invites ceaseless attempts to find a natural risk-free reference. Thus there is no expert dictum that would establish a property's unproblematic existence; and, consequently, the contractual terms governing its disappearance become endlessly litigable. The foundational claims of underwriting—its guarantee of stability and endurance over and against the vicissitudes of growth and obliteration—are a fantasy. The difference in states of value and possession that underwriting attempts to name assumes a perfectly accountable and traceable narrative to guide compensation.

Ultimately, the problem stems from the intrinsically textual work that insurance underwriting requires—to vouchsafe material loss (objective destruction) from the concept of absolute symbolic loss (nothing as a monetary value) through the mediating powers of texts and human trust. Caught in the gaps (or aporia) of contract law and regulatory codes, we are left with deconstructionist dispositions in the mouth of jurisprudence: "a concept which it is better to describe than attempt to define," and "definitions tend sometimes to obscure and occasionally exclude that which ought to be included." Still, it *is* effective. The obscure boundaries of property as text are the source of insurance underwriting's unknowable but capable foundation, its wavering grasp at stable axioms, its fuzzy but secure position within the nettles of legal undefinability.[45]

To the degree that the lack of materiality in the idea of the text (the underwriting as pure representation) presupposes the idea of material property (the underwritten), the two become linked by the method of underwriting and thus appear to be neatly dependent, cross-referential, and perhaps "classically" supplementary. But of course there is a silent narrative here that naturalizes a foundational relationship between property and text. The temporal sequence of the relationship divulges the underwriting's doubtful supplementarity, revealing the sense in which the insurance contract looms as a primary and defining value in relation to the property insured. Underwriting only seems to hold a deferred bonus to the intrinsic original worth of the material object (or subject, in the case of life insurance).

The structural design suggested by the compound term "underwriting" proclaims this: that is, written matter (a signature on an insurance contract) placed metaphorically and actually beneath some represented thing (valued property, now fully described) suggests, in the downward verticality of its logic, the cause/effect temporality of the relationship (see fig. 2). The combination of print standardization and signature authenticity is meant to suggest an original confirmation buttressing legal formalisms. As Walter Benjamin suggests when considering the relationship between original and mechanically reproducible texts, originality can take on a particularly intense objective guise: "The presence of the original is the prerequisite to the concept of authenticity" (2). Devices like the insurance contract are perfect examples of what Gerald Frug calls the "effectuating [of] 'subjective' constituent goals through an 'objective' bureaucracy."[46] The relationship between the originating object and the authenticating signature on the page of the contract indicates obligation and responsibility, one following the other, confirming mutual values.

The text, in temporal terms, is effective only after the eventuality of the object's loss, and after the reproducibility of the contractual life of its representation (that is, legal authenticity). This, too, can be seen to derive from the peculiar mixture of manuscript and print in the drafting of the contract. Benjamin writes:

The authenticity of a thing is the essence of all that is transmissible from its beginning, ranging from its substantive duration to its testimony to the history which it has experienced. Since the historical testimony rests on the authenticity, the former, too, is jeopardized by reproduction when substantive duration ceases to matter. And what is really jeopardized when the historical testimony is affected is the authority of the object.

This last sentence is true conversely, the object coming into question because of the fraught terms of the historical testimony of the contractual text. As we have seen, the function of the insurance contract is to offer the impossibility of property's final disappearance. The ground of the insurance contract's meaning, the source of its power, is the likelihood of the disappearance of the object that gives rise to its textual necessity. This is to say that the terms of the contract's effectiveness are in the remaking (via predictive testimony) of a practical truth into a falsehood. The commonsense view that anything might be lost at any time is now revoked by insurance underwriting, which lends, in the act of its defining, an imaginary permanence to the objectively transient.

At the same time, as if subject to the power of suggestion arising from itself, the rule of underwriting calls into importance that which it wants to banish (risk of loss). Priority is everything in insurance contracts. Indeed, prior invocation is the one essential mark of an insurance contract; insurance is required, by definition, to precede the event it names. François Ewald puts it concisely:

Insurance means covering a risk *before the fact*. This is what distinguishes insurance from assistance, which is the spreading of the loss burden *after the fact*. Once a risk has occurred, the option of insurance no longer exists [emphasis in original].[47]

An event not covered thus nullifies the possibility of conservation hypothetically promised by the contract. Insurance solves the problem of risk only by *being made effective* by risk; and the objects that risk endangers are given form and endurance in the contract.

This conserving artifice occurs in two places within the contract. The first is in the terms or conditions (including description of property, valuations, and limits of protection). To quote Edwin Patterson, "Conditions are not legally essential, since many contracts are made without them; yet they are highly important in insurance contracts, which are never made without them. The insured event . . . is the chief condition" (69). The second occurs in the place of the signature (where the terms are once again, and this time quite literally, underwritten). Taken in its totality as written matter, the contract effects a pres-

WHereas *Wm Willing & Morris*

as well in *our* own Name, as for and in the Name and Names of all and every other Person or Persons, to whom the same doth, may, or shall appertain, in Part or in all doth make Assurance and cause *themselves* and them and every of them to be insured, lost or not lost, at and from *Madeira*

To Philadelphia

upon the Body, Tackle, Apparel, and other *Furniture* of the good *Snow* called the *Sterling* of the Burden of Tons or thereabouts, whereof is Master under GOD, for this present Voyage *Samuel Howell* or whosoever else shall go for Master in the said Ship, or by whatsoever other Name or Names the said Ship, or the Master thereof, is, or shall be named or called, beginning the Adventure upon the said Ship, Tackle, Apparel, &c. at and from *Madeira* aforesaid, and to shall continue and endure until the said Ship shall be safely arrived at *Philadelphia* aforesaid, and until she be moored Twenty and Four Hours in good Safety. And it shall and may be lawful for the said Ship in her Voyage to proceed and sail to, touch and stay at any Ports or Places, if thereunto obliged by Stress of Weather, or other unavoidable Accident, without Prejudice to this Insurance. The said Ship, Tackle, &c. for so much as it concerns the Assured by Agreement made between the Assured and the Assurers in this POLICY, are and shall be valued *at Six Hundred Pounds*

without any further Account to be given by the Assured to the Assurers, or any of them for the same. Touching the Adventures and Perils, which we the Assurers are contented to bear, and do take upon us in this Voyage, they are, of the Seas, Men of War, Fires, Enemies, Pirates, Rovers, Thieves, Jettisons, Letters of Mart, and Counter Mart, Surprisals, Taking at Sea, Arrests, Restraints and Detainments, of all Kings, Princes, or People of what Nation, Condition or Quality soever, Barratry of the Master and Mariners, and all other Perils, Losses and Misfortunes, that have or shall come to the Hurt, Detriment or Damage of the said Ship or Part thereof. And in case of any Loss or Misfortunes, it shall be lawful to and for the Assured *their* Factors, Servants and Assigns, to sue, labour and travel for, in and about the Defence, Safeguard and Recovery of the said Ship or any Part thereof without Prejudice to this Insurance, to the Charges whereof we the Assurers will contribute each one, according to the Rate and Quantity of his Sum herein Insured. And it is agreed by us the Assurers, that this Writing or Policy of Insurance, shall be of as much Force and Effect, as the surest Writing or Policy of Assurance heretofore made in Lombard-Street, or elsewhere in LONDON. And, to we the Assurers are contented, and do hereby promise and bind ourselves each one for his own Part; our Heirs, Executors and Goods, to the Assured *their* Executors, Administrators and Assigns, for the true Performance of the Premises, confessing ourselves paid the Consideration due unto us for the Assurance, by the said Assured or *their* Assigns at and after the Rate of *Two Pounds* per Cent. and in Case of Loss, the Assured to abate Two per Cent.

IN WITNESS WHEREOF WE the Assurers have subscribed our Names and Sums Assured in *Philadelphia* the *Seventh* Day of *October* One Thousand Seven Hundred and Sixty *Six*

Memorandum. It is agreed by and between the Assured and Assurers, that no Loss shall be paid on any Average under Five Pounds per Cent. unless the said Average be General. And in Case of Loss, the Assured shall allow the Office Keeper or Broker, One half per Cent. for his Trouble in collecting and paying the same in due Time, and registring it in his Office.

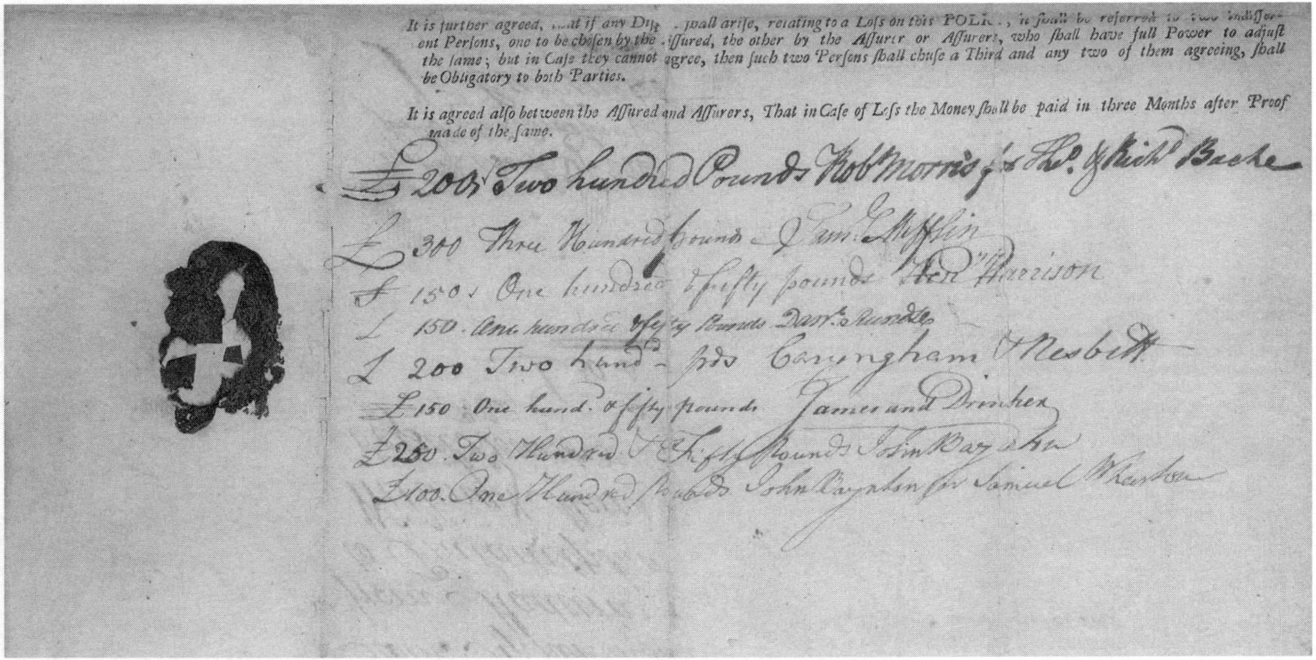

It is further agreed, that if any Di[illegible] shall arise, relating to a Loss on this POLI[illegible], it shall be referred to two indifferent Persons, one to be chosen by the Assured, the other by the Assurer or Assurers, who shall have full Power to adjust the same; but in Case they cannot agree, then such two Persons shall chuse a Third and any two of them agreeing, shall be Obligatory to both Parties.

It is agreed also between the Assured and Assurers, That in Case of Loss the Money shall be paid in three Months after Proof made of the same.

£200 Two hundred Pounds Robt Morris for Thos & Richd Bache

£300 Three Hundred Pounds Sam. Mifflin

£150 One hundred & fifty pounds [illegible] Harrison

£150 One hundred & fifty Pounds Davd Rundle

£200 Two hundd pds Caryngham & Nesbitt

£150 One hund. & fifty pounds James and Drinker

£250 Two Hundred & Fifty Pounds John Baynton

£100 One Hundred Pounds John Baynton for Samuel Wharton

FIG. 2. Marine Insurance Policy, 1765. Courtesy of the ACE Archives.

By the President and Directors of the Insurance Company of North America

No. 1322

Attest

Benj. Savard, Sec'y

WHEREAS *Petit Mayard*

as well in *their* own Name, as for and in the Name and Names of all and every other Person or Persons, to whom the same doth, may, or shall appertain, in part or in whole, do make Insurance, and cause *themselves* and them, and every of them to be insured, lost or not lost, at and from *Philadelphia to Madeira &c. & from thence back to*

Philadelphia

upon the *Body, Tackle, Apparel and other Furniture,* of the good *Ship* called the *Pacifn* _____ Tons, or thereabouts, whereof is Master, under God, for this present Voyage *Benjamin Maddith* _____ of the Burthen of _____ or whosoever else shall go for Master in the said Vessel, or by whatsoever other Name or Names the said Vessel, or the Master thereof, is or shall be named or called, beginning the Adventure upon the said Vessel, Tackle, Apparel, &c. at and from *Philadelphia* _____ aforesaid, and so shall continue and endure until the said vessel be safely arrived at *Philadelphia* _____ aforesaid, and until the be moored Twenty and four hours in good safety. And it shall and may be lawful for the said Vessel in her Voyage to proceed and fail to, touch and ftay at any Ports or Places, if thereunto obliged by Strefs of Weather, or other unavoidable Accident, without Prejudice to this Insurance. The faid Vessel, Tackle, &c. for so much as concerns the Assured, by Agreement made between the Assured and Assurers in this POLICY are and shall be valued

_____ without any further Account to be given by the Assured to the Assurers, or any of them for the same. Touching the Adventures and Perils, which we the Assurers are contented to bear, and take upon us in this Voyage, they are, of the Seas, Men of War, Fires, Enemies, Pirates, Rovers, Thieves, Jettisons, Letters of Mart, and Counter Mart, Surprisals, Taking at Sea, Arrests, Restraints and Detainments of all Kings, Princes or People, of what Nation, Condition or Quality soever, Barratry of the Master and Mariners, and all other Perils, Losses and Misfortunes, which have or shall come to the Hurt, Detriment or Damage of the said Vessel, or Part thereof. And in Case of any Loss or Misfortunes, it shall be lawful to and for the Assured, *their* Factors, Servants and Assigns, (and the said Assured on *their* Part agree and engage , by *Philadelphia Their* Factors, Servants or Assigns) to sue, labour and travel for, in and about the Defence, Safeguard and Recovery of the said Goods and Merchandizes, or any part thereof, without Prejudice to this Insurance, to the Charges whereof we the Assurers will contribute according to the Rate and Quantity of the Sum herein insured. And it is agreed by us the Assurers, that this Writing or Policy of Insurance shall be of as much Force and Effect as the surest Writing or Policy of Assurance heretofore made in any of the UNITED STATES of AMERICA, or elsewhere. And so we the Assurers are contented, and do hereby bind the Capital Stock, and other common Property of the Insurance Company of North-America to the Assured, *their* Executors, Administrators and Assigns, for the true Performance of the Premises, confessing ourselves paid the Consideration due unto us for the Assurance, by the said Assured, or *their* Assigns, after the Rate of *Two & one half p Cent*

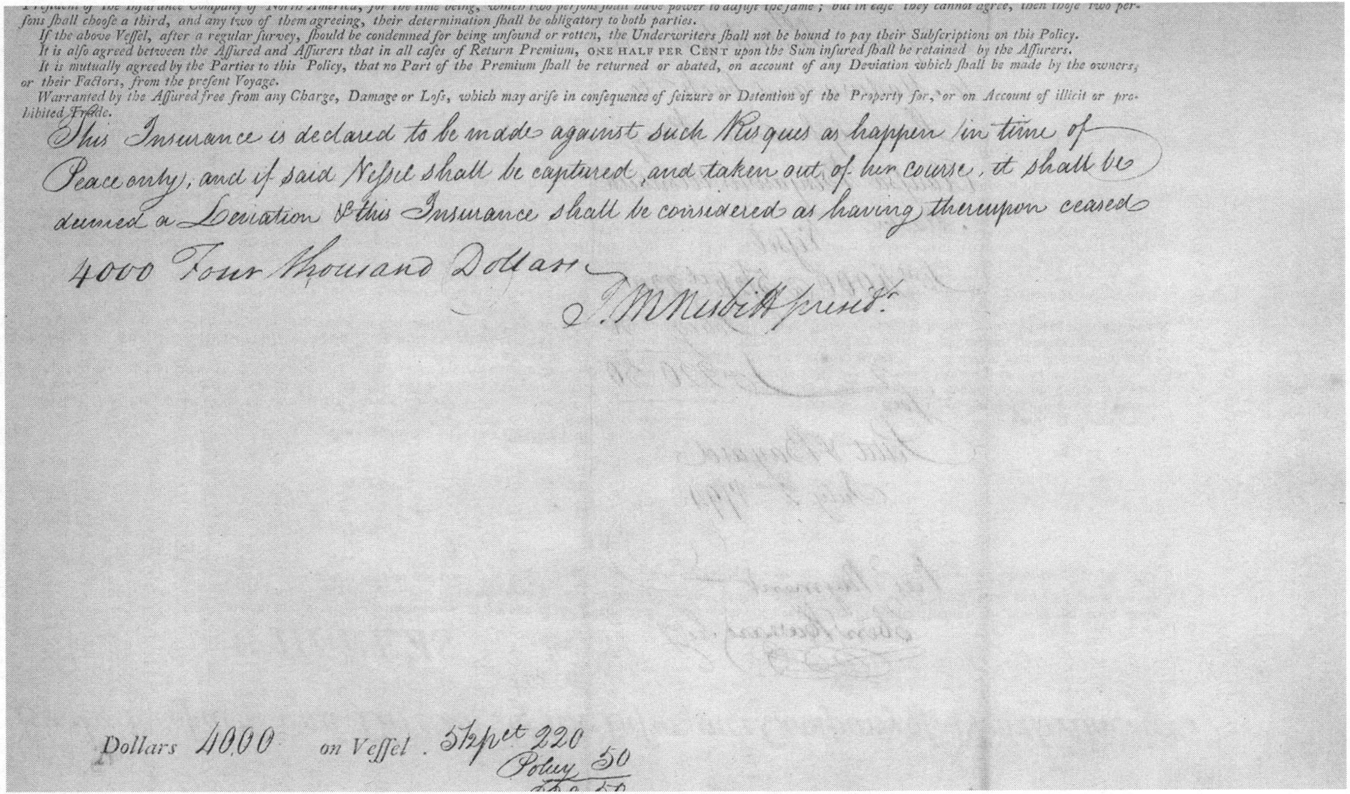

ſons ſhall chooſe a third, and any two of them agreeing, their determination ſhall be obligatory to both parties.
If the above Veſſel, after a regular ſurvey, ſhould be condemned for being unſound or rotten, the Underwriters ſhall not be bound to pay their Subſcriptions on this Policy.
It is alſo agreed between the Aſſured and Aſſurers that in all caſes of Return Premium, ONE HALF PER CENT upon the Sum inſured ſhall be retained by the Aſſurers.
It is mutually agreed by the Parties to this Policy, that no Part of the Premium ſhall be returned or abated, on account of any Deviation which ſhall be made by the owners, or their Factors, from the preſent Voyage.
Warranted by the Aſſured free from any Charge, Damage or Loſs, which may ariſe in conſequence of ſeizure or Detention of the Property for, or on Account of illicit or prohibited Trade.

This Insurance is declared to be made against such Risques as happen in time of Peace only, and if said Vessel shall be captured, and taken out of her course, it shall be deemed a Deviation & this Insurance shall be considered as having thereupon ceased

4000 Four Thousand Dollars

J. M Nesbitt presid.t

Dollars 4000 on Veſſel . 5½ p.ct 220
Policy 50

FIG. 3. Marine Insurance Policy, 1794. Courtesy of the ACE Archives.

ence, a completeness, that the text seems to deny the object (see fig. 3). (It should be remembered that underwriting began as a speculative venture, where the signatories often never saw the ships or cargo for which they claimed partial responsibility.) We are left to wonder which is real—which is the source of value—the confirming text or the thing confirmed? We observe here a strange twist on speech act theory, where the performance of an affirmative linguistic moment reverses what it intends. The ideas of risk and of loss have added something of value to the property so insured. Again, the text calls into presence that which would seem to not require its help—objective experience.[48]

↬

There are everyday instances in which this abstruse theorizing is borne out. In practical terms, insured things (or people) are more valuable than the uninsured; and, more often than not, things (or people) not insured are seen as worth less, if not "worthless." Underwriting guarantees the intrinsic, anterior status of property in the very act of its adding to the value of material property. It creates, moreover, through the alchemy of its promises, both fear and security with regard to the future.

But in the process, certain rights-based things go missing. Uninsured property does not exist as conventionally calculated economic reality, just as those without property (the homeless) do not exist as political actors. In this sense, property has borne out a deeply Lockean notion, that it exists coequal within the realm of rights "Lives, Liberties, and Estates" (II, §123). One's property, along with one's inclusion in the social contract, implies a set of naturalized capabilities—rights—that one may grasp or not, a matter of choice. The ideology of individualism guides the terms here, where a person is free to recognize the social and individual reciprocity that property demands. Louis Dumont has noted this Lockean transition in the meaning of property during the eighteenth century, an observation that seems to work, too, with the Emersonian innovations of individualism: "economics as a 'philosophical category' represents the acme of individualism and as such tends to be paramount in our universe" (34).[49]

Again, the description of the development of this economic individualism has the disturbing ring of truth in actual terms. Think only of the deliberate invisibility to American society of those who have no health, automobile, or home insurance. They exist outside the political sphere, where voting is tied to residency and driver's licenses, both of which are in most states keyed to compulsory insurance. The text has, in some very tangible sense, become the individual (the property or life) it underwrites; the property or life exists, politically and legally, to enact what words say about it. Assistance, after the fact, is devalued as an ethical option; private insurance companies call the public into politics on their own terms. Other legal fictions threaten to overturn the very terms of "life," as when employers seek to reinterpret the "lifetime" clauses of pensions to refer not to the lives of the workers the pension contracts cover but to the contracts themselves.[50] Whether this occurs in the electoral process or the financial realm, the individual being forced to live by the scripts of a privatized notion of the collective remains ethically dubious. Locke or Rousseau might sadly admit that we live implicitly contracted lives of a very strange sort.[51]

What this subtending deconstruction suggests is the power of artifice to be coextensive with the material world of capitalized and commodified entities even as it serves to exclude much of it at the same time. Deconstructing underwriting helps us to view property and texts referencing one another with imaginative authority, requiring the ever-growing networks of text and value that define modern commercialism and governmentality. We see the channels of representation broadcast between two closely related cultural and social transponders: the bureaucracy of finance and coinage that has arisen in close step with a specific notion of the imagination as expressive and transcendent (and which has at times been oppositionally arrayed against money and capital). The creative imagination is of course as much a product of property relations and its methods as insurance contracts. Deconstructing their dispositions shows us how they were connected with such force, despite the uncertainty of their endurance through variable types of risk.

Literati feel more at home than do businessmen or lawyers in the face of material challenges to textual certainty. Authors and critics base their ceaseless reengagement with artifice and narrative in the foundations of technique, genre, and authenticity, not to mention marketability and (ever-diminishing) profit margins. That ease with trying to capture the world as it is born and dies—as it becomes and passes away, as it is captured and sold, as it is manufactured and consumed—may stem from the religious aspects of literary rituals, both thematic and structural. But what literature shares with the deconstructionist logic of insurance underwriting is an abiding fascination with the reversible terms of existence—whole worlds and lives made convincing and valuable, indeed "real," in the forge of falsity.[52]

When seen in this light, literary pursuits are complicit with the labors of destruction they seem to defy. Like insurance, literature occupies the space between loss and permanence, and the discourse of genius and timelessness appears to satisfy that uncertain liminality. The "literary" thus comes into view as a function of a strangely circumscribed authorial confidence. Unlike business and legal writing, literary writing understands not only its necessary silences and invisible foundations but also the recursive textual basis of loss. Perhaps the most "enduring" literature is precisely that work which recognizes the double-edged labor of preservation that loss compels us to undertake again and again.[53] One is reminded of Robert Frost's great poem "Mowing," in which the scythe—like the signature or the contract or the poem itself—becomes collusive in the making of meaning, even as it destroys what it seeks to harvest, the fruits of labor, property:

> There was never a sound beside the wood but one,
> And that was my long scythe whispering to the ground.
> What was it it whispered? I knew not well myself;
> Perhaps it was something about the heat of the sun,
> Something, perhaps, about the lack of sound—
> And that was why it whispered and did not speak.
> It was no dream of the gift of idle hours,
> Or easy gold at the hand of fay or elf:
> Anything more than the truth would have seemed too weak
> To the earnest love that laid the swale in rows,
> Not without feeble-pointed spikes of flowers
> (Pale orchises), and scared a bright green snake.
> The fact is the sweetest dream that labor knows.
> My long scythe whispered and left the hay to make.

An understanding of the inability of underwriting to make a final claim on a foundation in the discourses of commerce and law may reside in etymology. The word "underwriting"—in its various and related forms—has come to mean what might legalistically be called "assuring" functions, all stemming from the root of preservation/conservation: endorsing, signing, funding, supporting, subscribing. The history of the word tells the story of the shifting demands of authorship, of both the reader's and the writer's responsibility to written matter, through the evolution of early capitalism. And, perhaps more tellingly, it illustrates quite precisely the shifting claims of what might count as a foundation, an unseen but stabilizing structure, for property and texts.

"To underwrite" is a relatively old verb. The *Oxford English Dictionary* (*OED*) cites 1433 as the first instance of the use of "underwrite" in its most literal sense, "to write (words, figures, etc.) below something, especially after other written matter." The variation "underwritten" goes back even earlier, to the fourteenth century, when it signified a portion of writing to follow—essentially a kind of verbal punctuation, a protocolon: "Of words, statements, etc: Written (out), expressed in writing below or beneath: following upon, coming after, what is already written."

The first citation of "underwriting" as a term explicitly applied to insurance, in 1622, is also the first time the term implies a monetary obligation: "To subscribe (a policy of insurance), thereby accepting the risk of insurance." This definition arose from the archetypal public-sphere practice of underwriting ships at Lloyd's Coffee House, on London's Tower Street. A merchant interested in obtaining insurance on a ship or cargo would circulate a description of the property to be insured as well as the names of the captain and crew, the destination, and the amount of insurance desired. Those interested in insuring the property would affix their signatures or initials beneath the description, along with the amounts they would be willing to be liable for should the ship be lost.

Around this appearance, in which "underwriting" came to signify "insurance" in the early seventeenth century, a variety of auxiliary meanings sprung up concurrently, each adumbrating the sense of obligation and contractual warrant: "to confirm or agree by signature," "to guarantee to subscribe or contribute (a certain sum of money, etc.)," "to guarantee or agree in writing to *do something*." Underwriting may be said to gain its commercial meaning by linking up with the words "insurance," "assurance," and "ensurance" in the course of the eighteenth century. "Assurance" in particular is a word that embeds within its etymology a struggle between religious meaning, the long-sermonized "doctrine of assurance" which goes back to John Calvin, and its evolving commercial denotation of mutual insurance, which come to dominate its usage by the late eighteenth century (refer again to figs. 1, 2, and 3).[54]

The *OED* cites 1858 as the first appearance of the word "underwriting" as a descriptively linguistic term where "underwriting" becomes a figure for original and authentic text within multiply layered textuality: "Writing lying below other writing: the first writing in a palimpsest." Such a literalist and yet suggestive meaning encoded the power of underwriting (especially in the form of contracts and policies) to denote deeper indisputable values, to sustain the imagined values layered over it by subsequent revisions, additions, and conditions. It is not until the late nineteenth century that the term comes to mean a specific form of corporate financing, a backup funding consequent to the public sale of stock: "to agree to take up, in a new company or new issue (a certain number of shares if not applied for by the public)."

This expanded and loosened set of meanings derives from the work to be done by textual resources against the material fact of loss (or its possibility). These meanings reflect the fundamental condition that the earliest practice of underwriting, in all its nuances, was meant to counteract, that of loss. For its part, the word "loss" has undergone a subtle but crucial transformation in its meanings: as capitalism emerges and insurance underwriting develops, loss moves from denoting the simple privation of something already possessed to the depriving of something expected and even the possibility of a particular deprivation. This new sense of loss is more unpredictable, less hierarchically stable, and more agent-driven in its relationship to narrative. The new, expanded notion of loss means loss of opportunity, where "opportunity" is a story in it-self.

Adam Smith's rumination in *The Wealth of Nations* on the sinuous implica-tions of loss occurs when he is discussing the risks associated with buying or not buying insurance. For Smith, loss generates a ripple effect in the economic calculations of commercial actors.

That the chance of loss is frequently undervalued, and scarce ever valued more than it is worth, we may learn from a very moderate profit of insurers. In order to make insur-ance, either from fire or sea risk, a trade at all, the common premium must be sufficient to compensate the common losses, to pay the expense of management, and to afford such a profit as might have been drawn from an equal capital employed in any common trade. The person who pays no more than this evidently pays no more than the real value of the risk, or the lowest price at which he can reasonably expect to insure it. But though many people have made a little money by insurance, very few have made a great fortune; and from this consideration alone, it seems evident enough that the ordinary balance of profit and loss is not more advantageous in this than in other common trades by which so many people make fortunes. Moderate, however, as the premium of insur-ance commonly is, many people despise the risk too much to care to pay it. Taking the whole kingdom at an average, nineteen houses in twenty, or rather perhaps ninety-nine in a hundred, are not insured from fire. Sea risk is more alarming to the greater part of people, and the proportion of ships insured to those not insured is much greater. Many fail, however, at all seasons, and even in time of war, without any insurance. This may sometimes perhaps be done without any imprudence. When a great company, or even a great merchant, has twenty or thirty ships at sea, they may, as it were, insure one another. The premium saved upon them all may more than compensate such losses as they are likely to meet with in the common course of chances. The neglect of insurance upon shipping, however, in the same manner as upon houses, is, in most cases, the effect of no such nice calculation, but of mere thoughtless rashness and presumptuous contempt of the risk.[55]

Smith comes to rest on the idea that the new projective calculation of loss ne-cessitates insurance of all types. Modern loss represents a proleptic iteration of what one possesses in the present, and insurance attempts to bind that prolep-sis in a way that short-circuits older Jobean notions of hardship, loss, and pri-vation. Anticipated deprivation requires a new concept of the human capacity to define property and to project individual stories of ambition, success, and happiness.

Smith is not alone in noticing the difference and preaching the utility of thinking through human experience as an algorithm based in the avoidance of negative values. Jeremy Bentham's *An Introduction to the Principles of Morals and Legislation* (1781), with its anatomy of utility as a property foreboding plea-sure or pain, may be read too as a retheorizing of loss: "By utility is meant that property in any object, whereby it tends to produce benefit, advantage, pleasure, good, or happiness (all this in the present case comes to the same thing), or (what comes again to the same thing) to prevent the happening of mischief, pain, evil, or unhappiness to the party whose interest is considered."[56] Bentham goes on to suggest the following heuristic for assessing future harm:

Sum up all the values of all the *pleasures* on the one side, and those of all the pains on the other. The balance, if it be on the side of pleasure, will give the *good* tendency of the act upon the whole, with respect to the interests of that *individual* person; if on the side of pain, the *bad* tendency of it upon the whole. Take an account of the number of persons whose interests appear to be concerned; and repeat the above process with respect to each. . . . The same process is alike applicable to pleasure and pain, in whatever shape they appear: and by whatever denomination they are distinguished: to pleasure, whether it be called *good* (which is properly the cause or instrument of pleasure) or *profit* (which is distant pleasure, or the cause or instrument of, distant pleasure), or *convenience*, or *advantage, benefit, emolument, happiness*, and so forth: to pain, whether it be called *evil* (which corresponds to *good*), or *mischief*, or *inconvenience*, or *disadvantage*, or *loss*, or *unhappiness*, and so forth.

For both Smith and Bentham, loss is fully situated within a modern notion of time, stretching in individualized lines past and future, shaped by social status. As Smith says in *The Theory of Moral Sentiments* (1761), placing modern loss in the anxiety-plagued realm of personality and its reputation (as opposed to placing it in the body) makes for a new kind of anxiety and a new species of pain: "The person who has lost his whole fortune, if he is in health, feels nothing in his body. What he suffers is from the imagination only, which represents to him the loss of his dignity, neglect from his friends, contempt from his enemies, dependence, want, and misery, coming fast upon him; and we sympathize with him more strongly upon this account, because our imaginations can more readily mould themselves upon his imagination, than our bodies can mould themselves upon his body"(42).

I would argue that rather than a diminishing of the importance of the body in relation to loss, what Smith's shrewd analysis exemplifies is the degree to which the body was fully subsumed into the public-minded interests of underwritten integrity. Smith writes, "The frame of my body can be but little affected by the alterations which are brought about upon that of my companion: but my imagination is more ductile, and more readily assumes . . . the shape and configuration of the imaginations of those with whom I am familiar"(41). Smith's displacement of words like "ductile" and "shape" from body to mind is striking. The body is not dismissed but given a new "shape and configuration," that of the mind in public, with the future before it. In this sense, underwritten holdings—the commodity form that includes real (body, house, cargo) and narrativized (status, opportunity, reputation) properties—exemplify J. G. A.

Pocock's observation that, as a result of the conceptual transformations of the eighteenth century, property was now "understood to exist within a historical process."

⤳

As I've suggested, the narratological implications of underwriting as a cultural poetics may be inferred from its distinctive contractual meanings. Mary Poovey's *A History of the Modern Fact* helps us to see how unique underwriting rhetorical practices were, especially when viewed alongside the other major textual breakthrough of modern business practice—double-entry bookkeeping. Poovey's focus is on how the innovative relationship between double-entry bookkeeping and rhetoric in the seventeenth and eighteenth centuries inaugurated a new form of factual reference. In its work of disciplining and discriminating among "audiences based on rank, education, and social character" (38), Poovey demonstrates the important civil functions of rhetoric. If rhetoric "helped uphold the status levels that governed the distribution of power," it was then preserving the social function that Aristotle first identified, and that John Bender and David E. Wellbery have more recently affirmed: rhetorical arts settled property disputes.[57] The new facts supplied by double-entry bookkeeping performed much the same kind of function.

A similar relationship between the conservationist functions of rhetoric and double-entry bookkeeping may also be at work in the rhetorical development of underwriting businesses. Both double-entry bookkeeping and insurance underwriting share conservation of property as a founding principle; it is worth repeating that almost all of the pioneering underwriters of colonial Philadelphia and Boston were originally notaries. There is a symmetrical function at work in the new business discourses that pivoted on the idea of mathematical conservation; double-entry bookkeeping premises its authority on the resolution of a zero-sum scheme, just as insurance underwriting hovers artificially above the principle of additive inverses. One might be tempted to say that business culture, as it evolves through the seventeenth and eighteenth century, is an elaborate set of social practices performatively arranged on the foundations of the mathematical conservation of the "new fact."

But it is in the realm of performative significance that underwriting differs from double-entry bookkeeping. Whereas double-entry bookkeeping never succeeded in making merchants equal to university men or clerics, underwriting may have made the social step up for them. Underwriting achieved what double-entry bookkeeping could not, because underwriters managed to fulfill the epistemological and narratological demands of the promise of the "new fact." How was this accomplished? Accounting is (or at least strives to be) transparent and documentary in its tabulations. Bookkeeping casts its gaze always backward and, using the results of its findings, establishes the new facts as emblems of virtue and trust, to be held in confidence by prospective customers or business partners. Insurance underwriting, meanwhile, employs the nearly magical operations of the new science of probability and relies upon an iterative event that makes declarations asserting the fiction of conservation, over and against the transparent fact of loss or gain. Underwriting is like rhetoric in the classical sense because it is a formulaic form of writing that anticipates variables of experience; it is enforceable through time.

The insurance contract purports to act upon the past, the present, and especially the future, come what may. Underwriting resonates (in much the same way that rhetoric resonates as a social performance) among disputed or fundamentally altered property interests. As such, underwriting is that form of money which consists of a store of value, an indenture to be redeemed and completed in the future. In his essay on Benjamin's notion of the "mystical foundation of authority," Derrida cuts to the core of such iterative practices: "It belongs to the structure of fundamental violence that it calls for the repetition of itself and founds what ought to be conserved." In other words, a social investment is made in acts that confer sovereignty and authority upon individuals who seek an underwriting endorsement and who may then, in turn, supply an endorsement. Put simply: only those who are first socially "licensed" may proceed to underwrite property.

But the crucial difference between underwriting and double-entry bookkeeping arises from even more specific aspects of their practice: double-entry bookkeeping is "memorialized," past-centered writing that offers no guarantees ahead of itself—indeed, it resonates weakly, if at all, as a predictor of future performance. It is the platform upon which social license—marked as it is by individual status, trustworthiness, and finances—is constructed. But that construction cannot do more than function as a background. It requires the signature of underwriting to make a contracted claim into and about the future. With double-entry bookkeeping, virtue is never displaced absolutely by certainty, as it is in underwriting.

By contrast, underwriting projects its claim of virtue (conserving value) forward, and in its guarantee it affirms what is essentially virtuous about it. Noah Webster's argument for the inherent virtues of consolidating the American language is a prime exemplar of this idea. Ownership—as a result of this textual performance—will always be assured, and it is this effect which becomes the cardinal virtue of what Geoffrey Clark has called the age of the "demographic investment." Indeed, underwriting extends the ledger into the future and the domain of ethical action, literally making, by textual declaration of probable truths, the "demographic investment." Underwriting thus manages a thoroughly modern displacement in which scientific methods of knowing and monetary instruments supplant, in the name of bourgeois virtue, an unprovidential God and a malign fate.[58]

Another good example of this practical, formally textual development is in the warranties made on marine insurance contracts. In the late eighteenth century, Lord Mansfield (an important personage in my discussion of Wheatley's manumission struggle) was the main figure in the modernization of the concept of warranty that had held sway in English courts under English common law. Warranties were made, according to Edwin Patterson, into a specialized legal instrument that departs in important ways from the colloquial sense of the term as a "guarantee."[59] Patterson explains:

> In the eighteenth century, a warranty was inserted in a marine-insurance contract when the underwriter wished to make sure that a particular state of affairs, past, present, or future, would, as the case might be, either exist as a factor tending to reduce the probability of the occurrence of an insured event or would not exist as a factor tending to increase the probability of the occurrence of an insured event. The warranty, even when affirmative rather than negative, seeks to exclude potential causes of an insured event; the exception excludes certain actual causes of an insured event [273].

The warranty functions as a rhetorical narrowing of the extent of an underwriter's exposure. It does this by extending the terms of insurability, defining and conditioning the proper bounds of risk and probability undertaken by the insurer. The method for doing this draws on narratable experience, assuming possible future states and proceeding to derive causes and effects that may impinge on credibility and trust, and thus the kinds of actions a person might take.[60]

↜

"I am alive—because / I do not own a House—" writes Emily Dickinson in #470, condensing many kinds of nineteenth-century critiques of modernity.[61] Beyond the writers I engage in this book, the claims of underwriting are met again and again in other canonical figures of ante-bellum literature—think of Nathaniel Hawthorne's *House of the Seven Gables*, the textualized dramas of ownership in Edgar Allan Poe ("The Gold-Bug," "The Fall of the House of Usher," and so forth), Emily Dickinson's repeated tropic concern with the financed space of domesticity, Harriet Beecher Stowe's domestically-based social morality tales, the manumitting poetics of Frederick Douglass—all are interested somehow in underwriting counterclaims to legal property and its implied burdens of historical loss and prospective uncertainties.

Slavery, especially in the American context, is a crucial component of an account of the rise of underwriting. It is oddly fitting that the great age of insurance underwriting begins at about the same time the abolition movement takes hold. For better and worse, insurance conceptually pressed the limits of defining human personages and possessions. Slavery, for instance, began to be seen in England as an acute moral outrage partly because of the Zong incident of 1783, in which a ship captain threw his sick slave cargo overboard in order to collect on the insurance.[62] As Edwin Perkins has shown, life insurance began as an offshoot of marine underwriting, where, in a strange mirroring of slave insurance, important and wealthy passengers were insured in case of piracy and ransom.[63] In many ways, slavery, especially insofar as self-ownership and manumission challenge textual boundaries, has given momentous force to the underwriting I trace in this book.

So, while the issue of slavery is obvious and ever-present in the case of Phillis Wheatley, it is perceptibly at hand in the entire study. It remains a codifying and disruptive subtext, from Franklin to Webster and on to Emerson and Melville. While it arguably enabled the viability of the slave trade in the first place, slavery increasingly becomes a legal difficulty for insurance—at the same time the abolitionist movement adds momentum in the late eighteenth and early nineteenth centuries. Life insurance as a marketable commodity slowly gains acceptance in the mid-nineteenth century while the nation moves to violent conflict over the morality of human bondage and the relative merits of different models of national economic development. This congruence reveals a common interest beneath violent contentions. One aspect of economic hegemony on which Union and Confederate partisans could agree lay in the underwritten assurances drafted on property. Perhaps it will come as no surprise, either, to learn that Robert E. Lee and Abraham Lincoln concurred on the prudence of property insurance for their homes (through the same company, The Hartford), with the Civil War imminent.[64]

Our own era is risk-obsessed, undoubtedly because insurance is one of the dominant corporate enterprises of our age. The fixation is in keeping with the millennial mind-set.[65] At the so-called end of history, in an age of capital's unquestioned dominance, with the presumptive safety of digital realities, latex sex, and the hope of genetic secrets and their newly textualized and rationalized defects, we fancy ourselves capable of absolute security. The virtual realities that are created by digital technologies (which themselves entail coded uncertainties and viral exposures) promise a world of nonmaterial, reversible possibilities, where real-world chance can be exorcised in an erasable, or at least "risk-free," domain (simulation technology, hypercapital[66], and so forth). Gene therapy and genetic testing seem to ordain the possibility of defeating diseases and disorders which have plagued humanity for centuries. In this case, science, as it has since the seventeenth century, becomes an explicitly underwriting practice, where the body may be mapped to actuarial advantage. All its imperfections and "problems"—from the superficially cosmetic to the molecular—might be anticipated or reversed by a written model of the great anterior subject, human material. The Human Genome Project is the supreme aspiration of such underwriting.

But with the escalation of promises, with the hope of closing the door on risk, we only seem to widen our exposure to loss and failure. By the quirks of representation, as Emerson correctly bemoaned, exposure is increased, not reduced, in the proliferation of modernity's fail-safe, redundant simulacra. In our mania to silence the alarms of chance, we hear yet more threats and become more fearful. What is it about the logic of insurance, somewhere in the heart of the underwritten gesture from the seventeenth century, that ensures more, not less, risk—that detracts from the security of a life lived in peace? This question haunts the literary imagination, in some form, from the early moderns to the postmoderns.[67]

Finally, I want to provoke historically informed questions about the ethics of corporate insurance underwriting. Presuming to dictate the value of the individual and of socialized collectivities, the insurance industry has managed to colonize vast spaces of modern life with its founding promises. We should understand why this topic has evaded ideological inspection. Insurance, and its associated logic, have endured through what François Ewald has called two "paradigms," that of "responsibility," in the nineteenth century, and that of "solidarity," in the twentieth.[68] That logic (simply put, a manner of thinking associated with a mode of writing) is, however, adaptable to multiple ideologies, and perhaps this is due to the mediating functions of the poetics I discuss in this book. It is adapting in ominous ways to what Ewald suggests might be a new "security" paradigm. To decolonize economic life requires, first, an understanding of the reach and quality of its logic, which could lead, perhaps, to a revised notion of how democracy and ethics are produced and compromised by private and public texts. And such assessments may be thrown back on the value and ethics of writing as an engine of imaginative identity and liberation.

Is there a way of following the logic from its historical invention to the manic complexity of our own hypertextual, hyperterrorized world? Today the logic of underwriting is almost exclusively at the service of postindustrial capitalism, and it continues to cultivate a species of imaginative writing under that authority. But I think the stories I tell indicate that there may be other turns in store for the poetics of underwriting, that new gift economies (as in software) can underwrite social innovation, that accidents and destruction can be made providential by pointing us toward the commons. Can we work to an understanding of the socialization of risk and loss that is no longer driven by the colonizing fictions of money, or by the marketing of private desires? Can we reconstruct the socializing patterns of money and texts to meet our needs? Stevens's Faustian mind, embodied in the questions we are left with, writes us forward.

CHAPTER ONE

Philadelphia

Fear in Hand: The Friendly Society, the Philadelphia Contributionship, and Other Projects

> As I have not read any part of the life in question, but know only
> the character that lived it, I write somewhat at hazard. . . . Should
> [the autobiographical lessons] even prove unsuccessful in all that a
> sanguine admirer of yours hopes from them, you will at least have
> framed pieces to interest the human mind; and whoever gives a
> feeling of pleasure that is innocent to man, has added so much to
> the fair side of a life otherwise too much darkened by anxiety and
> too much injured by pain. In the hope, therefore, that you will lis-
> ten to the prayer addressed to you in this letter, I beg to subscribe
> myself, my dearest sir,
>> etc., etc.,
>
> Signed, BENJ. VAUGHAN.

Benjamin Franklin was afraid, and it is Vaughan who gives him away. Indeed, the *Autobiography* refuses to admit that Franklin worries at all, manifesting a tone and disposition contrary to what his "hazarding" correspondent, Benjamin Vaughan, called "anxiety." Yet one discerns in the odd concern of Vaughan's entreaty a real concern: that perhaps Franklin's answering bravado would address a shared anxiety Vaughan wanted dispelled. In his response to Vaughan's plea for words—a reply drawn from a mind capable of putting pleasure where anxiety had once reigned—Franklin means to describe anxiety's opposing guise. He will incarnate a cool comfort with the mutable, hazardous world.

The *Autobiography* went on to fulfill that prescription. It underwrites his life with a contract-like stability, all terms and conditions manipulable and each outcome strategically foreseeable. In Franklin's world there are no surprises; at any point in the narrative, the future is welcomed, as a reasonably predictable function of his ability to meet it with reason and virtue. In the bargain, he gained a surface of calm in the present. This glossed the world he inhabited as a projection of his own self-willed mastering of (indeed, his aversion to) financial chance and mortal danger.

Franklin has become both a famous construction (for the critical-minded) and an inimitable essence (in the popular imagination), portraying for his readers an easy rider jaunting through turbulent times.[1] Critically speaking, the absence of the admission of fear in his writing—indeed, the optimistic momentum of the story of his life and of his collected views on how to live life prudently—suggests a narrative strategy that has psychoanalytic sources. Socially, it indicates the crafting of a new practical response to that which might cause anxiety, if not existential terror, in the public he cared about and sought to define.

Starting with D. H. Lawrence, many critics and biographers have noted Franklin's fearless, perhaps superficial, pose.[2] Michael Zuckerman provides a collation of such commentary, observing that Franklin "gave himself so utterly to the public that sophisticated commentators have questioned whether he had any interior existence at all."[3] Zuckerman points to Herbert Liebowitz's remark that the *Autobiography* "contains no intimations of neurotic behavior, no dreams or nightmares, no crises of spirit" (446). That lack of interior reflection translated quite well into the prescriptive demands of his social individualism. Larzer Ziff has shown how Franklin's exteriority helped pave the way for a new poetics of an externalized, representing identity that set off an anxiety he did not share. H. W. Brands declares with some finality regarding Franklin's surface and direction: "It was part of Franklin's credo to look forever forward, to dwell not on the past but on the future" (155).[4]

But few have wondered what that interior life might comprise and how the exterior craftwork of optimism may be viewed as a product of the interior. The particulars of the memoir's composition reveal just how much the finished story diverges from the angst-ridden terms of its production. Yet when that examination happens, we begin to glimpse inwardly. In words that evoke his worry about impending death, Franklin responded to the continued proddings of his friend the mayor of Passy, Louis Guillaume le Veillard, for the completion of his autobiography: "But considering now the little remnant of life I have left, the accidents that may happen between this and October . . . I have come to the resolution to proceed in that work to-morrow, and continue it daily till finished, which, if my health permits, may be in the course of the ensuing summer" (quoted. in Max Farrand, *Benjamin Franklin's Memoirs: A Parallel Text Edition*, xxii). Franklin's health was rapidly deteriorating as he undertook the third part of the *Autobiography*; he suffered from gout, an extremely painful bladder stone, and in December 1787, he fell down some steps, an accident that sprained an ankle and left him badly bruised. He made out his will shortly thereafter. This urgency in completing the autobiography arises from both obligation to his correspondents and an appropriate fear of the chances of time.[5]

Franklin's lifelong obsession with copying—as both metaphor for the attainment of virtue and practical insurance against the loss of important documents—betrays his worry about the relationship between personal fortunes and physical loss. Using informal circulation as a method of textual preservation, Franklin habitually sent at least two fair copies of important letters and documents to friends. The *Autobiography* is itself the best example of this fixation. His grandson Benjamin Franklin Bache was instructed to make two fair copies of the unfinished manuscript just before his death and mail one to Vaughan and the other to Veillard. Fear of loss (which stands in interesting contrast to Thomas Jefferson's inveterate burning of manuscripts) drove Franklin to safety measures that preserved the meaning of his life to the "rising generation."

The question of fear emerges critically, then, from a psychoanalytic intuition about Franklin's interior life and points beyond to the compositional methods and sociocultural contexts of Franklin's life. Other questions follow: How did Franklin manage to fashion such good-natured self-assurance out of the late-Calvinist culture of malevolent fearmongering in which he was reared. And how did he keep that optimism amidst the increasingly risk-obsessed society he sought to build?[6] As these questions would seem to imply, I do not claim in what follows to pursue a psychoanalytic discussion, laying bare Franklin's interior life. Rather, it is a series of readings that elicit a view of interior perturbations and represented assurances, a socializing preoccupation, based on what is ostensibly denied us as readers of Franklin.[7]

⌒

This chapter is also about the getting and losing of money, in keeping with the primary concerns of commercial underwriting. To discuss Ben Franklin's relationship to money has long been an obvious move. His fame, the most lasting effect of his representative self, is bound up in the modern story of money, and it has been told in many places and within many contexts. He was a major influence, beginning as early as 1729, in the debates surrounding the American colonies' decisions to adopt paper currency. And, as Max Weber famously contended, Franklin's moralisms about the "way to wealth" became the earliest cultural broadcasts of the doctrine associated with the post-Puritan capitalist work ethic. Finally (but not conclusively), Franklin capitalized persistently on his inventions and publications—he made a good sum of money during his life.

Yet the relationship between Franklin's musings on money and the specter of material uncertainty that the Enlightenment seemed determined to counter has gone largely unremarked. That is, Franklin and the idea of money and capital are used to demonstrate the telos of business ethics in American—indeed, global—culture without examining the strain placed on capital's triumph by the fact of loss. Franklin's view of money is seen as the pretext and model for the wave of individualism and capitalist dominance that was soon to break upon American cultural and business practices. Usually, the extent of the analyses runs to the level of the personal as a way to explore something else that only followed as an identifiable type later in history—that is, the work ethic. Or the investigations focus on the self-interest of a colonial printer, the inventor, someone who is discursively bound to the rules of capitalist practice (even as he is scripting them). Rarely is Franklin's relationship to money framed as an opportunity to learn more about American financial culture's emergence from the husk of virtue and the kernel of anxiety.[8] More unusual still is an examination of how Franklin the philanthropist was a product of Franklin the lone agent, or of how fearless self-interest carried deep postulates about the public good.[9]

For Franklin, fear—along with every other reaction to experience—is keyed to an optimistic faith in virtuous action. Without that faith, it would seem sensible that one *must* be beset by anxiety. Thus Franklin the optimist is also Franklin the man of virtue, and both personae are products of a lifelong experiment with chance. To understand the fate of virtue and action in a world promising both liberty and chaos (psychic, social, and natural) would be to test nothing less than the success of social progress under the new, often disordered, commercial ethos. If virtue depended on order, then the connection must be accounted for, underwritten by a rational textual device whenever possible. Thus I would suggest that Franklin, at some level, had to acknowledge and understand the problem of fear and, perhaps more important, become expert in learning how to contain and deflect its most debilitating personal and social effects. One way to accomplish this control, a way that was new but increasingly available to young men in early-eighteenth-century Boston, was to advocate for the practice and theory of public underwriting, especially insurance.

Which is precisely what Franklin did. In one of his earliest published pieces—written under the pseudonym Silence Dogood, and published in his brother James's *New England Courant* for the week of August 6, 1722—Franklin proposes a method of social underwriting based on a primitive form of life insurance. "Dogood" had been offering her opinions on a range of topics, from elegiac poetry to the merits of free speech, for about four months in the *Courant*.

The subject of the article served at least two superficial but telling purposes.[10] The first was to assault the presumed benevolence of the Puritan establishment with a non–clerically derived system of public/private social assurance that avoided the criteria of religious virtue in bestowing its benefits. The second aim was to buttress the authority of Dogood as a true widow writing on topics of interest to widows. Derived from the tontine of Italian (followed by French and then English) underwriting fame (Dogood claims to have learned of the tontine from "a Book" by an "ingenious Author," Defoe of *An Essay upon Projects*), the scheme was meant to benefit widows whose husbands had left them with little or no means of financial support.[11]

The ostensible concern in the tract is to keep the responsibility for providing for the city's destitute widows and their children from falling under the purview of the "Inferior Clergy, or of Shopkeepers and Artificers" (*Papers*, vol. 1, 33).[12] Instead of these patently unsystematic and ill-equipped—if not corrupt—methods of public relief,[13] Franklin asks us to

Suppose an Office to be Erected, to be call'd *An Office of Ensurance for Widows*, upon the following Conditions;

Two thousand Women, or their Husbands for them, Enter their Names into a Register to be kept for that purpose, with the Names, Age, and Trade of their Husbands, with the Place of their abode, Paying at the Time of their Entring 5s. down with 1s. 4d. per quarter, which is to the setting up and support of an Office with Clerks, and all proper Officers for the same; *for there is no maintaining such without charge;* they receive every one of them a Certificate, Seal'd by the Secretary of the Office, and Sign'd by the Governors, for the Articles hereafter mentioned [*Papers*, vol. 1, 33].

If and when one of the subscribers becomes a widow (provided that at least six months have elapsed from the date of her subscription) she files a claim and receives 500*l*. With the valuable assurance of an underwritten future, each woman would be obligated (but eager and happy) to pay a monthly premium in order to remain a good member in standing of the "society." There were two further eligibility standards, one related to a crude actuarial accounting and the other to a concept of social fairness, if not communal virtue. First, no sailors' or soldiers' wives would be allowed membership, owing to the extreme riskiness, or what Dogood euphemistically calls "the contingencies," of their husbands' employment. Second, no widow would be paid out who was left more than L2000 in her husband's will after clearing all debts, since the society was meant to "aid the poor, not add to the rich" (*Papers*, vol. 1, 34).

The question of eligibility, not to mention credibility and mutual trust, becomes a topic of great concern to Franklin.[14] He worries that women might be tempted to murder their husbands or cunningly marry older men sure to die imminently. Wills may also "be defrauded" to aid in collection and, in this way, would effectively "add to the rich." Thus trust has a close functional relation to a kind of commercial fear. The critical nexus between trust and the legal apprehension about fraud is ideally based in the all-purpose redemption offered by individual virtue: good women (and/or their husbands) will not attempt such fraud. But this is not enough for a proper underwriting enterprise, since the collective mutual trust presupposed by the voluntary nature of the friendly society cannot be undermined in any way by the possibility of unfair exposure. To this concern he has no answer but to be watchful and/or disallow such summer/winter marriages to be subscribed. Virtue, then, may be contractually accounted for, thus eliminating the worry about illegitimate underwriting.

Another objection he anticipates is that there appears to be no apparent "compulsion" to pay the premium. To this he answers that any compulsion to pay is, in reality, self-originating; in other words, it is utterly "voluntary," a kind of self-philanthropy that is entirely Franklinian in its hybridized "invisible hand" assertion that collective wealth can be generated by private interest. Interestingly, the payment of the premium may be viewed as a negative form of grace. Indeed, the whole scheme may be read as a counterdoctrine to the Calvinist conception of grace, which is, in effect, randomized though tantalizingly symbolized through possible tokens of predetermined election. In this context, grace takes on a distinctly Weberian bearing; it is a kind of capital, both producible and consumable. For Franklin, as early as the 1720's, virtue is both capital and product in the manufacturing of underwritten insurance against loss of life.

Even more to the point of underwriting seen as a procedure that contributed to the virtuous shape of property and its defining texts, Franklin's public presence in print is critical to understanding his scheme. Franklin was responding to a culture as much as he was innovating within it, and thus his underwriting media are polemically driven by an antipathy to the discursive limits imposed by Calvinism. Achieved through pseudonymic play, his countering rhetorical mask is worth exploring, since his newfound authority is crucial to describing the efficacy of subscription, persuasion, and trust.

The name Silence Dogood resonates with the concept of the Friendly Society in several productive ways. At its most obvious, it is a rebuke to internalized and austere notions of good work that continued to hold sway among early-eighteenth-century Bostonians. Indeed, the name may well be part of a counterargument to at least three of Cotton Mather's sermons from the previous decade. The first and most famous, *Bonifacius: An Essay upon the Good* (1710), is a much brighter, more proactive, and less angst-provoked piece on "doing good" than the later, more pertinent sermon of 1714, titled *Pascentius: A very brief essay upon the methods of piety, wherein people in whom the difficulties of the times have caused anxieties, May have a comfortable assurance of being at all times comfortably provided for.*[15]

The last of the apposite Mather essays is *Silentiarius: A brief Essay on the*

Holy Silence and Godly Patience, that Sad things are to be Entertained Withal, published in 1721, just before Franklin began writing his Silence Dogood columns.[16] Prompted by the deaths of Mather's daughter Abigail Willard and her infant child, it is a moving sermon on how personal loss can be converted to pious understanding. Beginning with the injunction that it is our biblical duty to hold our peace, he proceeds to break the peace in arguing for a pious reaction to Jobean hardship. In the end, though, there is no "device of good" (as he puts it in *Bonifacius*) that might be followed in reacting to the loss. Only silence. Anxiety will have to be voiced only by those with the status of Mather himself, and then only to counsel more silence.

For Mather, anxiety is an emotion that must be subjected to faith-derived cognitive will. Indeed, anxiety as a kind of affective deformation can be fixed by the resolution of a mind determined not to feel it. One does this tautologically, as it were, by resigning from dwelling on the material hardships of a life and redirecting such worries to the determination to "do good." Mather, interestingly, casts the affliction with public health consequences. Starting out with the scientific determination of a "physician" seeking to diagnose and cure the "epidemic" of psychological disturbance, Mather is sympathetic but clear in his task: "The distemper which I have under cure, is, the fear of want; a fear lest we shall not know how to live; a fear, lest thro' difficulties growing upon us, we shall not be able to live credibly or honestly among our neighbours; a fear, lest the means of our subsistence failing, we shall not be able to shift for living in the world." Mather's prescription for such disease is simple: "First. Our duty in hard times, is to trust in the lord, and to do good." What it means to "do good" for Mather is truly coextensive with "trust in the lord." God will assure such "do-gooding" with bread. Interestingly, Mather ends his essay by hinting that the day will soon come when enterprising young men like Franklin will take up the connection between material want and spiritual faith:

I do assure you, Your Compassionate Saviour will shortly shew you His Way, and will surely put you into a Right Way; and for the sake of a Number that are very dear unto Him here, the whole Country shall yet be most graciously Provided for. The most Likely Course to Sin away this Provision, and to defeat all Good Expectations, will be for People to go on in that Course of most Vile Extortion, in which there seems to be a General Purpose of our People to grow . . . upon One another. But our Good GOD, will put it into the Hearts of some Significant Persons, who aim at the Doing of Good, e're long to bring it about, that the Prizes of Necessaries may be brought under some regulation and Limitation, and the Wayes of the Oppressor shall have some Restraint upon them. GOD and His People will Bless those Happy Instruments [32–33].

Franklin's response to Mather announces a contrastingly willful and playful sense of virtuous action that "brings about . . . the Prizes of Necessaries" through "Happy Instruments."[17] For Franklin, displaying will in the face of bad luck and loss is not simply a matter of reasserting the goodness of God but of shifting authority and forging the possibility of rational blame—bringing it back to earth, as it were. The humility of virtuous action is transformed in both the nomenclature of the author and in the function of the Friendly Society itself. Doing good is now a matter of enterprising announcement, but subjected to the conditions of irony, satire, and contentious debate in a print forum. Doing good now had a "device of good."

Seen more specifically within the poetics of underwriting, Franklin's first pseudonym effects an intriguing species of announcement that is intricately bound up in the problem of loss. The Dogood Papers series begins on a pessimistic note that throws the pseudonym into the highly charged context of fortune and gender, for earlier in the series Dogood recounts how her "entrance into this troublesome world was attended by the death of my father, a misfortune, which tho' I was not then capable of knowing, I shall never be able to forget. . . . Thus was the *first day* which I saw, the *Last* that was seen by my Father; and thus was my disconsolate Mother at once made both a Parent and a Widow" (*Papers*, vol. 1, 9–10). Though young Silence still had a mother, she was bound over to a foster home and only later learns of the death of that mother. She loses her husband and is left to raise three children alone. Note, then, the conditions of his arrival in print: Franklin's appearance as a female character born of loss is premised on the very notion of loss that occasions the Friendly Society proposal. As such, he places himself in the shoes of one who would be most likely to feel the anxiety of financial and personal hardship that Mather advises on in *Silentarius* or *Pascentius*.

Hence the name "Silence Dogood" is an odd slogan of underwriting. It is a pairing of terms that signals a paradoxical entrance into both the world of print discourse and the world in which bad things befall us and, as a result of the misfortune, we begin to express ourselves. Moreover, in contrast to Mather's reactive sense of silence, Silence Dogood proposes the end of silence, as a prelude to doing good itself. Underwriting this entrance with an array of socially disruptive yet resourceful deflections from the straight narrows of Mather's world, Franklin makes his persona a tangle of conflicts already mediated: with pseudonymity, with gender-switching seeming to de-authorize masculine authority, with the influential echo of Addison and Steele's *Spectator* and *Tatler* (they had written detailed descriptions of the commercial scene at Lloyd's Coffee House twice, once in 1710 and again in 1711), and with a churlish slap at Puritanical piety in the sense of "do-gooding."[18]

Beyond this set of deflections (or intensifiers), Franklin's persona may be read as a name for the symbolically derived written encounter with social uncertainty itself, an encounter that was overly trumpeted by Puritan elders like

Mather as a question of submitting to exterior sovereignty (God) on questions of luck. Mather's advice begs tautological channeling of the force of individual action as always good—it is hard not to do good when there is but one direction to follow.

By contrast, "Silence Dogood" may be read as a device that efficiently offers us the pluralism of modern ethics—there is more than one way to do good. It does this by punning, oscillating between commonsense interpretations that may extend in multiple directions. Such indeterminacy affords pleasurable interpretive possibilities within the anxiety-inducing domain of chance. Indeed, the pseudonym—it is either noun and noun/verb or verb and then noun—encodes the moral "white noise" arising from the anarchy of needy lives. If it is the latter (where one *silences* a do-gooder), the act of silencing is conflicted and unstable, a method of self-effacement that sees peculiar power in its own disfiguring mutation, suggesting even a kind of hostility to "do-gooding." If it is the former (where one *is* a silent do-gooder) then it is no less ironic, since the very act of naming it renders the silent virtue no longer *silent*.

In either case, Franklin creates space for a new kind of authority.[19] "Underwriting" happens at manifold levels in Franklin's soberly proposed "real" underwriting scheme. To underwrite oneself in such obviously ironic and negative ways is to inaugurate a peculiarly businesslike style of understatement or neutrality. Here is a quality of self-effacement, noted by recent scholars,[20] which serves well the underwriting ambition. That ambition in turn seeks to deprive the social and material preservations made possible by print capitalism of the taint of individual human agency (fear, need) even as it takes that agency to new heights of efficacy and power.

Thus the appeal of "silent do-gooding." Underwriting in the new commercial sphere is apt to appear as silently good. Such business/writing is a precursor, as I've already suggested, to the invisible hand of Adam Smith's market. Smith's famous passage defines the indeterminate, causally anti-intuitive conditions for individual action that the Silence Dogood papers promoted:

He generally, indeed, neither intends to promote the public interest, nor knows how much he is promoting it. By preferring the support of domestic to that of foreign industry, he intends only his own security; and by directing that industry in such a manner as its produce may be of the greatest value, he intends only his own gain, and he is in this, as in many other cases, led by an invisible hand to promote an end which was no part of his intention. Nor is it always the worse for the society that it was no part of it. By pursuing his own interest he frequently promotes that of the society more effectually than when he really intends to promote it. I have never known much good done by those who affected to trade for the public good. It is an affectation, indeed, not very common among merchants, and very few words need be employed in dissuading them from it [*Wealth of Nations*, book 4, chap. 2].

In his underwriting projects, Franklin discerns this fundamental narrative of cause and effect, pursued by recessed ambition—a tacitly self-interested form of action that promotes, as Smith puts it, "only his own security." Moreover, by the suggestive terms of Smith's antitheological political economy, underwriting amounts to an omnipotent act in a time of an increasingly irrelevant God. The emergent power of texts and materialism allows men, not God, to design new circuits of social welfare; contra Mather, such goodness derives from the interests and actions of individuals. But perhaps more important than the theological, providential resonance in the connection between Smith and Dogood is the sense that both are promoting the inherent political morality of economic action.

The name "Silence Dogood" plays shrewdly with uncertainty—about virtue, about the ambiguity of identity, and about the contingencies of life that may require more "do-gooding."[21] In its relationship to that inextricably Franklinian topic, money and its value, "do-gooding" strains our credulity without severing the tethers of trust. The term "do-good" seems out of character, implying a disinterested act of individual charity that operates irrespective of monetary loss or opportunity cost. But of course it is not. What Silence Dogood's scheme illustrates so well is the onset of Franklin's quest to devise a method of representing the individual and his social interests so that he may sidestep misfortune. In his first underwriting, a distinctly Franklinian public comes into view.

Unde Malum? Misfortune and Money

About three years after the publication of the Silence Dogood papers, Franklin published "A Dissertation on Liberty and Necessity," what he would call in the *Autobiography* an "erratum." It is here that Franklin continues to mine the philosophical vein of anxiety and metaphysical uncertainty that seemed to have been of great interest in his early years. Larson cites this as the starting point for early Franklinian pessimism, and perhaps it is this self-consciousness of its running counter to his optimism that accounts for Franklin's view of the essay as a mistake.[22] The essay is radical in its logical rejection of the possibility for human virtue in the face of "uneasiness"—especially those painful external accidents that life incurs. (Larson claims that Franklin goes on to reject this view in the *Autobiography*.)

When seen as a further response to Mather's *Pascentius*, however, the essay secures virtue as a device that only seems pessimistic in its harsh determinism. Read in light of his unfolding and somewhat relentless method of underwriting fear, Franklin's pessimistic virtue here is but a necessary step to real earthly optimism, a way of shaking chance free from heaven's grasp. In the essay, Franklin sets about proving a series of propositions about the nature of God and the universe that lead inevitably to an Arminian discussion about the nature of evil and misfortune:

V. *If he is all-powerful, there can be nothing either existing or acting in the Universe* against or without *his consent; and what He consents to must be good, because He is good; therefore* Evil *doth not exist.*

Unde Malum? Has been long a question, and many of the learned have perplex'd themselves and Readers to little purpose in answer to it. That there are both things and actions to which we give the name of *Evil*, is not here deny'd, as *pain, sickness, want, theft, murder, &c.* but that these and the like are not in reality *evils, ills, or defects* in the order of the universe, is demonstrated in the next section, as well as by this and the following proposition. Indeed, to suppose any thing to exist or be done, contrary to the will of the almighty, is to suppose him not almighty; or that something (the cause of evil) is more mighty than the almighty; an inconsistence that I think no one will defend: And to deny any thing or action, which he consents to the existence of, to be good, is entirely to destroy his two Attributes of *Wisdom* and *Goodness* [*Papers*, vol. 1, 59–60].

Such radical restriction of individual free will is somewhat unremarkable. But he goes on to employ an argument about the intertwined roles of uncertainty, probability, and liberty to show why this limitation upon free will is logically consistent. It would be impossible, he reasons, to calculate the best moves to securing good fortune—the only computer capable of making the intricate calculus is God:

In order to know which is best to be done, and which not it is requisite that we should have on view all the intricate consequences of every action with respect to the general order and scheme of the universe, both present and future; but they are innumerable and incomprehensible by any thing but omniscience. As we cannot know these, we have but as one chance to ten thousand, to hit on the right action; we should then be perpetually blundering about in the dark, and putting the scheme in disorder; for every wrong action of a part, is a defect or blemish on the order of the whole. Is it not necessary then, that our Actions should be over-ruled and govern'd by an all-wise providence? [*Papers*, vol. 1, 62]

According to Franklin, it is "uneasiness" which characterizes the condition of human consciousness; indeed, it is its precondition. Organic life needs pain and uneasiness to be life itself. He goes so far as to call it "beautiful in its place." Taking the point further, uneasiness becomes the genesis of "desire"—the desire to be free from pain and the desire for more pleasure.

This becomes the basis for a peculiar method of sociological analysis derived in many important ways from Hobbesian human modeling, which is meant to separate the appearance of affective reactions like misery and unhappiness from the generalized reality of social misfortune (after all, the socially fortunate are often miserable).[23] But the significance of Franklin's approach goes even further than analytic separation. Fear, of uncertainty and social ruin, need not be linked with anything remotely having to do with reality:

And here let it be observ'd, that we cannot be proper judges of the good or bad fortune of others; we are apt to imagine, that what would give us a great uneasiness or a great satisfaction, has the same effect upon others: we think, for instance, those unhappy, who must depend upon charity for a mean subsistence, who go in rags, fare hardly, and are despis'd and scorn'd by all; not considering that custom renders all these things easy, familiar, and even pleasant. When we see riches, grandeur and a chearful countenance, we easily imagine happiness accompanies them, when oftentimes 'tis quite otherwise: Nor is a constantly sorrowful look, attended with continual complaints, an infallible indication of unhappiness. In short, we can judge by nothing but appearances, and they are very apt to deceive us [*Papers*, vol. 1, 67–68].

Critics have treated such theorizing as an aberration predating Franklin's concerted life of commerce, indeed as a contrary point (his admitted "erratum") against which Franklin later modified his views. But there is a way of reading this as entirely consistent with Franklin's economy of virtue (again, he regretted only the publishing, not the writing). For if appearances are unreliable, if God is the grand matrix for determining chance, then the best we can do is to ignore them and proceed as if the question of misfortune is entirely irrelevant. The true sources of evil are merely rhetorical, offering opportunities for the astute actor to strengthen his virtues in the midst of a tumultuous world. From such purging pessimism springs its powerful opposite, the optimism that Franklin saw as desire, now released from its dreary original conditions of pain and fear.

Life Is a Kind of Chess

There is another pretext worth looking at, his essay "The Morals of Chess" (1750). A source of lessons about the conditions and consequences for rhetorical forays, chess offers a metalesson, emblematizing the kind of precautioned optimism that governs Franklinian action. Two sides deploy differentially empowered forces, making intricately strategized moves in the hopes of vanquishing the other. Surprise in chess calls on the ideas of misfortune and anxiety only to tactically contain them. In the playing of the game, a premium is placed on the element of surprise, whether in the ability to stage it deliberately in an attack or to parry it in defense. Finally, chess portends the possibility of losing, and what one should do in its eventuality.

Franklin's essay offers a somewhat sporting version of his otherwise realistic battle with misfortune and the bad turns of strategic design. He writes that the game of chess is not merely an idle amusement; several very valuable qualities of the mind, useful in the course of human life, are to be acquired and strengthened by it, so as to become habits ready on all occasions; for life is a kind of chess, in which we have often points to gain, and competitors or adversaries to contend with, and in which there is a vast variety of good and ill events, that are ... the effect of prudence or the want of it.

By analogy, life is not merely a machine, nor a theological narrative of souls, nor even just a battle, but a game combining elements of all the above, played most effectively one to one. The game dictates a set of adversarial strategies that produce in turn a small universe of possible outcomes. Approached in this way, a complete life strategy becomes paramount. Virtue is less a matter of playing by the rules than of understanding them to one's advantage. And what really distinguishes Franklin's metaphor is the sense that chess is instructive because it models strategic thinking that is obsessed with danger, foreseen and unforeseen.

In characteristic fashion, Franklin is able to make of this observation a systematic and enumerated proviso. Franklin writes, "By playing at chess we may learn:

1st. Foresight, which looks a little into futurity, and considers the consequences that my attend an action ...

2nd. Circumspection, which surveys the whole chessboard, or scene of action:—the relation of several pieces, and their situations; the dangers they are repeatedly exposed to: the several possibilities of their aiding each other; the probabilities that the adversary may make this or that move, and attack this or that piece; and what different means can be used to avoid his stroke, or turn its consequences against him ...

3rd. Caution, not to make our moves too hastily. This habit is best acquired by observing strictly the laws of the game; such as, if you touch a piece you must move it somewhere; if you set it down, you must let it stand. ...

Franklin's strategic advice is as much the adoption of an attitude as prescription for advance. Restraint, caution, awareness—these are tools to master defeat and danger; they are not just matters of style and confidence.

Above all, when defeat and danger arise, as they inevitably do, one must maintain balance. Franklin acknowledges the inexorability of bad luck, and the appearance of a "bad ... state of affairs." But, as with "A Dissertation on Liberty and Necessity," Franklin is keen to dispel the notion that appearances account for the real condition of life, for appearances are but a snapshot, a moment divorced from the narrative possibilities that extend into the future:

And, lastly, We learn by Chess the habit of not being discouraged by present bad appearances in the state of our affairs: the habit of hoping for a favourable chance, and that of persevering in the search of resources. The game is so full of events, there is such a variety of turns in it, the fortune of it is so subject to vicissitudes, and one so frequently, after contemplation, discovers the means of extricating one's self from a supposed insurmountable difficulty, that one is encouraged to continue the contest to the last, in hopes of victory from our skill; or, at least, from the negligence of our adversary: and whoever considers, what in Chess he often sees instances of, that success is apt to produce presumption and its consequent inattention, by which more is afterwards lost than was gained by the preceding advantage, while misfortunes produce more care and attention, by which the loss may be recovered, will learn not to be too much discouraged by any present successes of his adversary, nor to despair of final good fortune upon every little check he receives in the pursuit of it.

This may be the most eloquent reply we find anywhere in Franklin to Mather's chin-up pessimism. In contrast to Mather's essays, agency in Franklin's essay is fully restored to the chess-playing actor, even though it may seem that one's adversary is "insurmountable." The idea that bad or good fortune still awaits is enough to keep one in the game. Despair is no option.[24]

The moral is put on written display in the *Autobiography* when Franklin discusses the death of his first son, Franky. It is squeezed, as it were, between seemingly more important strategic moves—an account of one of his first returns to Boston and a description of the Junto:

In 1736 I lost one of my sons, a fine boy of four years old, by the small-pox, taken in the common way. I long regretted bitterly, and still regret that I had not given it to him by inoculation. This I mention for the sake of parents who omit that operation, on the supposition that they should never forgive themselves if a child died under it; my example showing that the regret may be the same either way, and that, therefore, the safer should be chosen [Lemay and Zall, *The Autobiography of Benjamin Franklin*, 99].

Whatever Franklin may have truly felt with regard to the loss of his first and then only son, he has employed a dissociative rhetoric to talk about it in his autobiography.[25] There is something notably callous (and pitiable) about this embedding of personal tragedy into a discourse on public health; expressiveness is not to be found, but rather a rhetorical cushioning move. Franklin had no ability to account for sentiment. At least Mather acknowledged the presence of emotions that, regrettably, incite moral devaluation; Franklin sidesteps the matter. Such narration seems entirely in keeping with the methods of coping with misfortune that Franklin had been cultivating since he was sixteen.

Such lack of sympathy stands in marked contrast, as we will see in chapter 5, to Emerson's treatment of the loss of his son Waldo, or even to Wheatley's commissioned expressions of sympathy for eminent Bostonians. The difference is partly historical as well as one of temperament: for Franklin's pre-Romantic rationalism, loss is an occasion for strategy, and perhaps the rhetoric of deflection he exhibits above best expresses that; for Emerson, such personal loss is a profound call to self-reexamination and interiority. Interestingly and, I think, not inconsequentially for my larger argument about the cultural logic of insurance, Emerson comes around to a more Franklinian position later in life.

As he represents it here, Franklin's loss of a son was mostly a lesson about safety rather than a staring into the face of existential angst or a cosmic emblem of his own errors (as it would be for Emerson). It is as well a warning between progressive steps of life's journey and thus consonant with the strategies of chess, of widows' insurance, of the "Dissertation." The three essays—the Do-good paper, the "Dissertation," and "The Morals of Chess"—comprise a sort of completed jeremiad, a form of Bercovitch's optimistic social criticism that mandated improvement in the act of its very announcement, in the diagnosis it refutes and replaces, and in the new rules it prescribes.[26]

Lotteries

Luck, fear of misfortune, individual agency—thinking through and writing about such concepts was not enough to realize a healthy public. Franklin needed to act upon his strategies. Franklin's work to fund hospitals and fire pre-vention, often through organizing of lotteries, testifies to this. Lotteries com-bine elements of need, luck, and self-interest, catalyzing an endowment of pub-lic virtue. In Philadelphia, lotteries were used throughout the second half of the eighteenth century to transform "private" speculation into "public" benefit—roads, bridges, wharves, military batteries;[27] nearly all the components of what we now call "infrastructure" were, in some crucial sense, the products of the al-lure of good fortune—incentive public financing.[28]

There is a historical and conceptual relationship between insurance and lot-teries. Both public and private lotteries may be understood as existing along the same continuum as insurance companies. Ruwell points out that the "first American marine insurance company began as a speculative venture for a life insurance lottery, a tontine" (44).[29] Geoffrey Clark puts this relationship in terms of speculation and prudence:

[E]fforts to understand in formal economic terms why people can commonly be found both gambling *and* taking out insurance have been notably unilluminating. In fact, gam-bling and insurance need not be regarded as naturally antithetical but can appear as dif-ferent manifestations of the same basic aspiration for social security or financial ad-vancement. This point is often lost amidst the incomprehension with which some historians have greeted the mixed prudential and speculative motives so obvious in the eighteenth-century insurance market [23].

Barry Supple has also noted the "mixed motives" arising from common aleatory sources: "Insurance combines elements of gambling and of certainty—speculative hazard and the reduction or even elimination of chance by using the predictability of 'random' occurrences in large numbers of instances."[30] François Ewald has demonstrated that gambling and insurance only separated with the advent of an "insurance imaginary" meant to rationalize and make disinterested the new form of life insurance.[31]

The earliest forms of life insurance products (derived from Italian Renaissance tontines) were structured as lotteries. Within these schemes the chance of collecting was determined by the longevity of the subscribers. Writing about English regulation of life insurance, Clark asserts that the common and distinguishing link between gaming and insuring lay in the possibilities and blindnesses of aleatory science: "If the distinguishing feature of an insurance policy as opposed to a gamble is taken to be the presence of an insurable interest, which creates a capacity for loss, then the question of whether a given policy of insurance has an indemnifying or a speculative function rests on the *measurement* of that interest" (23).[32] It was life insurance, the underwriting that explicitly made human lives into valuable commodities, which finally set the relative ethical merits of insurance underwriting into the realm of political remedy and judicial consideration.

The attempt to manage risk by developing the science of statistical probabilism was a breakthrough for public modes of financing because it placed within reach a rational system of floating monetary credit and raising funds for massive projects based on numerical projections. Both insurance underwriting and lotteries share, along with a common genealogy in aleatory sciences, a similarly anomalous relationship with the emerging ideas of the public and private spheres. Lotteries encouraged individuals to chance their interest in a relatively accountable (because governmentally sanctioned) method of public development, allowing us to view the public sphere as a product of the circumscribed social text of chance. Through lotteries and insurance underwriting, the foundations of urban colonial life became profitable and secure.

Socializing private wealth had the allure of appearing voluntary; it still does. Insurance and lotteries challenge our received notions of the compulsory obligations of the discreetly bounded public sphere. As I suggested at the outset, Franklin also forces us to revise our sense of the distinctness of public virtue and private interest.[33] Franklin saw this as an opportunity to intervene in the print marketplace with a new concept of originality—driven by chance and prudent investment. It was driven instead by the events of life, as they occurred day to day. Franklin "owned" the eventualities of social life and redistributed them to the public in this way.

Franklin's "Proposals relating to the Education of Youth in Pensilvania" (1749) begins its advertisement to the reader this way: "It has long been regretted as a Misfortune to the Youth of this Province, that we have no ACADEMY. . . ." The public dimension of misfortune is primary. Indeed, the question of fortune as it relates to selling and credibility is everywhere in this document, consisting of two separate textual arguments. One is the ostensible plan to fund and build an academy or university that would take responsibility for providing a liberal arts education to young Pennsylvanians. The other is classic underwriting, in the mode of providing support, endorsement, and credibility to rectify and complete the void placed upon the city by "regrettable misfortune."

The year 1751 was remarkably productive for Franklin's underwriting the new public worry about loss and misfortune. It became apparent that Philadelphia was in need of a hospital to care for the growing numbers of sick who could not be attended to by the almshouse and/or lazaretto. Dr. Thomas Bond was the first to solicit funding but met with little success until Franklin was enjoined. Once on board, Franklin "not only subscrib'd to it [himself], but engag'd heartily in the design of Procuring subscriptions from others" (*Papers*, vol. 4, 109).[34] They had no trouble raising the money, reminding contributors that the commonwealth would match their donation. This scheme gave Franklin great self-congratulatory "pleasure" for his "cunning" "political manoeuvres" (*Papers*, vol. 4, 110).

One of Franklin's most eloquent fundraising statements appeared in its entirety in the *Pennsylvania Gazette*, August 8 and 15, 1751. In many ways it gives fullest voice to the underwriting methods, both rhetorical and monetary, that make Franklin's success unusual and worthy of emulation. He, like the poets, knows that human virtue is subject to "probability" and thus no amount of armor or safety can exclude defeat and loss:

> Pos obitum benefacta manent, aeternaque Virtus
> Non metuit Stygiis, nec rapiatur Aquis.

The old poets, how extravagant soever in their Fictions, durst never offend so far against nature and probability, as even to feign such a thing; and therefore, tho' they made their Achilles invulnerable from head to foot, and clad him beside in impenetrable armour, forg'd by the immortals, they were obliged to leave one soft unguarded place in his heel, how small soever, for destruction to enter at ... [*Papers* vol. 4, 147–48].

Given this preamble, with its arch use of Achilles' heel as a marketing tool, the public is urged to recognize individual vulnerability as a matter of empathy. And where there is empathy, there ought to be a social vision, answering of course to the ideal of public virtue. The public is, after all, the space of mutual habitation, a kind of interdependency that is peculiarly urban and modern:

We are in this world mutual hosts to each other; the circumstances and fortunes of men and families are continually changing; in the course of a few years we have seen the rich become poor, and the poor rich; the children of the wealthy languishing in want and misery, and those of their servants lifted into estates, and abounding in the good things of this life. Since then, our present state, how prosperous soever, hath no stability, but what depends on the good providence of God, how careful would we be not to harden our hearts against the distresses of our fellow creatures, lest he who owns and governs all, should punish our inhumanity, deprive us of a stewardship in which we have so unworthily behaved, laugh at our calamity, and mock when our fear cometh. Methinks when objects of charity, and opportunities of relieving them, present themselves, we should hear the voice of this samaritan, as if it were the voice of God sounding in our ears, TAKE CARE OF THEM, *and whatsoever thou spendest, I will repay thee* [*Papers*, vol. 4, 149–50].

Franklin annunciates the core of his mature public underwriting, using a manifold rhetoric to argue through to redemption as a matter of repayment for what is lost. Indeed, the cost of not repaying is, in this formula, a species of fear derived from the inevitability of one's own bad fortune.

⤳

Looking back on the accomplishments of Philadelphia during the previous century, Ebenezer Hazard (a Franklinian public man by any measure) wrote his "Address to the Citizens of Pennsylvania Upon the Subject of a Life Insurance Company" (1813), in which he lauds the city's peculiar blending of public institutions with private wealth:

It cannot but be a source of a pleasing reflection to you, that Philadelphia . . . stands preeminent over all her sister cities. This superiority of rank . . . has been the result of a combination of wealth and benevolence, of taste and public spirit, qualifications for which her inhabitants are highly distinguished. She can boast . . . an extensive hospital for the insane and infirm—a number of institutions for the education, support, and assistance of the poor and distressed—a dispensary for supplying medical aid gratuitously to the needy—an university—two public libraries—five banks—nine marine insurance companies—and three fire insurance companies [1–2].

Franklin's most telling capitalist and municipal schemes, so well represented in Hazard's persuasive list, were underwriting enterprises that deliberately tested the public "do-gooding" of private interest. His most enduring underwriting scheme took shape around what would become this triumphant civic narrative.

Two years after the initial offering to subsidize the building of what would become the University of Pennsylvania, and about a year after attempting to establish an insurance business as an offshoot of his local fire brigade, the Union Fire Company,[35] Franklin drafted "The Deed of Settlement of the Society for Insuring of Houses, in and near Philadelphia" (1751).[36] Philadelphia was becoming by far the most densely populated city in the colonies (the extrapolated 1760 census data has 15,000 people living in six-tenths of one square mile), and the hazard of catastrophic fire was serious.[37] Indeed, Labaree explains that the directors of the Contributionship asked Franklin to print in the *Pennsylvania Gazette* for December 24, 1753, a caution to policyholders that the fund would not honor claims which arose "if any such damage arises to such houses or

F I G . 4 . Franklin Fire Insurance Company of Philadelphia, engraving by Tucker. Courtesy of the Franklin Collection, Yale University Library.

stores, by the breaming of ships at their wharves, or by gunpowder stored in their buildings, contrary to the good and wholesome laws of this province."[38] Franklin saw not only the possibility for a new and expanded profit center but also the need for a regime of public safety that could derive energy from the underwriting impulse. In the nineteenth-century engraving by Tucker, Franklin sits safely circumscribed amidst the alarming chaos of Philadelphia on fire (see fig. 4). Such imagery epitomizes Franklin's recessed power, which paradoxically indemnifies him by settling his visage placidly into representations of the burning city.

In establishing what became the Philadelphia Contributionship, Franklin was keen to dismiss the notion that subscribers were mere investors interested only in personal gain. He saw the enterprise as one in the public service, addressing a dire need:

To all whom these Presents shall come; We whose Names are hereunto subscribed and Seals affixed do severally send greeting. Whereas, the Insurance of Houses from Loss by

FIG. 5. Philadelphia Contributionship Hand-in-Hand firemark, c. 1755. Courtesy of the Philadelphia Contributionship.

Fire hath, where the same has been practised, proved very useful and advantageous to the Publick; Now know ye, that we the said Subscribers hereunto, as well as for our own mutual Security, as for the common Security and Advantage of our Fellow-Citizens and Neighbours, and for the Promoting of so great and publick a Good as the Insurance of Houses from Loss by Fire, upon the most equal Terms, and apart from all views of private or Separate Gain or Interest; have of our own Motion offered each to the other, and have unanimously resolved and agreed, and by these Presents do covenant, promise and agree for ourselves severally and respectively, and for our several and respective Executors, Administrators and Assigns, to form, erect and settle an Office, Society or mutual Contributionship, by the Name or Stile of the PHILADELPHIA CONTRIBUTIONSHIP, for the Insuring of Houses from Loss by Fire, and to be and continue Contributors unto and equal Sharers in the Losses as well as the Gains and Advantages arising, accruing and happening in and by the same, upon the Terms . . . [*Papers*, vol. 4, 283].

As a representation of a business enterprise and its proposed field of profit, this passage reveals a great deal about Franklin's view of property and temporality—the discomfiture of the looming of events. On view is a modified optimism that secures prudent representative bravado, exemplifying an inviolable and mutually held credibility that would be sustained for the life of a dwelling.[39] Here we see how a socialized unanimity serves to measure out public "do-gooding." In Franklin's scheme, the subscribed subsume their names under a "nameless" corporate identity derived from the work of monetarized (contributed) consensus. This recessed agency projects the power of each subscriber's authenticity and their consequent depth of obligation to pay their monthly contribution.

The firemark that famously came to represent the Contributionship, the hand-in-hand (see fig. 5), demonstrates the anonymously embodied branding of property.[40] Indeed, these visible hands prefigure the remote limiting agency of Smith's invisible hand, mutually imposing rectangular order, increasing the security of the collective structure. Each hand comes to grips, presumably only after affixing its signature. And then a new signature is born. This truncated valorization of solidarity, subscription, and guidance ran to the construction of what amounted to the first highway billboards: the Contributionship set up milestones bearing the company seal and the distance remaining on the road from Trenton to Philadelphia. Capitalized public service could literally lead safely to commercial centers of power. This assuring stance toward what lies down the road is but another form of the contractual narrative style and motto-driven markers of the *Almanack* and the *Autobiography*.

The *Autobiography* and the *Almanack*

We are told that Franklin, on first arriving in Philadelphia, gave the owners of the boat which had delivered him to the city "about a shilling of copper"—some of his last coins. The owners at first refused it, probably taking pity on his visibly immiserated circumstances. They relented, according to Franklin, when he insisted on reimbursing them despite his penury. The moral to Franklin is bound up in the productive uses of anxiety: "A man being sometimes more generous when he has but a little money than when he has plenty, perhaps thro' fear of being thought to have but little" (*The Autobiography*, 24). That fear of perception driving not obligation but "generosity" sets the tone for many other public fears linked to private generosity, as well as private fears linked to public generosity. Philanthropy has at its root a version of anxiety.

This idea found expression in the mechanics of fundraising throughout Franklin's life. For example, the Quakers, one of the deal-breaking factions in Pennsylvania politics, posed a problem for public funding of Franklin's first fire company. This came immediately on the heels of New England's solicitation of a grant from Pennsylvania to buy gunpowder, a request denied by the Quaker-dominated Assembly, since it was meant for the purposes of war. What was crucial in the rhetorical fight was that the provision could not be granted under the common linguistic evasion "for the king's use." The governor, by way of spiteful response, went against the House by interpreting the phrase authorizing the purchase of "bread, flour, wheat, or *other grain*" to include gunpowder under the vague "other grain." Franklin saw the opportunity for the kind of linguistic play that could underwrite all manner of public projects:

It was in allusion to this fact [the expansively legalistic interpretation of commonsense words] that, when in our fire company we feared the success of our proposal in favour of the lottery, and I had said to my friend Mr. Syng, one of our members, "If we fail, let us move the purchase of a fire engine with the money; the Quakers can have no objection to that; and then, if you nominate me and I you as a committee for that purpose, we will buy a great gun, which is certainly a *fire-engine*." "I see," says he, "you have improv'd by being so long in the Assembly; your equivocal project would be just a match for their wheat or *other grain*" [*The Autobiography*, 114–15].

Franklin's subsequent discussion centers on the problem of fearing uncertainty and how this serves those who would codify their beliefs as public policy and those, like the Dunkers, who cannot publish or codify anything without sure eternal knowledge. Franklin offers to play a game with the language of the request, thereby serving his interests, the interests of the commonwealth, and of those who would circumvent the financial pacifism of the Quaker Assembly. On view here is a kind of updated "do-gooding" in which the punning of the first scheme continues to underwrite his attempts to secure public safety. The Quakers play the role of the straw man Cotton Mather, in their petulant high moral seriousness, impeding the design and implementation of public and private good.[41]

↜

Poor Richard's Almanack also can be viewed as a profitable way to underwrite security in the face of fear of future uncertainties. The *Almanack* is a celebratory pastiche of street and book wisdom as well as a compiler of public data from around the colonies, all in the name of a practical form of predictability. Indeed, there are moments in the *Almanack* when Franklin is keen to make his underwriting of anxiety about safety explicit.

One instance takes place in the 1752 edition, where Franklin makes liberal use of Richard Savage's 1737 poem "On Public Spirit in Regard to Public Works," quoting passages intact but also eliding lines, transposing and altering word sequences, and adding his own original lines.[42] For Richard, as for Savage, publicity is the quasi-mystical place that makes fertile the world of desire and possession:

> "On PUBLICK SPIRIT.
>
> Where never Science beam'd a friendly Ray,
> Where one vast Blank neglected Nature lay;
> From PUBLICK SPIRIT there, by Arts employ'd,
> Creation, varying, glads the chearless Void.
> By Arts, which Safety, Treasure and Delight,
> On Land, on Wave, in wondrous Works unite!
> Myriads made happy, Publick Spirit bless,
> Parent of Trade, Wealth, Liberty and Peace"
> [*Poor Richard's Almanack*, 1752, 150].[43]

According to Labaree, the last two lines are not in the original and therefore represent Franklin's tinkering for emphasis. Given the way in which "Safety, Treasure and Delight" are united, we might expect that the public at large would be the paramount beneficiary of such prudence. And, appropriately, we have "Myriads made happy," in which demographic notions of welfare are made the beneficiaries of security.

The emphasis on numerical chance and its relationship to suffering and danger is present as well in the almanacs of the late 1740's and early 1750's. Gambling, for instance, is dangerous in its addictive destruction—not that it is in and of itself wrong to incur chance as a means to speculation or profit, but rather that it is bad for public and familial welfare. It consumes time without paying attention to the price of time.[44] His admonition is hyperprivatized, emphasizing the way gaming affects the individual, offering a kind of mania that has little to do with public improvement. This is intimately linked to a view of freedom as always and already *public* freedom in Franklin:[45]

> From "Advice to Youth"
> Gaming, the Vice of Knaves and Fools, detest,
> Miner of Time, of Substance and of Rest;
> Which, in the Winning or the Losing Part,
> Undoing or undone, will wring the Heart:
> Undone, self-curs'd, thy Madness thou wilt rue;
> Undoing, Curse of others will pursue
> Thy hated Head. A Parent's, Household's Tear,
> A Neighbour's Groan, and Heav'n's displeasure fear
> [*Poor Richard's Almanack*, 1749, 56].

Meditations on the nature of life and chance continue in the almanacs of the early 1750's. One gets the sense that chance is useful for nothing so much as ego deflation; and, as such, it works neatly in favor of behavior that is frugal, industrious, thrifty, and so forth. And yet the converse is also true, that monetary riches, and real property especially, outlast the futility of human pretensions. Money outlasts the pride and plans of the high and mighty—accidents make sure of that. The conservation of property is thus a ridiculing memorial to human impermanence. All this is not in the manner of grave warning but of fearless chiding; the advice is almost devoid of anxiety, a sigh launching the weary wisdom of the long-lived:

> Ah, what is Life? With Ills encompass'd round,
> Amidst our Hopes, Fate strikes the sudden Wound;
> To-day the Statesman of new Honour dreams,
> To-morrow Death destroys his airy Schemes.
> Is mouldy Treasure in thy Chest confin'd;
> Think, all that Treasure thou must leave behind;
> Thy Heir with Smiles shall view thy blazon'd Hearse,
> And all thy Hoards, with lavish Hand disperse
>
> Should certain Fate th'impending Blow delay,
> Thy Mirth will sicken, and thy Bloom decay;
> Then feeble Age will all thy Nerves disarm,
> No more thy Blood its narrow Channels warms;
> Who then would wish to stretch this narrow Span,
> To suffer Life beyond the Date of Man?
> The virtuous Soul pursues a nobler Aim,
> And Life regards but as a fleeting Dream . . .
> [*Poor Richard's Almanack*, 1751, 130–32]

Similar in sentiment and tone to the above, the following, also from 1751, rehearses the fragility of material life. The human soul predates the house of life, taking residence there in the midst of violent change:

> Ere the foundations of the World were laid,
> Ere kindling Light th'Almighty Word obey'd,
> Thou wert; and when the subterraneous Flame,
> Shall burst its Prison, and devour this Frame,
> From angry Heav'n when the Keen Lightning flies,
> When fervent heat dissolves the melting Skies,
> Thou still shalt be; still as thou wert before,
> And know no Change when time shall be no more
> [*Poor Richard's Almanack*, 1751, 136]

But such warnings are always set off against the prospect of securing that fragility and warding off those dangers with scientific invention. In the 1753 edition of *Poor Richard's Almanack*, Franklin has a section on "How to secure

Houses, &c. from LIGHTNING": "It has pleased God in his Goodness to Mankind, at length to discover them the Means of securing their Habitations and other Buildings from Mischief by Thunder and Lightning" (215). Franklin's concern is to stress the need not to worry about the permanence of the soul, but to know the certainty of loss that awaits us. With such practical knowledge, anything might be underwritten.

(Under)Writing the Machine

In *Cotton Mather and Ben Franklin: The Price of Representative Personality*, Mitchell Breitwieser sets many of the key terms for appraisals of Franklin's purported ability to exemplify his age. Breitwieser writes of the relationship between Franklin's contribution to the science of electricity and monetized notions of the self. Located in his critique is a source of Franklin's ability to overcome anxiety:

> Franklin's greatest contributions to the theory of electricity . . . were his development of the law of the conservation of charge . . . and his insight into positive and negative charge, plus or minus, *amount* . . . It was a mode of representing the world of matter: the electrician could ignore, or transcend, the uniquenesses of things, and see them instead in a scheme of pure commensurability, as so much measurable presence or absence of electricity. As a mode of symbolization, the electrician's view enjoys the perfect clarity of number . . . [213–14].

Breitwieser's analysis takes this thoroughgoing claim for the meaning of Franklin's theory of electricity's integerization of the world and correlates it with money and its accumulation.[46] Using Franklin's advocacy of paper money as a revelation of a labor theory of value, Breitwieser integrates his notion of science, economy, and selfhood: "The traits Franklin discerned in the movement of the electrical fluid—subtlety, power of permeation, freedom from qualitative distinctiveness, abstract symbolization, the power to elicit a corresponding element from the particularity of its surroundings, and accumulation through unification—reappear in his discussions of money" (215). He summarizes the effects of such a connection as amounting to a kind of radical "transcendence" of the "peculiarities" of experience. Thus Franklin is able to alchemically convert life into a manipulable abstraction.[47]

It is not hard to see the connection between a life of writing spent in the optimistic mode and its beginnings in speculation on the wonders of electricity. Breitwieser describes the first stages of constructing an inviolable, irreducible representative personality, couching his analysis in the language of diagnostics:

> His life is to *be* a speculative treatise with extensive and meticulous application, so he has to ensure that his particular stances and opinions emanate from a single, explicit core. This diagnosis may provide him with a sharper than usual sense of the other definitions

of man implicit in the common sense of his time as adversaries with which he must compete, rather than as miscellaneous or indifferent options to be picked up or laid aside at convenience. As his diagnosis of human nature grows more explicit, reflective, and coherent, that is, his perception of aggregate or variety may be replaced by a polarity of purity and contamination [3].

We are told, furthermore, that as the "diagnosis" takes shape, the problems it is meant to discipline are associated with the notions of "aggregates" and "variety." Indeed, the diagnosis calls for a rigorous domestication, even expulsion, of the world of improbable circumstance, the "miscellaneous and indifferent options" that punctuate all lives, public and private. Franklin's narrative strategy—the telos of his underwriting representativeness—hits the mark, beyond even the age he sought to place his imprint upon. For much of what follows in Breitwieser's analysis constitutes an attempt to recover what Franklin so ardently wants us to recover—that core which has shunned the chaotic, the unanswerable, the contingent and chance-driven. His poetics of underwriting these contingencies—the experience of aggregates, accidents, misfortune—is the ground of his representative power, but it also has contributed to our missing this aspect of the socially conscious Franklin.

The needful promotion of a certain biographical tone and outline may be called optimism—an outlook that bodes a determinism which excludes certain trajectories. Optimism may be classified as a narrowing of narrative possibilities that excludes most bad news. More specifically, optimism sees this limited set of narrative futures as unfailingly benign and so brightly moves forward into them, without pause or hesitation (though not necessarily without calculation or precaution). Optimism and the representation of optimism in the personae of Franklin are part of a defensive construction hewed from a warehouse of limited narrative materials. The question arises: What is it that so threatens Franklin's self-construction? What generates the polarity of "purity and contamination" so necessary to the forward motion and so indicative of the Franklinian narrative which defines the subject? I would suggest that what Franklin cannot let us see, and what thus requires its own redemptive underwriting, is a peculiarly modern terror that Franklin did much to midwife.

Whence does that terror arise? The answer resides partly in the terms found in Breitwieser's diagnosis: from the aggregate, from variety, the incidental and accidental, misfortunes and bad luck—all of which arrive on the scene as natural electric corollaries of the new idea of society that has been charged with republican notions of virtue. Improvidence, which capitalist notions of monetary representativeness deprived its earliest believers and practitioners from explaining (as had been possible for Cotton Mather's generation, or for the new-wave Puritanism of Jonathan Edwards), required a new notion of historical narrativity, a new poetics of social fortune. In *Declaring Independence*, Jay

Fliegelman summarizes Enlightenment historicism in the following way: "Enlightenment challenges to a providential model of history further underscored the wishful insistence on efficacious agency by shifting much more accountability for the process of history onto individuals, not as witting or unwitting instruments of a greater or external will but as agents of their own moral volition" (141).[48] But, as he and Gordon Wood point out, there was a tendency to impose this positive aspect of humanist rationalism overmuch on the contingencies of experience that defy explanation or narrative coherence.[49] Franklin's engagement with insurance underwriting, and with manifestations of chance (lotteries, lightning strikes, and so forth), provides an opportunity to think through just where the Enlightenment fell short in its new histories and science, and where it succeeded.

⤳

Late in life, Franklin began to view slavery as an embarrassment to be abolished, and slaves as individuals unfairly deprived of the benefits of public as well as private life. In "An address to the public from the Pennsylvania Society for Promoting the Abolition of Slavery, and the Relief of Free Negroes," we see what happens to the individual stripped of any possibility for Franklinian assurance and credibility. In his assessment of the person of the slave, seen at the end of a life of dispossessed labor, Franklin puts in view the antithesis of the man who has the benefits of underwriting, broadly construed:

The galling chains that bind his body, do also fetter his intellectual faculties, and impair the social affections of his heart. Accustomed to move like a mere machine, by the will of a master, reflection is suspended; he has not the power of choice; and reason and conscience, have but little influence over his conduct: because he is chiefly governed by the passion of fear.[50]

Franklin's last point is revealing: A man reduced and exiled from the productive life of self-mastery is subject most of all to fear, and is thus, machine-like, "worn out." Under the reign of dread, the slave's personal agency has been so disabled that he cannot hope to withstand chance and uncertainty—"freedom may often prove a misfortune to himself, and prejudicial to society." Fear is the last passion of those who never got to exercise the first Lockean possession—the right to ownership of the fruit of one's labor. This recalls Burke's "On the Sublime and Beautiful," in which fear divests the rational mind, and leaves us in sublimity. But for Franklin, fear has no bonus aesthetic; indeed the lot of the deprived slave is to have his life remain unnarratable. The fearful do not deserve, nor can they truly enjoy, freedom; at the same time, the result of a life spent in debilitating, depriviliging fear is the most compelling argument Franklin can make against slavery.

It also brings us back to the logic behind Franklin's methods for governing the passions and interests of modern societies, ideally peopled. Fear is freedom's enemy and must be dealt with by both the individual and society in a way that keeps property stable and duly rewarding. A good life cannot tolerate fear's peculiar paradox, the logical cause and effect that has deprivation of appropriate human rights as its condition and end. This circular premise is much to the credit of republican humanism. Even so, underwriting leaves its commodifying trace: For whether it is a "machine" or a game or a narrative codified by the ideology of print, that life is always worth the money that represents it, and it is always, as he puts in the *Almanack*, "set on work."

CHAPTER TWO

Boston

Phillis Wheatley's Business: The Figures of Loss

> Tho' now the business of her life is o'er,
> Tho' now she breath[e]s and tunes her lyre no more . . .
> —Anonymous, "Elegy on the Death of a
> Late Celebrated Poetess," *Boston Magazine*,
> December 1784, on the death of Phillis Wheatley

The explicit topic of Phillis Wheatley's first published poem, "On Messrs. Hussey and Coffin," is not race. Nor is it in any obvious way a poem about slavery. And religion comes into play in the poem only as a response to an important, provocative occasion. To say this much is to demonstrate the dominant figure that delivered Wheatley to the themes for which she has become famous. The poem—which appeared in the *Newport Mercury* on December 21, 1767[1]— is very much about race, slavery, and religion, but only by virtue of its being concerned with the threat of physical loss.

A measure of fame followed publication of this poem. Wheatley went on to become well known as much for who she was as for the themes about which she wrote. She was among the first slaves to publish a book of poetry in America, and her renown as a prodigy and a racial exception (perhaps a "genius") defined her public reception. Today, critics probe Wheatley's approving poems about America and Christianity, searching for a key to what Betsy Erkkila calls a "double tongue"[2] that continues to confound readers. "On Messrs. Hussey and Coffin" makes apparent that slavery and theology are not the only places where critics should be looking. Perhaps the terms of bondage are held elsewhere, in the concepts of loss and redemption that were keys to the emergent commerce of underwriting commodities in the hulls of ships owned by the likes of Hussey and Coffin.

The poem is about the near drowning at sea of two friends of her master John Wheatley—the Hussey and the Coffin of the poem's title. Wheatley used her relatively privileged position of light servitude to listen in on their story of near catastrophe and felt compelled to inscribe a lyric moral about their experience. It is an extraordinary poem for someone no more than thirteen to have written, especially given its quiet irony. Wheatley's great subtext for the poem must have been the fearful dispossessing experience on the ocean voyage that was her middle passage from Africa. She traveled on her master's ship, *The Phillis*, almost six years before (imagine the grotesque power of being named for the ship which delivered her as cargo).[3]

Fear is rhapsodically invoked as a series of rhetorical questions (the question marks are scattered excitedly), offered with a knowing self-apprehension:

> Did Fear and Danger so perplex your Mind,
> As made you fearful of the Whistling Wind?
> Was it not Boreas knit his angry Brow
> Against you? Or did Consideration bow?
> To lend you Aid, did not his Winds combine?
> To stop your passage with a churlish Line,
> Did haughty Eolus with Contempt look down
> With Aspect windy, and a study'd Frown? [115]

Most interesting is Wheatley's use of the word "consideration." Signifying as early as the seventeenth century the contractual dimension of monetary compensation, "consideration" seems to pivot the poet's concern between the discourse of contractual obligation and that of providential care.[4] Wheatley strikes the note of accountancy and bookkeeping as a way of making tangible the prospect of annihilation and the fear that goes with it, while not losing sight of the merchants' primary nonlethal concerns. For Hussey and Coffin were lucky enough that consideration "bowed," taking into account what was owed, and thereby offering a kind of grace. This quasi-providential dispensation allowed the journey to continue with "aid" on loan and without the feared loss.

But loss, despite her best efforts and the assumptions of commercial success premised on the safe arrival of the merchants, is never not there in the poem. Wheatley attempts to dismiss her series of anxious questions with an abrupt refocus on the metaphysical dimensions of God and His design in the next two lines: "Regard them not;—the Great Supreme, the Wise, / Intends for something hidden from our Eyes" (116). God uses this fear as a deflection from the true destination of all lost things. The logic of loss—or, strictly speaking, the logic of the imagination of loss—seems to take hold in a completely new way, and so Wheatley invites us to imagine the worst: "Suppose the groundless Gulph had snatch'd away / Hussey and Coffin to the raging Sea; / Where wou'd they go? Where wou'd be their Abode?" (116).

The answer is the first in what becomes a persistent conceit for Wheatley's elegies. In a drama about belief determining the soul's very gravity, Hussey and Coffin will either ascend to Heaven or descend to "Beds down in the Shades be-

low." Caught ambivalently between the material and the spiritual, her meditation catches on its labor of signification. The poem seems to founder, as Wheatley is seemingly unsure about the proper end for these two men, merchants
concerned with cargo and its safe delivery:

> Had the soft gliding Streams of Grace been near,
> Some favourite Hope their fainting hearts to cheer,
> Doubtless the Fear of Danger far had fled:
> No more repeated Victory crown their Heads.

The doubtful pitch of her lyric seems to suggest either contempt or empathy for
the merchants—or perhaps both. Does she mean to say that in descending to
their deaths, Hussey and Coffin need not fear any longer, if they recognize the
saving power of grace? Or is she taunting them in the name of their own igno-
rance and fear—their inability to satisfactorily set aside the anxious fears she
presumably shared in her own passage near regions of imminent loss?

The last line is most puzzling, in part because it seems to send Wheatley into
a crisis of confidence. Indeed, the line "No more repeated Victory crown their
Heads" sounds anomalous, even with the somewhat confused lines preceding
it. "Victory" may refer to the galleon built in 1765 by the British, which went on
to great fame under the command of Trafalgar; or it may refer to the Olympic
custom of crowning the freeborn victors of the games; or it may gain force
from the scriptures' "O Death, where is thy Sting? O Grave, where is thy Victory?" (I Corinthians 55). All seem relevant, but none makes a definitive claim
on the sense of the line. Wheatley ends by breaking off her poetic conundrum
with a prose apostrophe to God, in which she despairs of her ability to satisfy
the goal of "tracing the Mark divine" in this meditation on near loss:

Had I the Tongue of a Seraphim, how would I exalt thy Praise; thy Name as Incense to
the Heavens should fly, and the Remembrance of thy Goodness to the shoreless Ocean
of Beatitude!—Then should the Earth glow with seraphick Ardour [116].

This inaugural poem serves as an apt introduction to Wheatley's poetics of
underwriting loss. The questions it raises are a kind of principal from which
one may draw analytic interest: Why does Wheatley's poem break off from its
narrative course? Is it a case of navigation gone awry at the behest of some unseen storm? What "victory" is at stake here, or how many different kinds? Such
questions suggest the idea of loss as a controlling metatrope for Wheatley. Loss
not only masks and exposes racial dispossession and religious triumphalism
(categories that remain so legible elsewhere in her poems) but also informs
them in ways that might not be readily apparent.

This chapter responds to these questions in two parts. First I show how
Wheatley was the object of an underwriting at the outset of her career, and then

I explain how she used that event as a poetics that rendered her, too, a kind of underwriter. Within this frame, we begin to see how Wheatley's career as a writer was begun, in literal and figurative terms, from within the condition of loss. We also see how that career never freed itself from loss, and that, rather than restricting her poetic capabilities, it became the structure of feeling that vested her work with "double tongued" meanings that critics are still puzzling out. Using loss as an underwriting poetic figure, Wheatley was perhaps the most economically astute poet in America at a time when economic tropes within poems were taken very seriously. That economic poetics bespoke underwriting in its varied guises. She exposed the shoreless margins of her exceptional condition by treating possession as an idea that answered to less obvious masters.

↩

To think of poetry in terms of loss, it pays to recall the analytic relationship between making things and losing them. This recollection should be even more acute in considering the poetry of a slave writing in the Lockean century that accorded authors definitive property rights over the products of their imaginations. It is not surprising, then, the popularity of the claim that Wheatley's work is more interesting when seen as a form of historically meaningful labor. Critics have been fascinated by Wheatley's labor of writing and performance, especially by how that labor is shaped by gender and the politics of Afro-American national identity.[5] They have sought that lyrical profundity with a variety of critical discourses; and, perhaps because of this, Wheatley stands as one of the most productive authors for critical interventions in the canon of eighteenth-century American writers.

For instance, Robert Kendrick has demonstrated the unique productions that were her "performative" elegies.[6] He denies that Wheatley's elegies perform the time-honored function of the elegy by "recover[ing] a lost Other" (44). Instead, the elegies—most emblematically "On the Death of the Rev. Dr. Sewell. 1769"—"exploit the presence of supplemental voices within the poem to lead the reader into an intersubjective and reflexive process of (re)membering his or her own position relative to another's" (44). Terrence Collins notes that it is in her poetry of annihilation that Wheatley makes an important semiotic slip between "religious escape and racial denial of the self" (157).[7] Hilene Flanzbaum makes a similar claim in her analysis of Wheatley's invocation of the muse, which paradoxically affords her "unprecedented liberty" within the aegis of permission to speak.[8] Kirstin Wilcox and Christopher Felker both recount Wheatley's struggle to achieve a transatlantic prominence within the public sphere of print-culture gentility, and how her struggles were augmented by a sense of the business she participated in.

In all these interpretations, Wheatley's poetry is read as an effort to achieve an agency that could be had only through symbolic labor. But one notices, too, in these critics an eagerness to absolve her of politically or racially ambiguous rhetorical positions. And in that eagerness is an accidental need to dehistoricize her, to make her a poststructuralist avatar rather than poet with a productively contradictory relationship to merchant life, religion, and political liberty. This is not to say that she does not exemplify a rhetorical cleverness that can be thrown into relief by theory, but instead that she does so only as a function of a set of eighteenth-century discourses about property and loss that remain underexamined. She seems to have understood those discourses quite well, and her poetic value, then and now, is the product of a unique skill in manipulating the moral aesthetics derived from those discourses.[9]

My outlook arises out of prior readings of Wheatley's elegiac voice as disruptive but seeks to place Wheatley within the commercial environment suggested by the legal terms of textual possession and physical loss, and of what that position might mean for one who strategized the terms of her manumission. This textual (here, poetic and commercial) link is in turn inferred from the economy of ship underwriting, so vital to Boston's economy in the late 1760's and early 1770's. My sense of her work is informed as well by the commodification of life and labor that is directly suggested by the conditions of slave economies. Indeed, for Wheatley especially, slave economies *were* shipping economies.

Seen in this way, Wheatley is supremely aware of the terms of artifice when it comes to her public presence. For Wheatley, artifice is ingeniously modified to fit the circumstances of the changing commodification from which she wrote. Thus, as with Franklin's underwriting names, it is productive to view "Phillis Wheatley" as a pseudonym, a character plied in public to achieve poetic effects. Not unlike Benjamin Franklin's fictional Silence Dogood of almost fifty years before, Wheatley learned of her capacity for writing well by reading in her mistress's library during the first years of her servitude. Wheatley's experience, of course, was real, rather than a productive pose; her condition of servitude shaped and made possible—while also limiting and squelching in crucial ways—the radically strategic artifice of her poetic expression.[10]

To say this much is also to say that the conditions of Wheatley's slavery have an impact on her poetic work. Naming those conditions accurately is the critical problem. Wheatley's case exhibits a moment in the history of textual labor when printing, ownership, and the restoration of lost value were truly contested. As a writer caught in the authenticating imprints of underwriting, Wheatley's is a poetics of compensation and redemption, where both words borrow from commercial and religious sensibilities.

Underwriting the Author

An elaborate and now famous set of prefatory pages accompanied nearly all of 1773's London and American editions of Phillis Wheatley's *Poems on Various Subjects, Religious and Moral*. They included the following attestation:

We whose names are under-written, do assure the world, that the poems specified . . . were (as we verily believe) written by Phillis, a young Negro girl, who was but a few years since, brought an uncultivated Barbarian from Africa, and has ever since been, and now is, under the disadvantage of serving as a slave in a family in this town. She has been examined by some of the best judges, and is thought qualified to write them [48].

This is, of course, one of the best-known underwritings in American literature. Henry Louis Gates is largely responsible for its exposure, and his strong interpretation of it as a text that tells much about eighteenth-century notions of race and writing is one that has resituated Wheatley's writing in the contexts of social power.[11] Thus the attestation has been read as an indicator of the displacements made by race within the two-headed concept of authenticity and individual talent.

But the attestation also serves as an ironic counterpoint to what Wheatley herself was up to in her poetry. Read alongside the poetry, the attestation tells a story about the match between property and text in colonial America, about how printed texts might be redeemed in the face of derivative doubts concerning the fundamental worth of certain kinds of property (slave writers). Indeed, the story of Wheatley's underwriting clarifies the methods by which Wheatley served a commercial function among the merchants and financiers of Boston and in turn exploited commercial language and techniques to her artistic and even legal advantage.

At its core, the underwriting was really advertisement (indeed, the letter from her master was called "An Advertisement").[12] Yet while this statement of authenticity was strictly meant as an advertisement for the book on the part of her publisher in England, Archibald Bell, and subsequently for her American publisher, Joseph James of Philadelphia, it also functions as insurance against a very public loss of expected value; it was meant to buffer the risk associated not only with an already proven marketing failure but also with an unprecedented market exposure. Representing an irrefutable compendium of signatures, the underwriting testifies to the truth of the author's status as black, woman, and slave, and thus to the text's resulting measure of "originality"—"that none might have the least ground for disputing" it.

The underwriters consisted of seven politicians, a group that included the governor and the lieutenant governor; three lawyers, among them John Hancock; seven clergy; and her owner, John Wheatley. It is hard to generalize about the occupational profiles of these signers except to say that all were public figures and all were white men.[13] What was the reason for a show of such overwhelming authenticating force? What was at stake? How did this securing text come about as a logical response to questions of authenticity and originality?

Critics have poured into the spaces left open by Gates. The story behind the attestation has been told recently by critics interested in examining Wheatley as a literary phenomenon within print culture. Most notable has been the work of Wilcox and Felker, whom I mentioned earlier. Both recount Wheatley's struggle to achieve a transatlantic prominence within the public sphere of print-culture gentility. But, for my purposes, they delineate a difference in British and American literary marketplaces by making clear that she was unsuccessful in fully subscribing a proposed 1772 edition of her book.

And so a London publication was schemed by Susanna Wheatley and, to lesser degrees, the Countess of Huntingdon and the Earl of Dartmouth. The proposal, or advertisement, which announced the first, unsuccessful Boston volume in the *Boston Censor* for Saturday, February 29, 1772 (reprinted on March 14 and April 11), constitutes a crucial underwriting moment overlooked by Gates and others. It was, as Felker points out, "almost certainly written by Wheatley herself" (86), unlike the advertising attestation written for the London publication. It reads:

A Collection of POEMS, wrote at several times, and upon various occasions, by PHILLIS, a Negro Girl, from the strength of her own Genius, it being but a few Years since she came to this Town an uncultivated Barbarian from *Africa*. The Poems having been seen and read by the best judges, who think them well worthy of the Publick View; and upon critical examination, they find that the declared Author was capable of writing them [Julian Mason, *The Poems of Phillis Wheatley*, 186].

Notably absent from this advertisement are any of the explicit assurances of the London recoupment. It lacks the ostentatiously patronizing lingo of "underwriting" and "assuring the world" that characterized the famous attestation of Hancock and others. Such absence indicates the unadorned power of the corroborating document underwriting her authority in 1773, something not directly and publicly available to Wheatley herself in 1772.

Both Mason and Wilcox speculate persuasively on the difference between the proposed poems in the Boston advertisement and the poems that found their way into the London edition. Many of the poems were probably deemed too local and too American in their focus on Boston's elite and their preoccupation with colonial concerns. Wilcox points out that the list of poems reads as an account of recent events in Boston, "particularly in the city's mercantile and Methodist circles" (14). As an incentive for subscribing, according to Wilcox, the book offers seeing in print "the shared experience of Wheatley and the reading public" (15). Wilcox ventures that the paragraph from the advertisement, attached after the list of proposed poems, was the work of Susanna Wheatley: "IT is hoped Encouragement will be given to this Publication, as a reward to a very uncommon Genius, at present a slave" (Mason, 188). Speculating that such encouragement is hoped for so that Wheatley might someday no longer be a slave, Wilcox goes on to say that the failed book project reflects on Boston's underdeveloped sense of itself as a print capital. Perhaps more important, the book's washout was a result of Susanna Wheatley's marketing error, made visible in her proposal's inability or unwillingness to trumpet the race of the author.

But Wilcox's adept analysis underplays the importance of Wheatley's failed Boston underwriting as a way of telling us what Wheatley was up to as a poet. For it is in the Boston edition that Wheatley truly begins to explore the connections between property and print culture and its markets. That exploration is brought about by her own prior underwriting, her attempt as a poet (within the generic limits accorded her by the elegy and its subjects) to guarantee her value above and beyond the liabilities of her condition, as a black female slave. She does this in the thematic particularities of her compositions, which seem to stress the very localism of her print emergence—the closeness of Boston's elite to her own sentiment.[14]

Sentiment is the emotional key to her figural transformations. Indeed, what is most striking about the list of proposed Boston poems is their tendency to be elegies; no fewer than twelve are specifically about someone else's death. Wheatley writes almost exclusively about losses within Boston's elite. By mediating the loss of white lives—white bodies, even—she manages to assert her claim to managing the transitions between material presence and the more legally and print-constructed concept of individual sovereignty, of self-ownership. Because of the controversy attending its initial publication in Boston—its too local cast—authentication may be viewed as necessary in order to reconceive it as a viable, uniquely alluring commodity in the highly competitive book market of 1773.

A letter dated February 24, 1773, written by Mr. Wheatley's friend, the merchant John Andrews, and sent to his brother-in-law in Philadelphia, the merchant William Barrell, demonstrates the precariousness of the volume's position as a commodity:

[Her printers] could not sell [the book] by reason of their not crediting ye performances to be by a Negro, since which she has . . . had [sic] a paper drawn up & sign'd by the Gov. Council, ministers & most of the people of note in this place, certifying the authenticity of it; which paper Capt Calef carried last fall, therefore we may expedit it in print by the Spring ships, it is supposed the Coppy will sell for L100 Sterlg [William H. Robinson, 27].

Andrews's breezy terms belie the seriousness of this process of underwriting: in the late-eighteenth-century public sphere of slaveholding Boston, in order for Wheatley to be acknowledged as an authentic producer of original poetry, she had to be certified by white money—or, as Andrews puts it, "men of note." Public doubt in Boston determined the need for recuperative advertisements in London.[15]

But this need in turn served multiple purposes. This underwriting was more than a simple affirmation; it implied a *self*-affirming challenge to the ability of public men (whether American or English) to certify the unlikeliest of literary products. Her lyrics would amount to nothing if they did not represent the conversion of a social property (Wheatley) into cultural distinction (for her, her master, and the underwriters). Its value, meanwhile, was likewise unique. Hers had to be poetry that bespoke a rare composite, an "original imitation" of eighteenth-century Augustan verse (Andrews refers to it in simultaneously accurate and demeaning terms as Wheatley's "performance"). It was to be a commodity with merit, to be sure, but not of the intrinsic sort associated with a purely "original" aesthetic artifact—not one whose worth derived from its formal perfections and virtuous content rather than from the unusual terms of its production.

Her originality and aesthetic value—here, two discrete things—thus arose out of a singular authorial position. Wheatley herself was, even more obviously and visibly than other authors in bourgeois print culture, a figure between property and text. In this sense, she presents a paradigmatic early case in the movement from common-law notions of copyright to newer, more fraught notions that attempted to balance the claims of economic liberalism with those of customary expectations and needs.[16] Because Wheatley's poems were offered by her authenticators as an unlikely phenomenon, and therefore valuable, the underwriting made a mess of the very idea of authorship (as Michael Warner has said of Walt Whitman). For Wheatley represented less the slave as artist than the "ascension" of capital underwriters into literary circles, a socially resonant show that demonstrated the flexibility and power of authentication through underwriting. If risk is categorically linked to exposure, then capital assured itself of its own print power over an exceptional instance of exposure—the possibility of false worth or, at the very least, diminished returns. The idea of "Phillis Wheatley" was a challenge and a triumph over a kind of authorial risk, a circumscribing method of ownership—and increasing value—in spite of fortune's "implausible" placement of genius.[17]

Witness the tone of triumph in the following announcement of publication for the London edition, printed in Boston and presumably written by Susanna Wheatley herself:

Proposals for printing *in London* by Subscription, A volume of Poems, Dedicated by permission to the Right Hon. The Countess of Huntingdon Written by Phillis, a Negro Servant to Mr. Wheatley, of Boston in New England [William Robinson, *Critical Essays on Phillis Wheatley*, 24].

William Robinson speculates that "Mrs. Wheatley may have run this advertisement-proposal notice in a pique of unchristian retaliation; the notice can easily be read as an announcement to fellow Bostonians that, despite their rejection of the 1772 proposals, Phillis Wheatley's volume would indeed be published, in London" (24). Thus the Boston failure throws into relief an antagonism between publicity, neutrally configured, and ownership as a kind of textual capital.

Her poetic presence in white English-speaking metropoles became the occasion for a command performance of instilling desirability through assigned value. Those who supplied the signatures granted their commercial imprimatur, their own metonymic proximity to money's public circulation and redemption, a domain of insurable symbolic exchanges, as proof of their integrity. What they saw in Wheatley was the valuable exception to the rule that a black female slave (terms sharing different degrees of risk) was incapable of linguistic mastery. This required a vouching that the rule was in place and that the exception was all the more remarkable, more worthy, given what one might have expected of a black slave. The value of her poetry for her sponsors resided precisely in what it was (by a black slave) and was not (by a white poet named Pope). The very idea of loss, embodied by the writing black slave, made profit and genius possible. Or so the underwriters thought.

↬

Not only did the poetry's value depend on niche marketing arising out of underwritten in-betweenness, it may also be argued that the poet's freedom arose from it. Wheatley's presence in England came on the heels of a monumental court challenge to slavery (well documented and amply discussed by Carretta, Felker, and Wilcox). The Mansfield decision of 1772 meant the beginning of the end for slaveholding in Britain (Scottish courts banned slavery soon after the decision). What this fortuitous event offered Wheatley was the context for rethinking how her print success might be related to her personal autonomy.

Vincent Carretta has astutely referred to Wheatley's gambit for manumission as an elaborate kind of "insurance."[18] He quotes Wheatley's fellow African Ignatius Sancho's evaluation of her public presence only to show the degree to which Wheatley herself underwrote her critical maneuvers. Sancho is critical to establishing a fresh understanding of the subaltern's negotiation of the terms of property and poetic genius:

Phyllis's [sic] poems do credit to nature—and put art—merely as art—to the blush.—It reflects nothing either to the glory or generosity of her master—if she is still his slave—except he glories in the *low vanity* of having in his wanton power a mind animated by Heaven—a genius superior to himself—the list of splendid—titled—learned names, in confirmation of her being the real authoress—alas! Shews how very poor the acquisition of wealth and knowledge are—without generosity—feeling—and humanity.—These good great folks—all know—and perhaps admired-l-nay, praised Genius in bondage—and then, like the Priests and the Levites in sacred writ, passed by—not one good Samaritan amongst them [quoted in Vince Carretta, "Phillis Wheatley, the Mansfield Decision of 1771, and the Choice of Identity," 218].

Genius in bondage is confirmed by the unworthy vulgar rich, who arrive at the agreement by deploying standards of taste purchased to underwrite the judgment. Here is the situation in all its bitter agony, as Sancho provides a somewhat familiar complaint about social standing and taste, shot through with the outrage of slavery.

But Sancho does Wheatley a disservice as well. Carretta rightly sees Sancho's evaluation as an underestimation of Wheatley's own self-confirmation. Carretta shows how Wheatley used the occasion of Susanna Wheatley's sudden illness as a bargaining chip in her attempt to leverage the post-Mansfield environment into her own manumission. Such maneuvering required what Carretta calls "an extra insurance policy" whereby Wheatley sent a copy of her manumission papers to Massachusetts's London agent, Israel Mauduit. The papers, probably composed by Wheatley herself, seek to secure her sovereignty over and against any subsequent claims by the Wheatley family: "The Instrument is drawn, so as to secure me and my property from the hands of the Executers [executors], administrators, &c. of my master, & secure whatsoever should be given me as my Own . . ." (quoted in Carretta, ""Phillis Wheatley, the Mansfield Decision of 1771, and the Choice of Identity," 219).

This textual struggle displays precisely the symbolic constraints and possibilities of Wheatley's entrapment between property and text. Given the delicacy of the slave safeguarding things she might not yet possess (freedom, her poetry, and so forth), we begin to understand what the fluctuating terms of human sovereignty meant under the law. In this sense, Wheatley was not unlike James Somerset, the slave petitioner in the case brought before Lord Mansfield (who also decided the Zong case and was instrumental in guiding the modernization of the law of warranties in insurance contracts). Teresa Michaels's analysis of the Somerset case illuminates the resemblances between the two situations:

In the landmark Somerset case of 1772, an archaic notion of inalienable property helped produce a popular rhetoric of inalienable liberty. . . . Behind this confusion lies the fact that to Mansfield and his court, James Somerset was neither an autonomous individual nor a piece of merchandise. Although these two alternatives may adequately describe the world of commercial relations, the common law traditionally offered a third option in a collection of persons who were also property, the objects of a personal dominion that did not involve commercial exchange. . . . While Mansfield was famous for adapting common-law principles to accommodate newer commercial practices, his inability to control the meaning of his ruling in the Somerset case reflects some of the tensions implicit in England's transformation to a commercial society [195].[19]

When the cases of Wheatley and Somerset are viewed as pursuing the same nexus between laws and human choice, they begin to announce as well the practices and ideas of underwriting. Using texts to account for property, whether in underwriting insurance against loss or using double-entry book-keeping, meant an opportunity to reconfigure the terms of slavery under the new regime of commercial property.[20] For underwriting enables us to see just how the "tensions implicit" in a "transformation to a commercial society" may be argued through by the very idea of commercial and legal artifice.[21] Michaels puts it this way:

Blackstone's *Commentaries* illuminate the shifting definitions of property and its relation to legal personality that underwrote this debate. In Blackstone, we see that the legal conflict over the status of English slaves was, in a sense, a conflict between competing notions of real and commercial property. The complexity of Blackstone's account of slavery reflects the complexity of the common law's understanding of how these different kinds of property constitute different kinds of persons [196].

This transformation in law and practice pivoted as well on the increasingly problematic realization that the relationship between slave and master had functioned as a contractless labor obligation. The common-law understanding began to change as the law of commercial property became more defined and specific.[22] This change in turn presented an opportunity for those interested in challenging the status quo not just within the discourses of race and law but also within the discourses of gender and law.[23] What Blackstone attempted to reconcile in legal theory, Wheatley and Somerset acted upon in the realm of discourse: poetry and legal action—textually disruptive and liberatory—gave shape to new arguments about property as a function of imagining personalities.[24] Both Wheatley and Somerset found the means not only to manumit themselves from slavery but also to underwrite in broader terms the incipient conventions of imaginative and legal humanism.

For Wheatley, these underwriting conditions assure authenticity and authority that challenge (via an elaborate rearticulation of the politics of passing) the bracketing categories of race and genius. Each poetic effort is a struggle to adapt the terms of her publicity, to underwrite herself, to repossess the possibility of material sovereignty through lyric figures. When Wheatley talks about new houses, it means something different from the elegiac invocation of heavily ironized celestial homes offered by Alexander Pope or Thomas Gray, or the excessively solemn sepulchers of Isaac Watts. Herself authenticated from a public liability into a positive redeemable value, she performed the trick for others. Wheatley's doubly underwritten poetry reversed the mystery of loss, figuring an assured continuity between life and death.[25]

Secular Resurrections

I conclude by returning to the beginning—to the poetic themes that guided her career and to the "property values" arising from them. As I've discussed, Wheatley's most important role as author was to underwrite death for Boston's elites, eulogizing the significance and ultimate redeemability of mortality. She was to mediate personal catastrophe with lyric expressions of grief that somehow contained loss and then replaced it.[26] Her primary means to allay the rising merchant class's fear of nothingness (a symptom of the simultaneous burgeoning of consumerism) was the time-honored tradition of executing a proper burial. Symbolically, the deceased had to be rehoused in a fantastic mansion. Wheatley endorsed the mortgage, a symbolic debt, with poetry that iconographically represented the lost ascending to "ethereal" and "empyreal" places with features that were recognizably domestic yet hard to purchase.

Witness the following from "To Mrs. LEONARD, on the Death of her HUSBAND." She proposes a "deathless mind" to assuage and reorder the chaotic separation of body and soul that came with physical death. Find the "native of the skies" and

> Thyself prepare to pass the gloomy night,
> To join forever in the fields of light;
> To thy embrace, his joyful spirit moves,
> To thee the partner of his earthly loves;
> He welcomes thee to pleasures more refin'd
> And better suited to the deathless mind [138–39].

It should be noted that this poem was occasioned by the death of the husband of Thankfull Leonard, daughter of Thomas Hubbard, one of her authenticity underwriters. Thus a double debt is paid by Wheatley: to one who helped her gain "authentic" presence in the public sphere, and a more conventional Christian exchange of body for spirit. At another level, the exchange can be described in the following way: one literary value (Wheatley the embodied author of verse) is catalyzed in the fiduciary authorial act into another (Leonard's disembodied value as a celestial inhabitant, the salvation of authenticity in the face of final annihilation). The property underwriter's law of conservation of value is affirmed through a kind of secular transubstantiation: an owned writer, a new kind of author, mediates the rehousing that leaves the soul's integrity undisturbed.

When Wheatley is seen to span the divide between heavenly houses and material contingencies, she becomes an especially compelling elegist. There are numerous examples of this throughout her poetry. Indeed, what strikes the reader most forcefully about Wheatley's poetry is its obsessive ethereality, its need to dwell in immateriality, which seems to go beyond even the most pious conventions of her time. This from "On the Death of a Young Lady of Five Years of Age": "Perfect in bliss she from her heav'nly home / Looks down, and smiling beckons you to come . . . " (58). Or, from "To the Honourable T. H. Exqu; On the Death of His Daughter," presumably the Thankfull Leonard of the previous poem, daughter of Thomas Hubbard ("T.H."):

> She leaves her earthly mansion for the skies
> Where new creations feast her wond'ring eyes.
> [. . .]
> To the same high empyreal mansions come,
> She joins her spouse, and smiles upon the tomb . . . [97].

Again, one wonders at the eager insistence on representing loss as a material place with obviously unearthly coordinates. An explanation for this may lie in her previously analyzed authorial position and function—an item of property herself, problematically generated as an authentic freethinking slave, revisiting older poetic models and imitating their styles. Everything about Wheatley as an elegist is fraught with the paradox of her authorial condition, and nothing more so than her eerie conviction of the realness of her disembodied locations for lost souls. Frank Shuffelton has called such elegiac moments a "communal vision of conversation and power in which the slave becomes masterly" (81).[27] I would add that a crucial component of these figures is the aesthetic notion of surrender—the surrender to communal and religious feeling and the surrender of one value for another, so crucial to the methods of possession, exchange, and loss.[28]

There is, finally, an aesthetic of surrender wielded in consistently surprising ways in Wheatley's poetry of loss. "TO A LADY ON HER REMARKABLE PRESERVATION IN AN HURRICANE IN *NORTH-CAROLINA*" (probably written sometime after the famously destructive hurricane of 1769) grappled with this notion of surrender and loss and so reengaged the enigmas initiated by her first published poem, "On Messrs. Hussey and Coffin":

> Though thou did'st hear the tempest from afar,
> And felt'st the horrors of the wat'ry war,
> To me unknown, yet on this peaceful shore
> Methinks I hear the storm tumultuous roar,

And how stern *Boreas* with impetuous hand
Compelle'd the *Nereids* to usurp the land.

To this point, the poem echoes, albeit in a statelier manner, the imaginative sympathies of "On Messrs. Hussey and Coffin." As the ship's demise becomes inevitable, we are told of the crucial preservation:

> But thee, *Maria*, a kind *Nereid's* shield
> Preserv'd from sinking, and thy form upheld:
> And sure some heav'nly oracle design'd
> At that dread crisis to instruct thy mind
> Things of eternal consequence to weigh,
> And to thine heart just feelings to convey
> Of things above, and of the future doom,
> And what the births of the dread world to come.

Once again, the poem matches the psychology of the earliest poem. Even absent the word "consideration" to direct the poetics of loss, the trope is one of reciprocity, as Wheatley imagines a "heavenly oracle" plotting to make Maria consider the "weight" of final self-annihilation in this world. Somehow this prayerful meditation is for Wheatley appropriately redemptive:

> From tossing seas I welcome thee to land.
> "Resign her, *Nereid*," 'twas thy God's command.
> Thy spouse late buried, as thy fears conceiv'd,
> Again returns, thy fears are all reliev'd:
> Thy daughter blooming with superior grace
> Again thou see'st, again thine arms embrace;
> O come, and joyful show thy spouse his heir,
> And what the blessings of maternal care! [86–87]

Note that the poet is empowered to "welcome" Maria to the safe shore—underwritten, that is, by God's command to "resign her." "Resign," as with "consideration" in the earlier poem, obtrudes as the interesting and strangely flexible word here. According to the *Oxford English Dictionary*, "resign" carries myriad connotations having to do with relinquishment of things, lives, offices, and so forth—especially so in the eighteenth century. According to Wheatley, Nereid was instructed to resign her possession, her right of capture, so that Maria might return in fulfillment of her imaginative consideration of what death means to her.

Preservation is ensured by the explicit instruction for someone else to let go, to surrender in exchange. God underwrites through the ventriloquence of Wheatley's familiar crisis. The terms of the poetic contract are now complete, and Maria is welcomed back to the pleasures of her daughter and husband. Similar operations are afoot in all these poems. She assures the commissioning survivors that a new habitation has been figured, that a contract has been completed by deed and exchange, that a represented value survives in glorious surrender to the tangible artifice of her poetic surveying.

It may be argued that such maneuvers are evident elsewhere in eighteenth-century religious elegies—indeed, that they are crucial to the genre. Seven of her authenticity underwriters were clergy—a significantly noncommercial bloc of signatures. But to see this poetry as exclusively generic or conventionally Christian is to ignore the terms of its production and its public presentation. It pays to remember the controversy surrounding her authenticity, how that might be thematically charged in ways that are unaccountable within given closed circuits of literary evaluation. For if, as many writers and political economists have observed, scriptural paper money elides the commodity, then underwriting does just the opposite with its inscriptions—it keeps the commodity forms always in view, translated and transposed, to be sure, but there in some anomalous way. For Wheatley, these conditions assure her of her authenticity and authority, her real place in imagined publics. Wheatley's ethereality can be read as an anachronism or as a challenging question that cannot be answered solely by the rules of property law: What does it mean to own something in this new public?

Wheatley's condition as slave and then manumitted ex-slave has provoked even more pointed questions that have nagged her critics: Whose interests did Phillis Wheatley serve, ultimately? Who really benefited from her necessary deferrals, her crafty (possibly unconscious) reinvestments in the figures of loss, the degree to which her imagination fed productively on the commercial world that produced her in turn? Walter Benn Michaels, in *The Gold Standard and the Logic of Naturalism*, makes a point worth considering in demystifying the paradoxes of property underwriting itself within the emergent symbolic economy of capital: "Identifying persons with money made money as irrevocable and unquestionable as persons. From this perspective, then, the logic of naturalism served the interests not of any individual or any group of individuals but of the money economy itself" (178).[29] While this may seem a formulation that amounts to Wheatley's invidious entrapment in a particular economic system, the logic of insurance suggests that it need not be viewed as necessarily so. Underwriting afforded her unexpected scripts. Wheatley served the economy that presented her with margins of economic and intellectual freedom—the poetics of underwriting revealed opportunities for challenging the methods of slavery.[30] In the business of her life, she exploited the techniques of dispossession and, by chance and by design, made good on the hope of a promise.

CHAPTER THREE

Hartford

Noah Webster's Foundations: Charitable Societies, the National Lexicon, Contracts, and Copyright

> INSURED, Made sure; assured; secured against loss.
> —Webster's *American Dictionary of the English Language* (1828)

> ... if the people of one country cannot preserve an identity of ideas, they cannot retain an identity of language.
> —Preface, *American Dictionary of the English Language*

> A foundation is a promise.
> —Jacques Derrida, "Force of Law: The 'Mystical Foundation of Authority'"

It is something of a mystery, even to the insurance companies that made the city famous, why Hartford became an insurance underwriting capital. Hawthorne Daniel, author of *The Hartford of Hartford: An Insurance Company's Part in a Century and a Half of American History*, attributes its importance in large part to a sense of intellectual "alertness" (7).[1] And no Hartfordian was as "active" and "alert" as Noah Webster, who, we are told by Daniel, did most of his early writing in Hartford. It was there, too, that Webster formulated, according to Daniel, "the very first really thoughtful plan for workmen's compensation and unemployment insurance" (7).

In truth, the plan was more like a charity, but with important features of conventional underwriting schemes. Like Franklin before him, Webster attempted to garner public support for the establishment of what functioned as a friendly society, but Webster insisted on calling a charitable society. In December 1791 he wrote an address to the people of Hartford, advocating for a fund which would be targeted to the needs of poor laborers:

TO THE CITIZENS OF HARTFORD

Poverty and want, in consequence of unforeseen and unavoidable misfortunes, are the lot of great multitudes of men. Sickness, wounds, fire, shipwreck, and other calamities, from which no man is exempt, frequently and suddenly deprive whole families of property and the means of subsistence.

The laws of Connecticut require that every town shall support its own poor. But there are, in every town, more especially in Hartford, great numbers of mechanics and other laborers, who do not fall under the description of the poor of the town, who, notwithstanding, have no means of subsistence but their daily earnings. Many of these are honest, industrious, and frugal, with large families. While the parents are in health, they are able by their labor to feed and clothe their families, and enjoy all the necessaries, and many of the conveniences of life.

Webster's concern here is to indemnify a part of society that had been left out of the social contract instantiated by Connecticut's ineffective regime of Elizabethan-derived poor laws. The scheme is in the theoretical self-interest of all classes of society. What happens to the working poor in the event of accident, illness, or loss not only is critical to avoiding burdening workers themselves, but such events also present an important obligation to the "overseers" of the poor. There is an understanding of the interrelatedness of social groups as well as an aggregated sense of the effects of exposure to risk, a kind of economic holism that was less a matter of social solidarity than it was pragmatic political economy:

But such people are as much exposed to sudden sickness and losses, as others, and more exposed to wounds which disable them for weeks or months, than people in easier circumstances. By such misfortunes, they are often reduced to want without fault of their own, and pride or modesty may prevent them from disclosing their distress and applying to the overseer of the poor for relief. Their families thus suffer, or they must contract debts for supplies, which debts afterward oppress and harass them. Instances of this kind happen every year, and within every man's observation.

In its rough outline, this appears to be an early form of disability insurance (it excludes the nonlaboring poor). A worker must "pay" into the social project with earnest labor before he can expect this form of charity. Whatever the precise protocol, and however primitive the mechanism, Webster was an early proponent of underwriting loss as a manifestly social benefit.

The attentiveness to social need and to the power of pooled private funds may be viewed as a necessary response to Webster's own provocation. After his antirepublican conversion, at the end of the 1780's, Webster evinced a damn-the-poor attitude that required, it would seem, subsequent moderation. In 1787, Webster had fretted for the preservation of property rights amidst radical republican debt repayment proposals, asserting the need for property's safeguarding within an increasingly chaotic political culture. By 1791, Webster saw fit to advocate a safety net. Indeed, this proposal constituted a recalibration to the social ramifications of his politics, undertaken as a public insurance proposal.

Despite the difference in attitude toward social class, there is a commonality between the Webster of 1787 and the Webster of 1791. Indeed, on view is a doctrine he held consistently throughout his life: the absolute sanctity of written contracts, of legal obligation and the commensurability of mutual interests as the basis for rational social cohesion:[2]

Instead of legal security of rights under governments of our own choice, and under our control, we find property at least unsafe, even in our best toned government. Our charters may be wrested from us without fault, our contracts may be changed or set aside without our consent, by the breath of a popular Legislature. Instead of a diminution of taxes, our public charges are multiplied; and to the weight of accumulating debts, we are perpetually making accessions by expensiv follies. . . .[3]

Webster was favoring a tilt toward the rights of individual property, an elitism of wealth and knowledge that reflected the rising power of commercial Hartford as an underwriting capital. With this switch to the interests of an early national elite, as well as his recognition of the baleful effects of economic boom-and-bust cycles, Webster adjusted his public philosophy to follow the prevailing directions of local civic life. But again, it is important to recognize, as David Simpson persuasively argues in *The Politics of American English*, that Webster refrained from altering fundamental concepts about what mattered most in public and commercial discourse. These continuities sent his public philosophy beyond the local, compelling him to envision the enlargement of social contracts into national ideas.[4]

Another good indication of this consistency is his later advocacy for a different charitable society, this one in 1803. Webster wrote to mechanics and seamen in New Haven, using as a rough template the plan for the fund he had written about in 1791. The difference was that workers themselves would pay into the fund according to the tested accounting principles of insurance underwriting:

The wise and humane policy of our ancestors has incorporated into our system of government a general provision for the poor of all descriptions, and the taxes necessary to carry the laws on this subject into effect, constitute no small part of our public burdens. But it is well known that the means of subsistence furnished to the poor by public bodies are often scanty. . . . In the vicissitudes of life, no man or family however prosperous and wealthy can calculate, with certainty, upon continuing in easy circumstances. Sudden losses at sea, or by fire; the death, sickness or inability of the head of a family, and various other misfortunes often reduce families from comfortable circumstances to real distress. . . .[5]

The answer for Webster was to set up a fund whose premiums would be paid by the subscribers "engag[ed] to pay, towards the common fund . . . and the interest to be used for the relief of such as may be in want, especially the families of subscribers" (Rollins, ed. *The Autobiographies of Noah Webster: From the Letters and Essays, Memoir, and Diary*, 172). In making his own gift investment in the society, Webster employed the core words he formed his public philosophy around—"bind," "authorize," "obligate," and "write": "For the purpose of encouraging an institution of this kind I will bind myself, my heirs, executors and administrators, and I do this by writing, thus obligate myself and them, to pay annually the sum of ten dollars, for the term of ten years, to such person as the society shall authorize to receive the same . . . " (Rollins, ed., *The Autobiographies of Noah Webster*, 172).

Webster's interest in providing for that segment of the public for whom sudden loss meant catastrophe was commendable on its own. But it is critical to recognize that it was part of Webster's greater effort to seek an ordering, stabilizing authority and underwrite it monetarily and linguistically. Webster took Franklin's underwriting stratagem and turned it into a hallowed commandment, redolent of the religious fervors that continued to inform public thinking in the early national period. Michael Warner provides an apposite statement about such constitutionalist thinking: "In the systems of positive law that characterize modern society—systems of law, let us say, not underwritten by God—law is defined by its derivation of authority from itself" (Warner, *The Letters of the Republic*, 106). Webster did not waver from the guiding logic of Warner's shrewd description of constitutional authority—that one must keep strengthening the self-evidence of national law by observing the sacral authority of contracted agreements between individuals.

↜

Hawthorne Daniel's assertion of Webster's and Hartford's "alertness" to social and cultural change seems to be right. Perhaps Daniel is more right than he knows, however. Webster's dual allegiance to the ideas of insurance underwriting and linguistic property was profound enough to invite us to inquire into the connection Webster exploited between commerce and words. Webster was alert to the intersections of language and commerce, and he made strengthening and extending those intersections the explicit project of his life's work. One might say that he was uniquely placed, ideologically and geographically, to capitalize on this idea, since his great project, the creation of a standard American language, was deeply vested in preserving and promoting creole English words and keeping them within proprietary bounds.

Webster was fixated on foundations, particularly foundations of language, government, and commercial activity. In keeping with a society structured around commerce and the emerging republican politics of print, such rudiments were to be sought most productively in the realm of commerce and through the proper deployment of words.[6] Witness the grounding, rigidly organized connotations in the title of his famous series of speller, reader, and grammar, *A Grammatical Institute of the English Language* (1784).[7] Or hear it in his rationale from the preface to his *American Dictionary of the English Language* (1828), "to unfold what appear to be the genuine principles on which these languages are constructed."[8] Or view its metaphorical reach in the following from his essay "Remarks on the Manners, Government and Debt of the United States": "Having raised the pillars of the building, [Americans had] ceased to exert themselves, and seemed to forget that the whole superstructure was then to be erected" (84). He writes to Joel Barlow of his systematized plans for national education: "My views comprehend a *whole system*, intended to lay the foundation of a more correct practice of writing and speaking . . . " (Unger, *Noah Webster*, 262). Grammatical "foundations" such as these were meant to give equal and mutually reinforced footing to both the collective (the nation) and the individual (the author and inventor).[9]

Webster's process of arriving at a dictionary also reflected the need to lay foundations of social action with more solid monuments to linguistic possessiveness. The ownership of American English as a public virtue would be the product of a campaign for cultural independence that followed the military and political struggles for independence. Webster's motivation for demarcating American, as against British, English was due not only to a perceived need for a patriotic cleansing of American identity of British corruptions and inefficiencies. His urgency arose as well from a sense that language was an ideal instrument to unify American identity and save it from the geographical inevitability of mutually incomprehensible localisms, and, indeed, the flourishing of regional European languages (German in Pennsylvania, French in Maine, and so forth).[10]

Hence language needed to be systematically elaborated in order for the education of American children, who would speak the words of a monolingual American identity, to be undertaken. Webster writes innocuously in the preface to his *A Compendious Dictionary of the English Language* (1806) in terms that suggest a broader scheme to his sequence of publication. The method would serve the ends of pure American English: "On the first publication of my Institutes of the English Language, more than twenty years ago, that eminent classical scholar and divine, the late Dr. Goodrich of Durham, recommended to me to complete a system of elementary principles, for the instruction of youth in the English language, by compiling and publishing a dictionary."[11]

Having taken Elizur Goodrich's advice, Webster built the foundations for a nationalized language in stages. One can view the progression as follows: the establishment of first principles in language (those of his *Grammatical Institute*, in the 1780's), the compiling of a compendium (1806), and the completion of a true dictionary (1826), culminating a completed textual monument to the rules and obligations of American English. With that closure in sight, the absolute design would be secured. In effect, Webster wrote a contract for the national language.[12]

The explicit sense of language and laws not only as foundational but also as something that could be systematically and progressively engineered from immutable principles is crucial to Webster's passion for continuity and uniformity.[13] Transferring authority from a Puritan and monarchical paradigm to a republican federation becomes for Webster a generalized civic problem of placing language within recognizable and preserving boundaries, and exploring that desired continuity's natural relationship to underwriting social practices. Throughout his religious conversions and philosophical revisions, Webster's alertness to the contractually underwritten claims of individual rights and obligations was one thing that remained constant. Copyright, contracts, and currency constitute the residuum in which that underwriting proposition may be read most clearly.

Backing Currency and Regulating Words

This fetish of solidity and foundationalism was most pronounced in Webster's substantial contribution to the national debate about currency, private lending practices, and public debt.[14] Webster took the side of a limited and well-regulated paper currency tied to proportional reserves of specie, his grounding principles for monetary policy residing in the sacrosanct nature of private contracts. Such specific concerns guided him to a nationalism that centered on the need for cultural consolidation, which in turn would derive its public and private virtues from religious and political prescriptions for individual and social action.[15]

Postrevolutionary debates about the role of banks, currency standards, and respect for contractual obligations generated a monetary conservatism that was coextensive with Webster's views about the necessity of a well-measured and common linguistic standard. (It was a time of inflation and worries about national solvency, given the massive number of government promissory notes issued to Revolutionary War soldiers.) In his fight against devaluation brought on by fiat currency, and for fixed exchange rates between currencies, Webster showed a steadfast belief in the commensurability of monetary values through time and across cultural and regional differences. Such concerns were brought directly into his linguistic project. His 1806 *Compendium* (following the model of John Entick's 1764 dictionary[16]) includes for the use of merchants a complete table of currency conversions and equivalences. Elsewhere in Webster's writing, the idea of monetary conversions and equivalences was articulated in ways that promoted specific policies designed to counter the devaluation and corruption of contracted promise that he saw enshrined into the process of debt redemption. For Webster, banks were important underwriters of social discourse, since they played a key role in securing public trust and maintaining healthy commerce through the issuance of circulating notes.

In the *Connecticut Courant*, during March 1791, Webster published three articles called "On the Utility of Banks" (interestingly, part of a larger series that included his first plan for a charitable society) which advocated the use of state-sponsored banks to underwrite a variety of public and private projects. One of the advantages of banks was that they could issue notes that obviated the imprecise need for barter—an odious practice for someone, like Webster, interested in the predictability and credibility of text-mediated conversions and exchanges.[17] Again, Webster remained consistent on the key functions of well-regulated banks. Late in life, he writes of solidly backing currency and of the innate value of equalizing money supply with levels of trade:

The Bank of the United States is to furnish a paper currency of universal credit throughout the nation. To accomplish this highly important purpose, in the manner most conduciv to the general welfare, and its own interests, two objectives are to be kept in view. One is, to sustain a currency equal, and no more than equal, to the exigencies of trade; and the other, to maintain this currency on the least possible specie-basis.[18]

The dual importance of specie and well-regulated currency surfaces again and again in his economic writing. Insofar as banks were the underwriters of national currency, they had a responsibility to be conservative with their ability to redeem in times of crisis. Writing in his "Remarks on the Manners, Government and Debt of the United States" (1787), Webster is keen to make the link between commercial/monetary folly and the "subversion" of "supports of social confidence":

Such are the sources of corruption in commercial intercourse. A relaxation of principle, in one instance, leads to every species of vice, and operates till its causes cease to exist, or till all the supports of social confidence are subverted. It is remarked by people very illiterate and circumscribed in their observation, that there is not now the same confidence between man and man, which existed before the war. It is doubtless true; this distrust of individuals, a general corruption of manners, idleness, and all its train of fatal consequences, may be resolved into two causes: the sudden flood of money during the late war, and a constant fluctuation of the value of currencies [Webster, "Remarks on the Manners, Government and Debt of the United States," in *A Collection of Essays and Fugitiv Writings on Moral, Historical, Political and Literary Subjects*, 107].

Here, Webster's brief for substantiated credibility and mutual trust is tied to the necessity for a stable currency backed by material value. An excess of purported value, albeit illegitimate and corrupt, drives concurrent degradation of individual and collective virtue. Even those "illiterate and circumscribed" observers see the symptoms.

A literate man, however, might see more than symptoms; he might find the source of the disease. It is not hard to see how Webster's philological pursuits delivered him to such origins. His linguistic philosophy, with its etymological and grammatical foundationalism, may be read back through his ""Letter to the Secretary of the Treasury, on the Commerce and Currency of the United States," which Webster refers to as an attempt to restore "solidity and prosperity to the commerce of the nation." His solution to the ongoing crisis of debt redemption in the new republic was to call upon a principle of mutual accounting and conservation of currency that would function as a trust-generating throttle on depreciating values and rising prices. Webster begins with a (characteristically false) show of humility:

What remedy can be applied to so great an evil, it is not for me to determin. But if I may offer my sentiments freely, I must acknowlege that I think no measure can produce so much mischief, as the circulation of a depreciated changeable currency. Let all our debts be placed on the footing of bank stock, and made transferable only at the treasury; or let the present evidences of it be called in, and new notes issued, payable only to the creditor or original holder; or let the securities be purchased at their current discount, let some method be adopted to draw them from circulation; for they destroy public and private confidence; they cut the sinews of industry; they operate like a slow poison, dissolving the stamina of government, moral principles [110].

Whatever the particular course of treatment, the effect ought to be simple and inviolable. Depreciation can be remedied only by a fully backed, reliably redeemable currency: "No paper should circulate in a commercial country, which is not a representativ of ready cash; it must at least command punctual interest, and security of the principal when demanded" (110). The hyperbole and sense of panic Webster employs suggest the foundationalism of his linguistic and copyright projects. Rather than arguing for specie-backed paper credit in terms similar to those of Hume, who counseled calmly against "encreasing money beyond its natural proportion to labour and commodities" (David Hume, "Of Money," 44). Webster saw wider stakes and used more potent rhetoric. Evil, as a socially derived force, is the product of representational insecurity, which has a deeper source (spiritual and semiotic) than a neutral policymaker might suppose. Indeed, if the public is corrupted in the social arena of money, it will not be long before similar corruptions spread to heretofore unaccountable areas of discourse, such as the grammatical underpinnings of language.

This depth theory of the importance of hard currency, secured by a stable and consistent form of collateral, found other, more vehement expressions. His terminology could inflate until it did the work of religious judgment. In his

1787 tract called "The Devil Is in You," Webster declares even more forcefully in favor of hard currency and makes explicit whereof he finds his legal arguments—in the theory of commercial contracts:

My countrymen, the devil is among you. Make paper as much as you please; make it a tender in all future contracts, or let it rest on its own bottom: But remember that past contracts are sacred things; that legislatures have no right to interfere with them; they have no right to say, a debt shall be paid at a discount, or in any manner which the parties never intended [Webster, "The Devil Is in You," in *A Collection of Essays and Fugitiv Writings*, 130].

The doctrine of money's tangible effect on the soul achieved its power from the sacredness of the written contract. Such inviolability went deeper than market exigencies or individual desires, and into the genetic spirit of the contract. Or, as Webster puts it in his unpublished 1787 essay "On a Discrimination between the Original Holders and Purchasers of Certificates," "It is the design of the contract, not the words, which should be pursued; for it must be remembered, that the design of the public has been counteracted" (*A Collection of Essays and Fugitiv Writings*, 379).

This may be perceived as promoting the opposite of stability, especially because Webster urges us to look beyond the "words" of a contract. But Webster's foundationalism saw the design of a contract arising in part from the limiting functions of tradition; "design" was a product of those bounded sets (of language, of money, of social order) that require a historical vigilance in the act of preservation. There is a recursive logic resulting from the contractual fetish: for Webster, contracts were sacred because language derived its authority and its restrictions from philosophical and philological doctrines that transcended the uncertainties of economic reality and partook of timeless moral truths. Language, like contracts in the financial realm, took its meanings from an almost objectively real structural and intentional "design," and all that flowed from such designs could be called justice and be perceived as tradition.[19] And, like money, language ought not be left to negotiation, speculation, or the free unauthorized circulation of paper. It should instead be anchored prudently, by a sense of property answerable to a nationalized social imaginary, made agreeable, stable, and lasting in the indemnifying contract.

Webster sought much of his philology in the work of Louis Moreau de Maupertuis (*Réflexions philosophiques sur l'origine des langues, et la signification des mots*, 1748), Johann David Michaelis (*Dissertation on the Influence of Opinions on Language and of Language on Opinions*, 1760), and Johann Gottfried Herder (*On the Origin of Language*, 1770). What resulted from his study was a composite linguistic theory, which placed its faith in a reductivist notion of etymology and colloquial democracy. Linguistic legitimacy derived from original generative meanings and from the most rational and widespread current deployment of those meanings.[20] In that composite one discerns the homology to faith in hard currencies and the contractual stabilizing of value.

For instance, we are told by Webster that all languages can, in the end, be distilled to universal principles and even a common set of verbs—thirty-four, to be exact. Webster's fascination with the hard laws of linguistic generation echoes his belief in the natural and inviolable laws of contract and metal-backed currency. Both tend to generate value in only one direction, and only insofar as they are legitimated by proper rules of use and etymology. The appeal to authority also stands parallel with Webster's insistent belief in the power of the designing, well-educated author (Webster foremost among them) to effect the constancy of language. That this would be done through the sale of his books was all to the better. In keeping with the notion that all contracts need endorsement, these books in turn would not be self-evidently worth using but needed their own collateral approvals. The 1790 (second) edition of his speller came complete with three pages filled with the names of forty-one eminences (including Ezra Stiles, Benjamin West, and Timothy Dwight) supporting the book. Such endorsements bespeak as well the urge to use the power of an individual signature—an underwriting name, with the authority that supplants debate or any surplus declarations of value—to take the place of the French tradition of philology he drew on.[21]

Indeed, what is so important about spellers, grammars, and dictionaries is that, like banks, they represent fixed stores of meaning that social activity tends to cheapen. They stabilize the exchange differentials within and between languages that are predisposed to devalue words over the course of time. Repeatedly, in his prefaces to both the compendium and the dictionary, Webster asserts the need to correct errors of usage, not only in the halls of academe but also in common writing and parlance. Such correction is not pedantic, by Webster's view, any more than bankers' enforcement of good monetary policies could be seen as unnecessary or foolish. Rather, such punctiliousness assures national functionality, continuity, and a kind of preservation of that which would be chaotic and subject to loss. Webster's principle of social order makes primary the virtue of contracts with language and contracts with debt. This contractual view of language and, ultimately, nation raises a question that derives from the theory of insurance contracts and monetary devaluation.[22] How might the nation—as an idea, and in its organizing languages and social practices—be used as a hedge against both financial and cultural risk?

The new republican nation can be analyzed as a particular response to a new financial formation. As Ruwell, Fowler, and others have noted with regard to the rise of insurance underwriters in the 1790's, one of the great consolidating aspects of nationhood came with the development of American-based financial markets.[23] Such markets could only arise and be shaped once there was a sufficient pool of capital, made available by Alexander Hamilton's development of banks, the concerted floating of national debt, and the quickly accumulating capital pools of the insurance industry.

Webster offers a way of approaching this crucial question of cultural and commercial interaction. After the revolution, financiers were the strongest voices lobbying for the levying of taxes and a national bank; they wanted to fix and stabilize available credit and have the proliferation of increasingly devalued paper money be in some way redeemed. Webster's views on the role of the national government in the regulation of money and capital markets are somewhat hard to generalize about. But in the end they may be resolved to a public-mindedness that understood the power of private money to accomplish collective goals. Looking back on the Revolutionary period, Webster wrote to James Kent (a member of the New York Supreme Court) on October 20, 1804, that

the neglect of New York and Rhode Island to comply with the measure of a general impost, the popular tumults and discontents in New England in 1783 and 4 on account of the half pay and Commutation, which menaced Connecticut with a revolution, the total loss of public credit, and the ruinous state of our commerce, induced me, tho then young in political affairs, to take up the pen. In a series of papers, published in the [Connecticut] Courant in 1783 and 4, I combated the spirit of popular discontent under the signature of "Honorious," &c. and in February, 1784, in a series of papers under the title of the "Policy of Connecticut," which were intended to persuade the legislature to empower Congress to lay and collect an impost, I introduced the subject by endeavoring to evince the absolute necessity of enlarging the powers of Congress, or rather of creating a supreme power adequate to the purposes of a general government. I was much flattered by the success of my essays . . . [Rollins, ed., *The Autobiographies of Noah Webster*, 91].

Webster used similar terms to argue for the private financing of public amenities, such as museums. These investments would be public-private ventures and have the primary virtue of being exceedingly safe investments for both the public and the individual investor: "Such useful establishments [museums, libraries, and so forth] will always experience encouragement from the state legislatures, and all wise governments, by donations of land, grants of lotteries, or special privileges, so that the undertaker will obtain a large interest for his capital without any risk, by getting the building and its contents insured against fire or other accidents."[24] Taking on such projects would be well worth the risk of loss involved for an entrepreneur, since the public, through its governments, stood ready to contribute to their mutual satisfaction. Underwriting with collateral or lotteries was a kind of investment without the dangers of loss.

Debt, whether individual or collective, was another matter. National debt was inherently risky, since it is a form of unwanted exposure to a potential loss of value. But debt involved a series of textual promissory obligations that Webster thought highly of, despite the risk of loss involved in unstable, time-sensitive markets. Over and against risk, the ability to promote monetary obligation based on contracted values constituted a kind of national bookkeeping virtue writ large. Such virtue was to be promoted on a national scale, through the use of national time to repay creditors, and the use of national assets (in effect, national economies) to leverage debt. The ability to do it at all was to be a sign of strength, an indication that valuing the word as bond could redeem and even reverse natural tendencies to political and economic corruption.

Debt is thus a form of national possession, underwritten by material promises and by what one might call "public equity." Nations are underwritten as a series of publicly agreed-upon equity provisions by the prospect of future redemptions. Webster's view held that debt ought to be as freely distributed and negotiated as possible. But, in accordance with the orthodoxy of Smith's theory of market action, Webster bridled at the thought of government interference in setting the terms of fair credit, holding instead that the market was sufficient to decide reasonable terms of interest. Webster writes in "The Injustice, Absurdity, and Bad Policy of Laws against Usury" (1789):

> Money is a species of commercial property, in which a man haz az complete ownership, az in any other chattel interest. He haz therefore the same natural right to exercise every act of ownership upon money, az upon any other personal estate; and it iz contended, he ought to hav the same civil and political right. He ought to hav the same right in trade with money az with goods; to sell, to loan and exchange it to any advantage whatever, provided there iz no fraud in the business, and the minds of the parties meet in the contracts. The legislature haz no right to interfere with private contracts, and say that a man shall make no more than a certain profit per cent on the sale of hiz goods, or limit the rent of hiz house to the annual sum of forty pounds [*A Collection of Essays and Fugitiv Writings*, 304].

Webster advocates less for the market as the real setting of contractual health than for something slightly different, and it is more ideological than metaphorical. He means to acclaim the natural contractual freedoms of private individuals, a set of actors and rights that exist prior to the marketplace (an article of faith among contemporary libertarians). Markets are merely sites operating under the rules of classical economics, the zone of activity encompassing the rights and interests of private actors and the generation of public welfare; as such, markets tell us only a partial story about what is supposed to happen there. Contracts are what truly matter, since they are the individualized nexus between private and public within the market; contracts between individuals also imply obligations to the public and to the inherent designs of language. Negotiating contracts ought to be as free as private interests desire; but, once signed, contracts are subject to the demands of the public.[25] The designs of the private are indebted to the public.

Private money had public virtues, but public opinions and documents (though the products of private minds who were otherwise entitled to copyright protection) belonged to a kind of national treasury. While Webster viewed money as ideal when it circulates autonomously (albeit in regulated underwritten amounts) within the nation, he defaulted to a more stringent, conservative position with regard to public discourse; this he viewed as a national treasure to be compiled and safeguarded against loss, one of the methods of republican public spirit. Such an arithmetic view of national well-being is implicit in a comment made in the preface to *A Collection of Essays and Fugitiv Writings*: "I am attached to America by berth, education and habit; but abuv all, by a philosophical view of her situation, and the superior advantages she enjoys, for augmenting the sum of social happiness" (x).

Augmenting the sum of social happiness recalls the work of social underwriting that pervaded Webster's archival projects. The case of Webster's relationship to the New York publisher, merchant, and broker Ebenezer Hazard is instructive. Hazard was, among other things, an important figure in early national thinking about texts as part of a public record to be preserved and safeguarded.[26] Hazard had contact with Webster in the painstaking labor of putting together his two volumes of American "state papers" and his *Historical Collections: Consisting of State Papers and Other Authentic Documents; Intended as Materials for an History of the United States of America* (Philadelphia, 1792–1794).[27] Hazard was also one of the first Americans to propose tontines as an early form of life insurance. The first American marine insurance company was started as a side business for a life insurance lottery, or tontine (named after the Italian banker Lorenzo Tonti). The tontine worked on the premise that subscribers would purchase shares in a lottery, and the last remaining subscriber would receive the remaining principal after the fund paid out prorated amounts based on length of contribution. Hazard would become the instigator and later the secretary of the Philadelphia Tontine. That Webster and Hazard had their hands in the development of both insurance schemes and in the meticulous preservation of historical American texts is in keeping with the underwriting premise I have been elaborating. Their mutual pursuits share the idea that collective loss is recoupable only through the action of individuals choosing to compile stakes in the fate of the text, whether state archives or life insurance policies.

Public records and insurance came together elsewhere in Webster's career. In

1802, Webster published the first history of the U.S. insurance and banking industry, a "Sketch of the History and Present State of Banks and Insurance Companies." It comprises a rather dry compilation of the essential figures, policies, and histories of each major American bank and insurance company over the preceding twenty years. His final paragraph, however, is telling. Webster extols the generation of finance capital by the successful growth of banking and insurance enterprises. Credit, trust, and institutional durability have marked the dual fate of the country and the companies:

> Within twenty years, in a young country, just emerged from the depression of a colonial state, we have seen thirty three public banks organized and put in operation, with capitals amounting to more than double the sum of circulating specie in the United States. ... We have seen these banking institutions and the insurance companies, so well conducted, that their credit has remained unimpaired. ... These facts, while they inspire confidence in the credit of the institutions, evince a degree of ability, diligence and integrity ... to the commercial character of the United States.[28]

Underwriting the Copyright

Insurance comprised a conceptual boundary in the new nation's textual landscape, marking with its contestations and growth how texts might be circulated and interpreted. As we have seen, the underwriting of money and contracts also helps us to distinguish how Noah Webster viewed the manifold functions and contexts of language. For Webster, some texts were the product of private and individual interest (for example, an investment in a private bond), some were the products of the public or the nation (for example, dictionaries, grammars, historical documents), and some were both/and (for example, insurance tontines, Webster's dictionaries and grammars, Hazard's historical compilations). In all cases, such writing does the work of underwriting, connecting notional symbols with material property and economic privileges in a way that has the urgency of moral necessity.

Martha Woodmansee suggests that the study of copyright entails considerations of the historical and metaphysical trends unique to eighteenth- and nineteenth-century legal contexts: "The notion that property can be ideal as well as real, that under certain circumstances a person's ideas are no less his property than his hogs and horses, is a modern one."[29] Just how modern is hard to fix, but one might productively look to the colonial American situation, where the real and the ideal were in flux between Lockean and yet more utilitarian notions of authorship and language.[30] A nation as well as its laws, commerce, and cultural spirit were shaped by the explicit question of whether property was solely real or a mixture of imagined and material claims.

Webster's ardent advocacy for copyright in the new nation provides an excellent example of the arguments entailed by copyright. As any professional writer or intellectual-property attorney will confirm, copyright is a protection that seeks to balance the virtues of free circulation of ideas within a given society against the rights of the author to marketplace protection and the nurturing of individual innovation. Indeed, copyright, as a legal performance and textual mark, may be viewed as the process of underwriting property that is subject to theft and piracy. Specifically, the affixing of copyright assures the writer against a form of property loss that has been maliciously brought about. In so doing, it makes explicit the long-held legal view of property as a bundle of rights—in this case, a right of prevention that presupposes potential alienation rather than a timeless, immutable, and immanent claim on a material entity. In this regard, Marshall A. Leaffer puts it precisely: copyright "connotes a negative right, the right of the owner to prevent copying of his work" (Leaffer, *Understanding Copyright Law*, 3). As such, the ideological impetus behind the practice is derived from broad notions of social and cultural welfare rather than from the power of the author to claim an immanent entitlement.[31] Perhaps more than any other legal doctrine espoused constitutionally, copyright law explicitly merges collective goals with individual rights and powers.[32] It is, no less than contract law, the legal site for the delicate explication of underwriting property with assurances.

Insofar as copyright debates, from the British Statute of Anne (1710) onward, have centered on the term of copyright possession, copyright has been a way for authors to accrue the state-sanctioned benefits of property insurance. Wordsworth used precisely this terminology when he defended copyright in his 1838 letter to the editor of the *Kendal Mercury and Westmorland Advertiser*: "A conscientious author, who had a family to maintain, and a prospect of descendants, would regard the additional labour bestowed upon any considerable work he might have in hand, in the light of an insurance of money upon his own life for the benefit of his issue. . . ."[33]

Webster's view of copyright was a mixture of the two poles of copyright doctrine; he understood it as combining immanent rights of property with a robust sense of adding to public benefit. His effort on behalf of authors in the promotion of copyright was balanced, for instance, by the collective spirit embodied in his dictionaries.[34] Webster made distinctions between linguistic properties as common and individual. "The language of a nation," he writes in the introduction to *An American Dictionary of the English Language* (1828), "is the common property of the people, and no individual has a right to make inroads upon its principles." Linguistic principles were untouchable, but contributions *about* language were commodifiable. His work to establish the right of copyright was an outgrowth of his philosophy of language and the kinds of works he himself published—grammars, compendiums, and so forth.[35] Indeed, such work would go on to be the object of much contention well after the federal copyright statute of 1790.[36]

Webster's views on money and linguistic conservation appear at one level to be complementary, flowing from a common understanding of structural foundations and the regulation of change. But, taken hand in hand with his resolute view of copyright as a material and ideal right—the view that the author's claim to copyright was absolute and perpetual over all forms of copying[37]—Webster's logic begins to seem a bit shakier.

In other words, money was not equally material and ideal but was a controlled distillation of the two. By contrast, underwritten property is conceptually nothing more or less than its market value, whether a house or a literary text or a language collectively held. That is, the contracted value of the property is ideal, but it is also real and exchangeable in definite ways. Similar logic informs Webster's view of the qualified nature of the franchise (and his later dislike of Jacksonian democracy), where the belief in private interest generating public welfare was tethered to the possession of objective property. Webster maintained until the end of his life in 1843 his belief in the original constitutional requirements of property holding to cast an informed and appropriately interested vote in electoral politics.[38] What is common to his view of imagined property, real property, the franchise (a term of property, in fact) and money is that all rely on the sacrosanct nature of property itself.

Property (whether land, currency, book, or bond) in the postrevolutionary period was in constant danger of fractionalization, devaluation, or dispossession. With the advent of the Revolution and the resulting judicial separation, American authors no longer had the copyright protection of the Statute of Anne. Moreover, in the early 1780's, Webster became particularly affected by the law, since his reading system, embodied by what he was calling *The American Instructor* and what would later become *A Grammatical Institute*, was soon to be a bestseller. From 1783 to 1785 Webster traveled the colonies, petitioning legislatures to pass copyright protection for authors. He started in Hartford and moved on to New York and Massachusetts, gaining renown as a key figure in the movement to secure property rights for authors, above and beyond common-law protections: "In October following I went to Hartford, with a view to petition the Legislature of Connecticut, then in session in that place, for a law to secure to me the copyright of my proposed book. The petition was presented. . . . " Eventually Webster was able to impress upon James Madison the urgency of having the Continental Congress pass copyright recommendations to the states, proposing a grant of fourteen years' protection.[39] The lobbying was not finished, though, for Webster saw fit to trek the colonies to assure passage. Two years later he was still at it: "In May, 1785, I undertook a journey to the Middle and Southern States, one object of which was to procure copyright laws to be enacted. . . . " It was only with the ratification of the Constitution that copyright protection would be enshrined in article I, section 8, clause 8 as an individual right and a spur to social progress throughout the states.

Forty years after his initial legislative successes, Webster learned that the British had passed further protections in their copyright law, and he decided to bring the same to the United States. He wrote to Daniel Webster (a distant relative) in 1826, imploring him to promote a right of perpetual ownership over intellectual property:

. . . I sincerely desire that, while you are a member of the House of Representatives in Congress, your talents may be exerted in placing this species of property on the same footing as all property as to exclusive right and permanence of possession.

Among all modes of acquiring property—or exclusive ownership, the act or operation of *creating* or *making* seems to have the first claim. If anything can justly give a man an exclusive right to the occupancy and enjoyment of a thing, it must be the fact that he made it. The right of a farmer and mechanic to the exclusive enjoyment and right of disposal of what they make or produce is never questioned.

What, then, can make a difference between the produce of muscular strength and the produce of the intellect? If it should be said that as the purchaser of a bushel of wheat has obtained not only the exclusive right to the use of it for food—but the right to sow it and increase and profit by it, let it be replied, this is true; but if he sows the wheat, he must sow it on his own ground or soil. The case is different with respect to the copy of a book—which a purchaser has obtained, for the copyright is the author's soil, which the purchaser cannot legally occupy [Harry R. Warfel, ed., *Letters of Noah Webster*, 418–19].

Webster's strategy is at once a subtle dig at the yeoman pretensions of republican property theory and an argument that resonates in appropriately Lockean ways. Property, whether the result of mental or physical labor, is assigned rights of ownership by whoever stands at its figurative or literal center—the symbolic difference between physical centers and imaginative ones being moot for the purposes of law. The republican commercial virtues that Meredith McGill has shown to have driven the antiauthor bias of the antebellum book trade were trumped for Webster by the invariable "principles of ownership":

Upon what principles, let me ask, can any fellow-citizens declare that the production of the farmer and the artisan shall be protected by common law, or the principles of natural and social rights, without a special statue [sic], and without paying a premium for the enjoyment of their property, while they declare that I have only a temporary right to the fruits of my labor, and even this cannot be enjoyed without giving a premium? Are such principles as these consistent with the established doctrines of property, and of moral right and wrong among an enlightened people? Are such principles consistent with the high and honorable notions of justice and equal privilege which our citizens claim to entertain and to cherish as characteristic of modern improvements of civil society? How can the recent origin of a particular species of property vary the principles of ownership? I say nothing of the inexpedience of such a policy, as it regards the discouragement of literary exertions . . . [Warfel, ed., *Letters of Noah Webster*, 419].

Without intellectual property rights encoded in the social contract (that is, statutory law) the nation suffers in proportion to the suffering of the author or inventor.[40] To preserve such rights against piracy is to demand a premium for the use of such textual creation. More to the point, personal rights underwrite public needs and desires in ways that are neatly logical but not easy to argue. One might view this as a version of Franklin's public-private dynamics, where public and private exist in productive tension with the countervailing forces of narrative certainty and accidental experience. Copyright merely crystallized an unresolved aspect of what print was capable of and how long the benefits of property might last. The controversy over copyright as a perpetual right lasted for much of the rest of Webster's life and well into the nineteenth century.

Copyright could no more be perfectly rationalized than could the insuring function of any financial instrument—contract, debt, or money. The logic of underwriting—using stable value to insure the endurance of that value—found its negative paradoxes expressed in the practice and theory of copyright. That kind of paradox, one that suffused the linguistic and educational realms as well as the commercial, did not go unnoticed by Webster. In a letter written one month before the letter to Daniel Webster, Webster wrote to DeWitt Clinton. He added a postscript to the body of his letter, bemoaning the negative effects of copyright as an organizing principle in the educational marketplace. It constitutes an awareness of the convergence of commercial ideologies and his linguistic project, while at the same time betraying deep anxiety about the disordering tendencies of the unalloyed market-based society that "compels" competitors to betray "charters":

P.S. I had intended to notice a remarkable coincidence between our education and our commerce. The *competition* for the sale of schoolbooks has already nearly destroyed all certainty, systems, or uniformity, in instruction and in language—just as *competition* has compelled companies to abandon their business and give up their charters. I sincerely hope, Sir, that a wrong direction may not be given to our scheme of republican education, a scheme which shall raise the pride of men without furnishing the means of supporting it.[41]

Commerce and education find mutual interest in the strengthening and perpetuation of "certainty, systems, and uniformity," qualities that make ownership, both public and private, possible. And yet commerce and education are hard pressed to survive the very market forces they need to remain transcendently necessary in the structure of American society. Ownership is, in Webster's ideal republic, an unabridgable and reciprocally underwritten activity, like the insurance contract, always referring to and profiting from its own objective virtue. When that view of possession is lost, support for the national foundation, its contracted design, is lamentably corrupted.

CHAPTER FOUR

New York City

Jupiter as against the lightning rod: Melville's Properties

> New-England hath been a countrey signalized with mischiefs done
> by thunders, as much as perhaps most in the world. If things that
> are smitten by lightning were to be esteemed sacred, this were a sa-
> cred country. . . . To enumerate the instances of damages done by
> thunders in this land—houses fired, cattel slain, trees pull'd a-
> pieces, rocks pulverized, bricks vitrify'd, and ships mortify'd-
> would be to fill a volume.
>> —Cotton Mather, *Magnalia Christi Americana*

> Where the political state has achieved a full development, man
> leads a double life, a heavenly and an earthly life, not only in
> thought or consciousness but in actuality. In the political commu-
> nity he regards himself as a community being; but in civil society
> he is active as a private individual, treats other men as means, re-
> duces himself to a means, and becomes the plaything of alien pow-
> ers.
>> —Karl Marx, "On the Jewish Question"

> Where does Vulcan come in as against Roberts & Co.; Jupiter, as
> against the lightning rod; and Hermes, as against the Credit Mo-
> bilier?
>> —Karl Marx, "A Contribution to the
>> Critique of Political Economy"

One might say of Melville's stories that opportunity and misfortune—accidents, in short—highlight the individual's exposed and inconstant relationship
with property. This axiom could function persuasively as a description of his
most pessimistic fictions, from the risks involved in chasing Moby-Dick to the
hapless self-dispossession of Bartleby. And yet, as a class of events rather than
as occurrences in themselves, accidents also serve a constructive purpose. They
suggest, for Melville, a critical refuge in a volatile nation bent on disavowing the
uncertain while asserting sovereignty over the "unclaimed." They pose the possibility of figuring comfort in ownership.

Melville's revisionary understanding of accidents is on view in his short story "The Lightning-Rod Man" (1854), which satirizes the discourses of safety that find their way into the home of a rural property owner. This focus places "The Lightning-Rod Man" at a pivotal moment in Melville's career—a period in the 1850's when he faced genuine crises of ownership.[1] Having purchased, with the help of his father-in-law, Lemuel Shaw (who by no small coincidence is acknowledged as one of the most important figures in the expansion of American tort law),[2] a house in Pittsfield, Massachusetts, Melville found his luck taking a turn for the worse.[3] With the failure to make a reliable profession of writing, the strain of holding real estate increasingly became a thematic concern. Moreover, Harper & Brothers, Melville's principal American publishers, was the scene of a catastrophic fire in 1853, several months before Melville composed and then published "The Lightning-Rod Man" in *Putnam's*.

"The Lightning-Rod Man" thus may be read as an important part of his evolving decision to leave the commercial world of writing—first novel writing, then magazine writing (and then prose altogether). Perhaps more important, the story represents a foray into the meaning of writing and safety, given the instability of personal and commercial exposure. At the core of the problem in "The Lightning-Rod Man" (borne out subsequently by Melville's "exile" to the Holy Land) is the question of Providence's continued value in a fully commercialized world of material uncertainty.

Nothing less than technology-driven capitalism becomes the challenge for Melville to understand and accommodate. Ben Franklin emerges as a major pretext, given his role in the invention of both lightning rods and modern commercialism. Indeed, Franklin's lightning rod, from the moment of its invention, challenged theological understandings of the rule of Providence;[4] even more to the point of this book, Franklin's underwriting poetics are grist for Melville's revisionary play.[5] For Melville, that scientific challenge provided by Franklin had been degraded by its attendant discourses of safety; he shows the selling of lightning rods, taken to their end logic, as commercial absurdity, the narrative form of the ringing bell that signals the rod's benign functioning.

With this satire in view, the story dares to be doubtful about the society of sales and safety. Indeed, the story represents the final inversion of Franklin's optimistic and inventive capitalist ethos; Melville's lightning rod is an emblem of a thoroughgoing skepticism, of all that cannot be satisfactorily secured and underwritten. The story asks us to consider the meaning of skepticism for a man who could not, despite a resolute will, make a home from the labor of his imagination. Part of what makes the story unique in Melville's body of work is that the idea of pessimism about property is tested in the story as he had not tested it before—on land, in a scene of domesticity, without the shadows of tragedy.[6]

Again, I want to stress that Melville's pessimism[7]—charged by the underwriting discourse of Franklin's dual invention (prudent optimism *and* the light-ning rod)—is both surrender and redemption. While denying the aggressive nature of possessiveness and salesmanship, Melville points us toward an ethic of ownership that subverts conventional underwriting and denies the discourse of safety that gives underwriting its epistemological force. Underwriting, as a commercial poetics, is there in his exposé of the absurdity of scientific or reli-gious remedies for wanton chance; the story is one of Melville's most direct satires on safety and all that lies beneath its structures and discourses.

When viewed as a comedy about underwriting—the interpretive and prac-tical procedures that attempt to sell and safeguard property—"The Lightning-Rod Man" becomes an aggressive inquiry into the very logic of extracting profit and evading loss. What underwrites the home, if not the lightning rod salesman and his science? What texts underwrite Melville's attempt to offer an alterna-tive?[8] Can pessimism be hopeful?[9] Can the void beneath private (and, on occa-sion, public) spaces—the modern home, in short—be comforting?

This chapter is about a particularly tragicomic case of the figurative and practical effects of underwriting. A writing business (whether involving a writer, a publisher, or an insurer) involves the articulation of a repeatable nexus between property and text, seeking profit and security in the imaginative capa-bilities of the text. The obligations of a text tethered to the properties and the owners it names presupposed a bourgeois stability that insurance both fostered and took for granted. By 1854, though, such obligations were becoming as prob-lematic for Melville as the stolid illusion of linear narrative logic; randomness, accidental logic, and enigmatic characters filled his fiction with a new urgency. "The Lightning-Rod Man," in addition to his two great satires of commercial life, "Bartleby the Scrivener" (1853) and *The Confidence-Man* (1857), is a good example of this response. Melville satirizes hucksterism's tricky language even as he knows that his own fictional counter-underwritings are caught within the managed risks of book production and book selling.

∽

As Marx (in my epigraphs) and Melville both seem to imply, safety is an essen-tial watchword in discursively sketching the distances between heaven and earth. The modern will-to-safety and the atomizing civil society that cloisters private from public are the invasive agents within property's logic, and, once in-fected, we become like Marx's "playthings of alien powers."[10] As we shall see, Melville displays a cunning awareness of this invasiveness and of countering ef-fects of playfulness in the story. What makes "The Lightning-Rod Man" so mis-understood[11] is the extent to which Melville offers a response to Marx's critique of the self-alienating effect of capitalist forms of property. As a response, and in keeping with the playful nature of his critique, one might say that Melville sees

Marx's critique and then raises it.[12] For, in stark contrast to Marx (or Emerson, for that matter), this subjection to the underwriting logic of ownership and capitalism is, at its core, weirdly comic.

The need for protection and safety invites a comic response, whether in the age of fates and oracles or in the age of probabilism and insurance. Safety's claim is not hard to burlesque, what with the feverish calamities it asks us to imagine. Nonetheless, safety also sobers us in useful ways with its predicates and promises. Safety is the name given to the satisfying result of intricate negotiations undertaken with chance. It is a steadying nexus between the individual and all that lies beyond—from actions in society to encounters with nature. Safety is also a secondhand story about the brittle alienation lurking in society and about the possibility of nature's malevolence. But any calculation of safety is pregnant with the harsh possibility of error and thus becomes an irresistible element of fiction's representational lesson to reality. Such doubleness also suggests a generic duality: the moment a narrative focuses on safety, it will generate tragedy or comedy.

Melville's updating of the roles of chance and safety, given newer and more practical discourses and paradigms, is not his alone. Risk has been most notorious in its challenge to scientific narratives of human experience. In *The Emergence of Probability: A Philosophical Study of Early Ideas About Probability, Induction, and Statistical Inference,* Ian Hacking shows how Blaise Pascal, the father of probability and statistical analysis, attempted to make science accommodate chance, while David Hume, with his theory of induction, provided similar conceptual cover.[13] The idea of chance nonetheless remained an empirical irritant and thus became the precipitate for a commercial discourse of safety. The accident—a (usually) negative result of chance playing out in reality—has suggested, to those who would limit its appearance in the world, the dark side of juridical and personal claims to sovereignty, control, and rights.

The deep source of its comedy may reside in the presence of radical narrative incongruities within a common frame. Comedy requires surprise. Surprise happens when play puts pressure on determinism, and some necessary entropy determines that the unpredictable—the playful error—must surface every so often. This anarchic quality has narratological and rhetorical implications, giving jokes and puns their delicate calibrations within measures of time and accent. Play demands a narrative syntax that is exceptional yet natural-seeming; "X" must happen, but the event, "X," is unusual, thereby fixing in its place that which should not have a place. Scientific predictability can only name accidents as negative results, or aberrations, from the curve produced by a system of smooth plots. Play is always on the other side of safety's discourse of power and control, and accidents are the moment—both in actuality, and as part of a narrative poetics—when the ongoing tension of control dissolves while leaving grammatical and narrative sense intact.[14]

Experience confirms that there is no natural or scientific right to safety—or at least that it is futile to make the claim absolutely that one is "safe." By the same token, to acknowledge the role of chance is to accept what cannot be understood. Thomas Kavanagh, in *Enlightenment and the Shadows of Chance*, describes chance (*hasard*) as "an activity carried out against the backdrop, not so much of an almost physical danger, but of a radical silence, a fundamental inability of human thought to understand and dominate that which can be neither accounted for nor explained by the various narratives of reason" (3). For Kavanagh, chance suggests the limits of reason. I would propose that in the post-Enlightenment shadings of Emersonian thought, which placed reason in poetic relation to power and will, chance also represents the limits of a determination to exercise reason.

The new world of probability demands a response to reason—more precisely, a new disposition toward the world as it is revealed by reason. Chance challenges not only a reasonable world but also a world in which humans can be willfully reasonable. Thus it seems at once a threat to, and an opportunity for, new valuations within the controlling logics and discourses of capitalist practice. Chance constrains in this way because it toys with the edges of human theoretical capabilities, forcing us into a recursive game, a scene of radical play. In this place, the unknown compels thoughts of safety, which itself is a strategic attempt to thwart accidents. With its strategies of control, safety posits the individual alone—self-reliant but without a guarantee—in a maze of irrevocable choices that effectively mock him. Risk thereby suggests an even darker shadow, an ominous determinism, whereby the individual awakens to the futility of even attempting to avoid the dead end, the unfortunate turn, the irrecoverable loss.[15] Safety is the last fiction.

To be released from the injunction to be reasonable and safe is to be underwritten by comedy rather than by science. But it is also to worry about the efficacy of words in their relationship with the stable material world. Melville shows us precisely this. When the will is diseased or disabled, one can mourn it rhetorically with aphorisms in the manner of the earlier work of Emerson, or one can show how the conflict between chance and human determination is darkly funny and absurd, as in "The Lightning-Rod Man." A fire taught Melville that lesson.

❧

The publishing house of Harper & Brothers suffered a devastating fire—perhaps the largest commercial fire in New York City history to that point—on or about December 10, 1853. The *New York Daily Times* of December 12 treated the fire as a sensation worthy of the following headline: "DESTRUCTIVE FIRE, The Establishment of Harper & Brothers in Ruins, Over $1,000,000 of Property Destroyed!" The fire struck in spite of Harper's best efforts to make its printing complex as safe as possible. The *Daily Times* devotes the second paragraph of its story to the extraordinarily prudent lengths that Harper's had taken in safety design. The passage is notable for its discourse of safety, which is resolute and tragic, by contrast with the facts at hand:

Having suffered from a fire some ten years since, the Harper's had taken extraordinary precautions to prevent the recurrence of such a calamity. They had a large steam boiler in the cellar; but, with this exception, no fire was ever allowed to be used about the building in any form. The gas lights were so arranged as to be perfectly safe. All the buildings were heated by steam pipes, which had been carried, at an expense of over $6,000, into every part of them; and instead of the charcoal furnaces generally used in bindery establishments for heating the tools, gas-burners had been provided to take their place. Under these circumstances, a fire was impossible, but for one of those accidents which cannot be foreseen, and against which, therefore, no provision can be made.

In spite of the precision and certitude of design safety, it all burned. The conflagration was a result of the need to clean the ink rollers with an inflammable substance called camphene. Even this cleaning process was accounted for in the safety design, for it was accorded a separate room "carefully lined with zinc, and [with] all the precautions taken which seemed necessary to insure its safety." And yet a careless plumber is blamed for having ignited the blaze.

According to Jay Leyda, a complete inventory of Melville's book losses in the fire was sent to him on October 6, 1854, but surely Melville must have been alarmed.[16] The *New-York Herald* of December 12, 1853, reports on the "particulars as to the loss of the Messrs. Harper's, and the insurance on the property": and the *Daily Times* is exhaustive in its explanation of the wonder that textual masters survived the unprecedented destruction:

The amount of property destroyed by this conflagration is very heavy,—larger, probably, than any single establishment in this City has ever before been called to sustain,—and larger, it is not improper to add, than many others could sustain without utter ruin. The buildings and everything which they contained, with such trifling exceptions as scarcely to be worth mentioning, were totally consumed. Fortunately the stereotype plates, which next to their stock of books, constituted the most valuable single item of their property, were stored in vaults which extend under the pavement in Cliff-street, in front of all the buildings of the concern. The Harper's, as an invariable rule, stereotype every book they publish,—being able thus to work off new editions as they may be required. . . . It is believed they are all saved.

What is important about the reporting I've cited is that it clarifies the intimate relationship between safety and written property—indeed, makes spectacular its spatial connection for an interested public. An architecture of written safety—that is, literally and physically, the safeguarding of words by de-sign—is exhaustively detailed by such reports. While the building that rises into the air is inherently prone to fire and accidents, all that is underneath, because of its position, is saved. The safety of being underground, beneath the reach of fire, is thus affirmed—indestructible master texts avoid the ephemerality of traditional paper texts and preserve property past and future. In effect, these master plates, in their placement outside the circuit of destruction effected by the accident, underwrite the building destroyed above.

The article details, with elaborately displayed sidebars, the dollar amounts lost in property destruction as well as the property saved. Immediately follow-ing this, we are told that Harper's was insured only up to $250,000 "so that the net loss to the Harper's will not be much short of a million of dollars." Part of the problem seems to have been that no single insurer was willing to incur the risks associated with the multiple hazards of a publishing house—its enormous inflammable inventories, its combustible chemical processes, and the closeness of its separate quarters.

The Harper & Brothers fire exemplified a great problem when it came to in-suring the industry of book publishing. As an industrial and commercial enter-prise, book publishing became almost uninsurable. But, ironically, the indus-try's aesthetic and intellectual property was more durable, since the authoritative texts necessary to the reprinting and reissuing of books survived.[17] This provided little consolation to Melville, however. Hershel Parker speculates that news of the fire must have sent Melville into fits of "agony over the loss of the plates of his books," and he adds that, while disappointments related to the publication and sales of *Pierre* and *The Isle of the Cross* were "misery beyond calculation," this loss meant, in effect, having "his career wiped out abruptly and absolutely."[18] Parker goes on to retreat from the melodrama of this specu-lation, noting that the news of December 12, recounting the safety measures taken by Harper & Brothers that had preserved all of Melville's book plates, probably provided a modicum of relief.

Still, a good portion of his unsold book stock was destroyed, and Melville is said by Parker to have felt nearly in financial ruin. The passage is from an 1856 letter to Lemuel Shaw: " 'Before the fire, the books (not including any new pub-lication) were a nominal resource to me of some two or three hundred dollars a year; though less was realised, owing to my obtaining, from time to time, con-siderable advances, upon which interest had to be paid.' " In closing his account of the fire, Parker editorializes starkly on its effects:

As the defeated Melville came to see, the coolly avaricious Harpers in effect blamed him for the fire, charging him all over again for their new costs, costs which they had already deducted from his account before paying him any royalties. Honest men would have cut their losses and not charged Melville double. . . . For Melville, the fire was less than catastrophic only because his books were already selling very slowly and much of his income, for the last months, had been from stories, which he could continue to sell to the Harpers for their magazine as well as to *Putnam's*. Even as he took the advance for *The Tortoise-Hunters*, Melville was beginning to be known as a magazinist [Hershel Parker, *Herman Melville: A Biography, 1851–1891*, 188].

Melville's career went in new directions after the fire, to magazine writing and poetry. "The Lightning-Rod Man," seen in this light, becomes a step toward reconceiving writing as communicative practice and career. His turn toward *Putnam's* may in this case be a direct result of his postfire relationship with the Harper brothers.[19] The story stands as a thematic guide to Melville's exasperation with bookselling and, in a deeper sense, the idea of loss.[20] Melville's security, the material survival of his marketable texts, lay beneath the buildings of Harper's—or, more accurately, beneath the public spaces (sidewalks) fronting the buildings. Yet the potential for destruction haunted the venue that would promote and sell his work and thereby secure the financial stability of his home. How, then, to record the relationship between the industry of publishing and the threat it poses to domestic privacy and happiness? Part of the answer to this question involves the invention of the salesman of "The Lightning-Rod Man." His visitation responds to the social and economic implications of the Harper & Brothers fire for Melville's disease of certainty—his sense that property is always under threat of earthly destruction or heavenly recall.

⌐

"What grand irregular thunder," begins the verbally overloaded, comically self-reliant narrator of "The Lightning-Rod Man."[21] He attributes the "glorious[ness]" of the sound to the topography of the "Acroceraunian hills" in which he lives. What makes the thunder associated with this storm particularly irregular is the punctuation it gets from a knock at the door. This knock is made with the flesh of the hand rather than the conducting metal of the knocker—a detail derided by the narrator, somewhat ironically, as "unmanly." To not employ technology now is to be inhuman—indeed, to sound like an "undertaker"; by the same token, given the potential hazards of employing the conductive knocker, to use one's hand is a sign of womanly fear.

Such interpretive ambivalence so early in the tale begs questions: On what terms—rationality or foolhardiness, masculinity or femininity, consumption or asceticism—is bravery to be constructed? More broadly (and with equal relevance to Emerson), we might also ask: Which paradigm is wisest—safety and reason, or solitary comfort and self-reliance? Can the owner be mythically heroic as against the shrunken Jupiter of the modern age?

The focal point of the argument that might settle such hovering agonism between the homeowner and "Jupiter Tonans"[22] is the fireplace (ironically, the site of Promethean containment amidst vulnerable property). The practical question of the narrative is: Should one who is wet be near the warmth of the fire or be far from its conducting chimney? The question is the kind of fool's trap that underwrites the psychology of homeownership: Damned either way, who is to know the correct answer for keeping oneself safe on one's own property? It is a matter of chance, and only the dueling rhetorics of sales and domesticity seem to fuel action on a decision. The dialogue which makes up the bulk of Melville's narrative serves to burlesque both aristocratic tradition and contemporary hucksterism:

"Sir," said I, bowing politely, "have I the honor of a visit from that illustrious god, Jupiter Tonans?" So stood he in the Greek statue of old, grasping the lightning-bolt [119].

Or rather, more accurately, we might say that Melville slyly shows how hucksterism, in a more precise revision of Marx's aphorism, ridiculously appropriates aristocratic and classical ideas.

Ridicule seems a natural outgrowth of the tremulous scene of numbers-driven jeopardy. Jupiter, in response to the owner's grandiloquent imploring that he sit near the fire, answers by throwing down an actuarial gauntlet:

"Sir," said he, "excuse me; but instead of my accepting your invitation to be seated on the hearth there, I solemnly warn you, that you had best accept *mine*, and stand with me in the middle of the room. Good Heavens!" he cried, starting—"there is another of those awful crashes. I warn you, sir, quit the hearth" [119].

What makes Jupiter's discourse so remarkable here—indeed, so absurd—is how the will-to-safety and its allied sales pitches seem to disintegrate the real world they aim to conserve (or at least to insure through an exchange of value). By "disintegrate," I mean a comic degeneration of the object of the sales pitch—to such an extent that Jupiter loses sight of his sales script, the attempt to trade his words for the homeowner's money.

As a tactical matter, Jupiter has lost some control. He is reduced to a somewhat silly tug-of-war, centered on a dispute about positions in the room, rather than pursuing what he seems so good at (language deployed deliberately in the service of logical persuasion). Melville is indulging in nonsense here, but for a purpose, intended to demonstrate the slippery *dis*positions of language when intensified by common situations of modern anxiety. In the dialogue of Melville's story, we begin to see how certain modes of language, the "safe" and "sensible" kinds, when put in the service of commerce and scientific probability, are especially susceptible to a literary reductio ad absurdum.

Melville's comic strike must be linguistically centered. As a stable source of meaning and purpose, language is in jeopardy under such conditions, at least as much as its sheltering referents are a source of anxiety. For this language, which seems to destabilize Jupiter's intentions, has the strange ability to supplant the material (read as an easily decidable and sensible) world. Jupiter's trivial argument, meanwhile, obscures the goals of his visit—selling the rod, saving the house, improving the value of the property through its certain survival. Thus does property—the object to be bought as well as the house to be saved—fall out of view in the degradation of the sales pitch. Now it is an exchange of invitations (yours versus mine).[23]

Surprisingly, though, this comic devaluation of language has the paradoxical effect of making the homeowner more, not less, stable. The homeowner, echoing the most affirmative moment in "Self-Reliance," when Emerson commends the man who "knows his worth, and keeps things under his feet," replies that he "stand[s] very well here" (119). His self-reliance is a prelude to a direct challenge, cutting to the quick with the salesman, an attempt to restore a sense of reality and proportion to the grandiosity of the rhetoric (120): "Sir, will you be so good as to tell me your business? If you seek shelter from the storm, you are welcome, so long as you be civil; but if you come on business, open it forthwith. Who are you?" The stranger's response is both direct and fragmented, constructed as a collage of artificial fear (120): " 'I am a dealer in lightning-rods,' said the stranger, softening his tone; 'my special business is—Merciful Heaven! What a crash!—Have you ever been struck—your premises, I mean? No? It's best to be provided,' significantly rattling his metallic staff on the floor,—'by nature, there are no castles in thunderstorms; yet, say but the word, and of this cottage I can make a Gibraltar by a few waves of this wand. Hark, what Himalayas of concussions!' " The absurd persistence of mythological tropes playing out in the humble techniques of salesmanship is accented by the spectacle of Jupiter no longer vengeful but now cringing, afraid, brashly exploiting his own diminution.

Even more interesting in these exchanges is how hyperbole in the name of safety and sales appears to blur the line between play and reasonable action, the very threshold of the mind interpreting accidents.[24] So Melville ratchets up the play in this scene of "probable" disaster. Indeed, Jupiter has become the harbinger of a threefold intensification of anxiety, each level being served by its own context of playful destruction: Jupiter's own accidental (random) descent upon the hermit, fortuitously in the midst of a thunderstorm; his description of the inevitable (though unlikely) disaster and what it will mean for loss of property; and, lastly, his discourse of linguistic destruction, whereby the nominative force of words is inevitably scoped out of sight and significance. "By nature . . . no castles in thunderstorms"—the words impart potency out of proportion to content. Irony is too genteel a word to describe the semantic disparity between threat and logic—how his salesman's terror makes language's practical communicativeness seem beside the point.

It seems appropriate that the salesman seeks to revoke nature's ordinations by his customer's mere "word." With that he will make a "Gibraltar" that is all too quickly threatened by "Himalayas." There is no place to stand, and certainly no place to call home, under this assault. An agent of the market invokes nature and no sooner finds his own terms faulty and overblown, Gibraltar trumped by Himalayas. In this manner the story plays mercilessly with the scale of distances between heaven and earth, between heaven's churlish caprice and earth's stolid necessity. Gibraltars swell and shrink, Providence spares and inflicts, depending on the salesman's bellows. But the salesman's trifold accidents are gradually exposed in the story by the experience of the homeowner ("Of what use is your rod, then?"), who has an acute sense of the use value of commodities (120).

The homeowner's commonsense verbal punctures, coupled with his cool resistance to the language of sales, eventually defeats Jupiter. The final exposure begins when the homeowner finds out that the salesman has recently sold twenty-three rods in the town of Criggan. The homeowner remembers that the church's steeple, "the big elm, and the assembly-room cupola were struck" (120). The salesman admits that one of his rods was on the church steeple but blames the destruction on his "workman," "not my fault, but his" (120). Melville satirizes both religion and science, reducing the arguments of Jupiter to a feverish simulacrum of reason. He continues in this vein as the homeowner mockingly describes an accident in Montreal in which a "servant girl [was] struck at her bed-side with a rosary in her hand; the beads being metal" (120). Despite her dialogue with the heavens—indeed, because of it—that working girl is no longer. So too the church that tried in vain to supplement its religious underwriting, an attempt to swell its influence toward heaven in the form of a steeple that has as well the scientific assurance of a lightning rod.[25] The homeowner is now on to Jupiter: "For one who would arm others with fearlessness, you seem unbeseemingly timorous yourself" (121). Neither religion nor science can placate fear, but neither can they manufacture it. Only capitalism can.

↝

Kant writes, in the *Critique of Practical Reason*, "Nothing happens through blind chance." Kant's stolid dictum may be read in the nineteenth-century context of the theory and practice of money as a darkly ironic aphorism: "nothing" is indeed a real product of the new world of probabilism and its capitalized systems of knowledge. If there is a valid theory of surplus value, then there is a systematic surplus charge in the political economy of lightning—and that system is fearful or absurd, depending on one's position in and susceptibility to the rhetoric of sales and safety. Jupiter is counterinterrogated by the homeowner, who once again tries to make the sales pitch into a series of dispositions rather than a medium for intentional, objective persuasion:

"Presently. Something you just said, instead of alarming me, has strangely inspired confidence."
"What have I said?"
"You said that sometimes lightning flashes from the earth to the clouds."
"Aye, the returning-stroke, as it is called; when the earth, being overcharged with the fluid, flashes its surplus upward."
"The returning-stroke; that is, from earth to sky. Better and better" [122].

The homeowner's last words are comforting to him but disquieting for everyone else (Jupiter and readers). "Better and better" than what? Whose revenge is suggested by this enigmatic response? Could it be that Melville is exposing—via a non sequitur functioning as a wink to the knowing reader—the theoretical allegory implicit in his own tale? Probably not. But it is clearly, if not a tip-off to other, quite definite references, a wry in-character comment on how one might address "unreasonable" contingency with words and, in effect, confuse the salesman and so win the argument.[26]

The homeowner's response makes evident how much he enjoys the absurdity of the salesman's discourse and its hard-wired reprisals. I call the reprisals "wired" because the sales rhetoric itself always already suggests its own comic annihilation. Mitchell Breitwieser has noted that it was Cotton Mather who wrote of lightning in relation to an ontological "self-annihilating stroke," and that it was Franklin who made lightning's "return stroke" a mark of conservation in both electrical and monetary discourses.[27] Both the scientific phenomenon called lightning and the *fear* of lightning entail "return strokes" that suggest just how senseless the commercial pitch has become: lightning always returns to its origins, always burns its casters. This is, in its allegorical relation to language itself, the lesson of rhetorical self-cancellation that Melville obliquely points to. That, and more. For the homeowner's comment is based on the great paradox of the counting, arithmetic, actuarial age: all things of value—all things, in short, that can be said to "exist"—are dependent upon the arithmetic concept of a countable series leading out from the grounding idea of zero.

As Brian Rotman has shown, modern markets have been fundamentally dependent on the idea of nothing, and this dependence was no more apparent than in the 1830's and 1840's in debates over the predominance of paper money as against metal specie.[28] So the preoccupation with the relative value of linking material substance with the idea of nothing is likely to have been familiar to Melville. After all, the salesman stands as an ideal figure through which to circulate the idea of nothing: salesmen are counters in every practical sense of the term; they determine their success or failure by numbering consecutively and, perhaps more important for our purposes, invoking confidence and cultivating market trust based on the countable and measurable values attributable to the things their products hope to underwrite (that is, lightning rods underwrite safety, vacuum cleaners underwrite cleanliness, and so forth). And lightning rod salesmen are even better, since the metal rod is the designated destination for the immaterial power of electrical destruction, paralleling, however roughly, the metal specie/representational currency of the money debates.

Lightning rods and their salesmen are perfect emblems of this marketing apparatus. The rods are, in effect, underwriting mechanisms for a material domain that has been toted up and exists in ceaseless fear of a return to a baseline zero—the return stroke that sends a home to ashes on the ground. Counting men rely on lightning rods to drive their numbers upward from zero. Meanwhile, "The Lightning-Rod Man," as a rhetorical document, demonstrates a comfort with the counting subject—indeed, a comfortably contemptuous view of the salesman and his wares—because it recognizes the comedic force of zero.

But just how is "zero"—evocative of the possibility of loss—part of the comedy of Melville's story?[29] As a convention of underwriting practice, property is soberly underwritten by a text fortified against an artificially valuable idea of loss, that is, nothing. The closed set of things known as property excludes—and gains identity by contrast with—the null set, the managed notion of loss that insurance stands for. Why does "it" get "better and better"? Because both Marx's surplus (or Ricardo's, or the salesman's—theoretical surpluses, in short) and lightning's surplus (natural surplus) are really nothing more than imaginative constructs that are assigned values through rhetorical and textual excess. All of these surpluses/excesses in the circuits of value are charged by a human (imaginative) construct, the vanishing point of chance (nothing) that is entirely within our control.[30] We are led back to the proposition that modernity, with its discourse of safety, has curtailed and constrained, for those alert to the truth, the will to be reasonable. We may go only so far in thinking our way through to stable logic and safe lodgings. The radical irony of surpluses built upon fictions of zero can only get better and better, crueler and crueler.[31] The idea of nothing, in short, requires an ever-increasing world of discrete *some*things to give it meaning, and vice versa.

Thus this difficult irony, residing at the core of all Jupiter's admonitions, derives from the danger of materiality. The nub of Jupiter's argument is this: Human contact with the tangible world is dangerous. The touch of a live body to any conducting element, whether oak floorboards, bell pulls, window bars, or, more ominous and profound, another human being—and, even worse, a crowd —is risky, inviting heavenly punishment. The logic of risk strips the self-reliant man of the social buffer that might save him. Moreover, it asks each of us to become singular, to isolate ourselves, to be destroyed by our own hellish fantasies (123): "Do I dream? Man avoid man? And in danger-time, too."

To the homeowner, Jupiter conveys the satire within his own person—he is a conductor of heavenly punishment, the devil invading the life of the homeowner. "Jupiter," the now ironized figure from the age when the mortals and gods mingled blood, is in the age of risk assessment. He is pervasive, and at the same time he is nowhere. For Melville, the rejoinder to Marx—like the homeowner's answer to Jupiter—is simple: no sale; this home *will* be in danger, since lightning rods and scientific underwriting are laughably empty gestures. If property needs safeguards, then to be really safe means to be social, to launch humanist quests, to move away from commercial materialism.

∽

How does the story of property and fire in Herman Melville's life during the 1850's address the epistemological underwriting drama playing out between safety and chance? It helps to see the story as a working through of the emotional strains and anxieties of Melville's labor and craft. He writes a parable about the effects of certain kinds of danger on the self, wherein the individual is made relevant to the social, not in the claims of safety, but in a self-trusting resistance to safety. Melville must have sensed this new possibility for turning skepticism into comedy when he witnessed the ephemerality not only of the property he struggled to keep as home but also of the books he lost to fire in the months before writing "The Lightning-Rod Man."[32]

Indeed, the need for figurative escape or comic redemption was irresistible, in spite of Melville's bad luck with conventional economies of matter and possession. The antihumanist message of probability science and commercialism contrived to return Melville to a humanism that was oddly underwritten by the very antihumanism it rejected. The underwriting that seemed true and comforting consisted of a story which told of the possibility of a physical escape from the demands of commerce and its self-degrading logic. Such underwriting, a literary mixture of linguistic play and evasion, might have pointed out new kinds of physical and social sanctuaries—whether a public space beneath Cliff Street in Manhattan or a providential tour through Palestine.

The commercial discourse he disputed was informed by a stricter, property-centered underwriting practice that required owners of real estate to be, like Jupiter, antisocial. It required a fierce determination that insistently warned of the inevitability of the improbable. It bred anxiety that proved fertile ground both for sales and, in the hands of Melville's counterlogic, for the clever undermining of the language of sales. But in the life of a professional writer, the tensions of such discourse were too much to bear. Melville ridicules the protocols of anxiety and obsessive safety that forever preclude real security, realizing that in the face of comic tortures, property will never feel like home. Melville's burlesque stands as a last-ditch denial of pseudodeterminism and calculated heroism—poses that can no longer, from 1854 forward, withstand commercial misfortune.

"You are going to lose"

Melville has at least two other stories that address safety and commercial responses to it. One—"Bartleby the Scrivener: A Story of Wall Street" (1853)—precedes "The Lightning-Rod Man"; the other, *The Confidence-Man* (1857), comes after. They are also important metaworks about writing, seeing the eighteenth century's logics of liberation and print through to their grimly comic nineteenth-century destinations.[33]

For instance, Bartleby, both the character and the socially emblematic story about him, is nothing less than a Franklinian nightmare. It is also (and necessarily, given its Franklinian negations) the nightmare of the probabilistic world, narrating modern anomie as a sad but, in the end, random and negligible anecdote. This story is where the masses amount, precisely, to nothing. Turning Franklin's optimistic and mechanistic conception of the transmission of virtue on its head, Melville provides the story of imitation as little more than a dead-letter office.

Bartleby's very vocation is that of "imitation." He is a copyist who derives neither pleasure nor virtue from his craft. Moreover, Bartleby, we are told by his boss, the narrator, defies biography, precluding any such Franklinian models to be rescued from the past and passed on for the learning of the "rising generation": "I believe that no materials exist for a full and satisfactory biography of this man" (13). The reason is that Bartleby is without a paper trail—there is no underwriting document to lend ballast and legibility to his narratable life.

The irony is not lost on the narrator, who speaks of Bartleby's anonymity as a "loss" which cannot be replaced: "It is an irreparable loss to literature. Bartleby was one of those beings of whom nothing is ascertainable, except from the original sources, and, in his case, those are very small" (13). He is without sovereignty, even less than a slave, who would at least have the bills of sale to establish a rudimentary life story. The narrator is reduced to an impressionistic account of Bartleby, the consequence of which seems to be that he is a character who will start to recede at the very moment the story of his end begins.

For his part, the narrator is, interestingly, eminently Franklinian in his personal style. We are told that he is a believer that "the easiest way of life is the best" (14), even though he is, as a lawyer, part of a profession which is "energetic and nervous," even "turbul[ent]" (14). In many important ways, the lawyer has been Franklin's perfect pupil: like Franklin, he is the type to betray no anxiety (he boasts of his "cool tranquility"). This is, we will see, a corollary of his wearily sensible worldview, which understands virtue as a product of contented realism. It also has the added benefit of making him a good lawyer, for he is "considered an eminently *safe* man" (14; emphasis in original). Implicit in the statement is the idea that safety is a word that pertains both to emotional balance and to the legal circumscribing of property.

But the narrator is not all Franklinian. He is not a public man, preferring to draw profit from a privatized "snug retreat" (though he was public while holding the title of Master in Chancery). And though admittedly vain, we can be sure he does not use it as an engine of self-promotion. Moreover, he projects a despairing sense of social futility that is hard to find in Franklin. That desperation may stem not so much from Bartleby's particular fate as from the observation the narrator makes in his epilogue: "The report was this: that Bartleby had been a subordinate clerk in the Dead Letter Office at Washington, from which he had been suddenly removed by a change in the administration. When I think over this rumor, hardly can I express the emotions which seize me. Dead letters! Does it not sound like dead men? . . . On errands of life, these letters speed to death" (45). Writing here bodes not just social disintegration but an inability to provide consolation or counterweight when things go wrong. And in both the narrator's world of commercial disputes (the Master in *Chance*ry) and Bartleby's world of degraded imitation and dispossession, things always go wrong.

꙳

It is, by the same token, not much of a stretch to view *The Confidence-Man*'s main character as a fleshing out of Jupiter Tonans in "The Lightning-Rod Man," an observation first made by Daniel G. Hoffman in *Form and Fable in American Fiction* (1961). Both Jupiter and the confidence man are hucksters, itinerant and gifted with a sinister power to persuade.[34] Even more important, the novel extends the Franklin critique found in both "The Lightning-Rod Man" and "Bartleby the Scrivener." Melville interrogates Franklin on the advantages of identity shifting and anonymity as well as on the perils of vulgar heroism and urbane superiority: "Every great town is a kind of man-show, where the novelist goes for his stock, just as the agriculturalist goes to the cattle-show for his" (317–18).

The final damning targets left by the Franklinian legacy are of course the overweening commercial enthusiasms of mid–nineteenth century America and, what is even more essential, the fiction of mutual trust suggested by the benign public man Franklin constructs. The voice of Franklin is evident at several key points in the novel as Melville manages to capture Franklin's wry wit, all the while subjecting it to the irony of the confidence man's amoral actions. The moral universe of *The Confidence-Man* is antithetical to that of the *Autobiography*—all action redounds unexpectedly, and virtue is rarely rewarded. The world is, in the end, to be endured, to be survived, despite our best attempts (contra Webster and, as we will see, Emerson) to condition it with contracts and character.

Toward the end of the novel, the Cosmopolitan holds forth on the protective value of the Bible, in a passage that combines sarcasm with a quiet sense of wise futility about the anxieties and dangers of modern life. Reading this, we know that the Cosmopolitan would have been a match for Franklin:

Though this is a theme on which travellers seldom talk to each other, yet, to you, sir, I will say, that I share something of your sense of security. I have moved much about the world, and still keep at it; nevertheless, though in this land, and especially in these parts of it, some stories are told about steamboats and railroads fitted to make one a little apprehensive, yet, I may say that, neither by land nor by water, am I ever seriously disquieted, however, at times, transiently uneasy; since, with you, sir, I believe in a Committee of Safety, holding silent sessions over all, in an invisible patrol, most alert when we soundest sleep, and whose beat lies as much through forests as towns, along rivers as streets. In short, I never forget that passage of Scripture which says, "Jehovah shall be thy confidence." The traveller who has not this trust, what miserable misgivings must be his; or, what vain, short-sighted care must he take of himself [334].[35]

But safety, we know from "The Lightning-Rod Man," is a matter of social, human trust, not of faith in the symbols on church steeples or in the scientific wares of Jupiter. Melville's character is not to be trusted on the matter of trust. Contracts, novels, even the Bible offer faint comfort.

The point is memorably made with the final scenario involving the Cosmopolitan (who calls himself, in a nod to Silence Dogood and Franklin's subsequent incarnations, "Philanthropist, and Citizen of the World") and the distrusting barber, who, in his wager, demands a written guarantee against loss (of his own faith in mankind). The conclusion to the novel that this sequence comprises may be read as a densely layered meditation on the themes I have discussed in this chapter, and indeed in the book as a whole. Melville's confidence man, in his last incarnation, reprises the debate between the homeowner and Jupiter in "The Lightning-Rod Man," a comic struggle over who (and what) is to be trusted and thereby counted as "real." The confidence man is the man picked at the "man-show," some strange cross of lawyer, gambler, and insurance agent. I will quote at length:

"Now, then, for the writing," said the Cosmopolitan, squaring himself. "Ah," with a sigh, "I shall make a poor lawyer, I fear. Ain't used, you see, barber, to a business which, ignoring the principle of honour, holds no nail fast till clinched. . . . I won't put it in black and white. It were a reflection upon our joint honour. I will take your word, and you shall take mine."

"But your memory may be none of the best, sir. Well for you, on your side, to have it in black and white, just for a memorandum like, you know."

"That, indeed! Yes, and it would help *your* memory, too, wouldn't it, barber? Yours, on your side, being a little weak, too, I dare say. Ah, barber! how ingenious we human beings are. . . . But to business. Let me see. What's your name, barber?"

"William Cream, sir."

Pondering a moment, he began to write; and, after some corrections, leaned back, and read aloud the following:—

"AGREEMENT
between

FRANK GOODMAN, Philanthropist, and Citizen of the World, and

WILLIAM CREAM, Barber of the Mississippi steamer *Fidèle*.

"The first hereby agrees to make good to the last any loss that may come from his trusting mankind, in the way of his vocation, for the residue of the present trip; PROVIDED that William Cream keep out of sight, for the given term, his notification of 'NO TRUST,' and by no other mode convey any, the least hint or intimation, tending to discourage men from soliciting trust from him, in the way of his vocation, for the time above specified; but, on the contrary, he do, by all proper and reasonable words, gestures, manners, and looks, evince a perfect confidence in all men, especially strangers: otherwise, this agreement to be void.

"Done, in good faith, this 1st day of April, 18—, at a quarter to twelve o'clock P.M. in the shop of said William Cream, on board the said boat *Fidèle*.

"There, barber; will that do?"

"That will do, said the barber, "only now put down your name."

Melville has parodied, by making comically recursive, the very idea of the insurance contract that insurance law and state legislatures at the time were having monumental difficulties making stable.[36] The challenge to underwrite the very idea of underwriting—regulating the threat of an exposed world without credit, trust, or socially directed confidence—is thus posited and set up to be subjected to subsequent doubt and uncertainty, qualities that reside within the contract itself. There is no better or more ironically loaded example of Emerson's prophecy in "Self-Reliance" that the insurance office only makes for more accidents:

Both signatures being affixed, the question was started by the barber, who should have custody of the instrument; which point, however, he settled for himself, by proposing that both should go together to the captain, and give the document into his hands—the barber hinting that this would be a safe proceeding, because the captain was necessarily a party disinterested, and, what was more, could not, from the nature of the present case, make anything by a breach of trust. All of which was listened to with some surprise and concern.

"Why, barber," said the Cosmopolitan, "this don't show the right spirit; for me, I have confidence in the captain purely because he is a man; but he shall have nothing to do with our affair; for if you have no confidence in me, barber, I have in you. There, keep the paper yourself," handing it magnanimously.

"Very good," said the barber, "and now nothing remains but for me to receive the cash." . . .

"You speak of cash, barber; pray in what connection?"

"In a nearer one, sir," answered the barber, less blandly, "than I thought the man with the sweet voice stood, who wanted me to trust him once for a shave, on the score of being a sort of thirteenth cousin."

"Indeed, and what did you say to him?"

"I said, 'Thank you, sir, but I don't see the connection.' "

"How could you so unsweetly answer one with a sweet voice?"

"Because I recalled what the son of Sirach says in the True Book: 'An enemy speaketh sweetly with his lips'; and so I did what the son of Sirach advises in such cases: I believed not his many words."

"What, barber, do you say that such cynical sort of things are in the True Book, by which, of course, you mean the Bible?"

"Yes, and plenty more to the same effect. Read the Book of Proverbs."

"That's strange, now, barber; for I never happen to have met with those passages you cite. Before I go to bed this night, I'll inspect the Bible I saw on the cabin-table, to-day. But mind, you mustn't quote the True Book that way to people coming in here; it would be a violation of the contract. But you don't know how glad I feel that you have for one while signed off all that sort of thing."

"No, sir; not unless you down the cash."

"Cash again! What do you mean?"

"Why, in this paper here, you engage, sir, to insure me against a certain loss, and—"

"Certain? Is it so *certain* you are going to lose?"

"Why, that way of taking the word may not be amiss, but I didn't mean it so. I meant a *certain* loss; you understand, a CERTAIN loss; that is to say, a certain loss. Now then, sir, what use your mere writing and saying will insure me, unless beforehand you place in my hands a money-pledge, sufficient to that end?"

"I see; the material pledge."

It is worth pausing to consider the great fun Melville is having with the word "certain." Melville's play with the idea of certainty—at once the absent assurance that, ironically, makes accidents certain, and the secured precondition of a contract—shows us just how tricky and, indeed, untrustworthy the world of contracts and experience can be. Clearly, this will not end in mutual satisfaction. The haggling continues:

"Yes, and I will put it low; say, fifty dollars."

"Now what sort of a beginning is this? You, barber, for a given time engage to trust man, to put confidence in men, and, for your first step, make a demand implying no confidence in the very man you engage with. But fifty dollars is nothing, and I would else you have it cheerfully, only I unfortunately happen to have but little change with me just now."

"But you have money in your trunk, though?"

"To be sure. But you see—in fact, barber, you must be consistent. No, I won't let you have the money now; I won't let you violate the inmost spirit of our contract, that way. So good-night, and I will see you again."

"Stay, sir"—humming and hawing—"you have forgotten something."

"Handkerchief? —gloves? No, forgotten nothing. Good-night."

"Stay, sir—the—the shaving."

"Ah, I *did* forget that. But now that it strikes me, I shan't pay you at present. Look at your agreement; you must trust. Tut! against loss you hold the guarantee. Good-night, my dear barber!"

With which words he sauntered off, leaving the barber in a maze, staring after.

But it holding true in fascination as in natural philosophy, that nothing can act where it is not, so the barber was not long now in being restored to his self-possession and senses; the first evidence of which perhaps was, that, drawing forth his notification from the drawer, he put it back where it belonged; while, as for the agreement, that he tore up; which he felt the more free to do from the impression that in all human probability he would never again see the person who had drawn it [312–16].

Gaming Franklin's representative self gives way in the end to Noah Webster's nightmare: no longer are the moral outlines of a person's identity or a nation's credibility given value by the transcendent design of contracts. There are no more "material pledges." Given this, it is hard not to read these final pages apart from the multiple contexts of loss and writing, safety and surety, which had been accumulating in Melville's life. Despite Webster's efforts at rescinding in-terpretive chaos (or Franklin's manufactured comfort with anxiety), there was nothing stable or particularly comfortable about (under)written properties.

For Melville, this instability is both friend and crisis; loss—like drama and insurance—is Janus-faced. The phrase "nothing can act where it is not" suggests its positive, that actions can take place anywhere the imagination chooses. As with a confidence man, there is the strange ability of the writer to contrive value or stories ex nihilo, and then just as easily to restore that nothingness by whim of words. Such hard-to-locate agency promises to return our "senses" and "self-possession." But one hears also the undertones of Webster's conservative lament for a foundation of written certainty ("material pledges") that Melville, try as he might, never found. His America was becoming a place averse to acknowl-edging tragedy, that grim ceremony being cheerfully usurped from art by the profitability of insurance. Melville lets the logic of insurance speak at the end of what is perhaps his most bitter and comic novel about artifice and loss. He never published another.

CHAPTER FIVE

Boston

Beauty Is an Accident: The Insurance Office and Ralph Waldo Emerson

> Accident, n. a property of a thing, that which comes to pass without being foreseen.
>
> —Noah Webster, *A Compendious Dictionary of the English Language: A Facsimile of the First (1806) Edition*

> Accident, n. [l. *accidens*.] 1. A coming or falling; an event that takes place without one's foresight or expectation; an event which proceeds from an unknown cause, or is an unusual effect of a known cause, and therefore not expected . . . 3. An unfortunate event, occurring casually, and involving no guilt in the parties concerned. [This is the most common use of the word.] 4. In *logic*, a property or quality of a being which is not essential to it; as, *whiteness* in paper.—5. In *grammar*, something belonging to a word, but not essential to it; as, gender. . . . —Syn. Chance; contingency; casualty; misfortune.
>
> —Noah Webster, *An American Dictionary of the English Language*, 1850 edition

> Accident, . . . p. pr. of *accidere* to happen; *ad* + *cadere* to fall . . . 1. Literally, a befalling; an event that takes place without one's foresight or expectation; an undesigned, sudden, and unexpected event; chance; contingency; often, an undesigned and unforeseen occurrence of an afflictive or unfortunate character; a casualty; a mishap; as, to die by an accident. 2. (Gram.) A property attached to a word, but not essential to it, as gender, number, case. 4. (Log.) (a) A property or quality of a thing which is not essential to it, as whiteness in paper; an attribute. (b) A quality or attribute in distinction from the substance, as sweetness, softness. 5. Any accidental property, fact, or relation; an accidental or nonessential; as, beauty is an accident.
>
> —Webster's *Hypertext Gateway*

Almost a year before his beloved son died suddenly, and about thirty years before his house burned down, Ralph Waldo Emerson wrote about insurance. This peculiar instance (but not isolated in the course of his writing) comes near the end of "Self-Reliance," where Emerson blames modernity's throttling of human vitality on a variety of social institutions and events, among them the "accidents" caused by the "insurance office":

The civilized man has built a coach, but has lost the use of his feet. He is supported on crutches, but lacks so much support of muscle. . . . His note-books impair his memory; his libraries overload his wit; the insurance office increases the number of accidents; and it may be a question whether machinery does not encumber; whether we have not lost by refinement some energy, by a Christianity entrenched in establishments and forms, some vigor of wild virtue.[1]

Recognizable in its Enlightenment genealogy, the narrative of loss that trails modernity's progress is familiar enough. In this social history, modernity ponderously and clumsily replaces the past in fits of destruction that also supplant individualized true experience. An inverse relation can be drawn: As society grows larger and more coercive, we become smaller and more ineffectual.[2]

Yet Emerson's jeremiad is a crucial revision of Rousseau's "natural man" (and, as we will see, Lockean notions of "personal" property) because it is so peculiarly specific. Why name the insurance office? And just how does this site, meant to limit unfortunate turns of chance, paradoxically "increase the number of accidents"?[3]

In attempting to answer these questions, this chapter takes its epigraphs from Webster as underwriting moments in themselves, marking the limits and suggesting the unforeseen possibilities of meaning. For Emerson, accidents, in their controversy with human potential, are intrinsically about properties both grammatical and material.[4] Accidents, as they have been represented by the underwriting force of the dictionary, lead us into the description of a reverse deconstruction. In this representational controversy, Emerson first rejects and undoes the socially underwritten world of property and then moves through the experience of loss and accidents until he finally accepts the insuring poetics of underwriting. Underwriting establishes itself as a way of socializing capital and sharing information and risks of the most private kind. Underwriting presents a challenge to the "early" Emerson precisely to the degree that it involves a social, if not communal, alternative to the radical individualism of major early essays like "Self-Reliance."

In certain microeconomic ways, this concluding chapter is about the struggle for a renovated idea of the modern "world" and the everyday engagements we make with the regulation of its inconstant turns. Emerson's contention is as much with the enervating underwritten terms of modernity as it is with the painful fact of accidental loss. I follow Emerson's process of acceptance of the underwritten world, and, more specifically, of the representative techniques by which social enterprises attempt to mediate change and certainty. I trace the procedure as a theoretical restoration of a particularly commercialized notion of representational power, keeping in view the biography that corresponds to and shapes Emerson's shifting positions.

Starting with the thoroughgoing critique of "Self-Reliance," and moving through his journals, letters, later essays (such as "Experience," "Poetry," and "Fate,"), and the great poem "Threnody," this story is equally about the poetics of money as a historical entity and the relation of Emerson to particular misfortunes. Indeed, Emerson's approval of underwriting comes to dominance in a way that bespeaks the wider nineteenth-century American cultural and social acceptance of the insurance office as a means to greater comfort in a world of utilitarian individualism, of commodified property and statistically risky lives. What Emerson offers is an emblematic and fitting concluding case in the cultural history of insurance underwriting, wherein the representational relationship between accidents and property emerges as a result of what befalls the theorizing and grieving mind.[5]

ᔐ

Emerson's target in 1841 might seem too obvious until we press a little deeper into what he means by indicting it. For the insurance office is not merely one of many equally degrading activities, listed neutrally and without order of significance. The insurance office, as culminating scapegoat, does the work of extending the gradually expressed nexus between technologies of public expression and features of private selfhood ("notebooks" and "memory," "libraries" and "wit") into a vigorously social and hotly pursued domain. The insurance office provides the grammar for generating ever-larger calculations of loss and defect without really making a safe place for the nonconforming self. So it is there, for Emerson, in the theory and practice of the humble insurance office, that the modern self fully comes into public view; and then it appears as a slave.[6]

But a slave to what? Answering that question returns us to the theoretical foundation of underwriting; it is that foundation which seems to trigger Emerson's argument. The argument Emerson builds his jeremiad upon demonstrates once again that the progress of a writing civilization is a mutually unfolding story about property. For Emerson, the capitalized and socially defined link between writing and property has the effect of a shackle in which the human is forever caught. The dual pursuit of writing for the articulation of an expansive self (the self-conscious and literate bourgeois) and for the purpose of propertyholding is somehow counter to a deeply held human faculty for freedom. The two modes of writing are mutually incompatible.

I want to argue that such a critique is at the heart of the creed of "Self-Reliance." Property's strike at the foundation of a particular form of the self, contingent on a specious notion of social and historical progress, has yielded a world that defeats the self in the name of "Property." This capitalized monolith puts us to work each day: "And so the reliance on Property, including the reliance on governments which protect it, is the want of self-reliance" (281). The seeming flatness of the idea here is deceptively nuanced. In a sentence explicitly concerned with materialism, Emerson ironically constructs his aphorism with the subtending metaphor of lack, the want of some spirit in spite of having some thing; it is a lack of something within that describes the disease of wanting things external and material. The need for this kind of possession, and the consequent laws necessary to defining and safeguarding it, are for Emerson nothing more than a sophisticated response to a lost understanding of the complete self, sufficient to its own will and desires.[7]

We soon learn that this lack of a locatable self sufficient to itself—an entity usurped by property—is the ground from which real resistance to the acquisitive onslaught might be launched. In realizing the chance nature of possessing things (and its consequent displacing and hollowing out of the self), the self-reliant man conceives the basis for an anticonsumerist response to capitalist social change:[8] he "hates what he has, if he see that it is accidental. . . . But that which a man is does always by necessity acquire, and what the man acquires is living property, which does not wait the beck of rulers, or mobs, or revolutions, or fire, or storm, or bankruptcies, but perpetually renews itself wherever the man breathes" (281).

Withstanding property's colonization of the self arises out of a conceptual bifurcating of the term "property" into inward and outward forms. For Emerson, property of the negative sort—dead, unnatural, and external property—is only deceptively a Lockean product of labor; really, it is had by accident. But a different kind of property—a kind of naturalized self-property—is incidentally made rather than accidentally acquired.[9] The deep paradox of Emerson's critique is that it expresses property's iniquity by describing a fundamental dispossession that is, literally, a theft of something rightfully proper to an individual. Bad property, for Emerson, seems to steal.

↪

This theory has a directional component, providing an important link to the poetics of insurance that Emerson seems so vigorously to resist. All accidentally acquired property—property gained as an adjunct to the self—is outwardly directed and thus exposed. With enlargement of the self, the individual looms larger in the sights of malevolent chance: exposure. Exposure is a feature of social and institutional practice; the condition of exposure is the condition of the writer who sends outside the proper—asocial—bounds of the self his own inscriptions and assertions. Every writer is vulnerable (because wrong, because a misunderstood genius) when exposed to the accidents (malevolence, faulty understanding) of criticism. This tenuous situation invites the logic of insurance underwriting in the generalized form of conformist thinking—to wit, one would be well advised to direct one's writing to the social consensus. Put another way, if a writer prudently thinks and expresses himself as others do, he is underwritten by a confirming network of mutual thinking.

By contrast, one who writes of the self as though the activity were a corollary of breathing can never—to his credit—truly be underwritten. Obviously, this is a difficult corollary to put into practice. But it is an idea that the younger Emerson rarely tires of making real with his own suspiring inscriptions. To delineate the all-important difference between writer as poetic seer and writer as propertyholder was the distinction he worked toward.

Such is the nub of the distinction Emerson draws at the beginning of "Nature," when he describes the difference between property and landscape: "Miller owns this field, Locke that, and Manning the woodland beyond. But none of them owns the landscape. There is a property in the horizon which no man has but he whose eye can integrate all the parts, that is, the poet" (9). Perhaps it is no coincidence that Emerson places the poet ascendant over Lockean property.[10] The difference between prudent writer serving the ideology of Lockean property and all-encompassing Poet serving the transcendent ideal of organic integration resolves into two different kinds of sovereignty over a landscape that in turn offers figurative possession or integrative freedom.[11]

In "Self-Reliance," the distinguishing trope between poet and conformist, between poet and underwriter, is even more personalized and inwardly directed than it is in "Nature." The involuntary act of respiration—the chemical surplus on the material world that is the breath—makes a kind of intelligent wealth adhere to the self. This inward, unexposed accretion to the self is therefore always unregulatable. Such property ignores the conscious will of a subject; it is, rather, silently constitutive of the individual. As in Marx's famous Milton-as-silkworm trope, the worker/writer spinning out of intuitive necessity is a man who understands what is properly his own: he "know[s] his worth, and keep[s] things under his feet" (267).[12] Though the silkworm directs its work outside its being, this is not a self-alienating severance from what it must do to remain free; put another way, worms are not underwritten by anything other than their own essence.

⟩

This is, to put it mildly, a problematic theory of property, in part because it appears to be so semantically derived. Indeed, it is the product of a written essay, mutually apprehensible to both reader and author—it is an exposure. The argument seems to easily provoke its own deconstruction—Emerson is a writer, after all, and his written work is his property. With only a little nudge, the territorial trope, signifying the ground under one's feet, begins to slide of its own gravity. And so, as we have seen, Emerson seems to hedge, eager to make certain forms of writing free from the idea of loss altogether. Thus all property is not Property. Property can be good or bad, natural or unnatural, depending upon how it stands in relation to the self and the propertyholding aims of written expression.

The unnatural (exposed) sort is derived from the following logic: Accidents are in the nature of material, especially capitalized, property; property invites accidents, just as accidents of fortune, known otherwise as good luck, bestow property, a claim he makes clearly and forcefully in "Politics": "One man owns his clothes, another owns a county. This accident . . . falls unequally . . . " (560). For each individual, transcendence of that situation is a distinct possibility, and a glorious one at that. But when we begin to think of human will as a social entity—a collective condition primarily visible when written material is shared— it is inevitably a victim of the insured dream of linking writing and material property. Mobs, governments, revolutions, banks—social or juridical instruments or written declarations of any sort—cannot rectify or underwrite the fundamental instability of property. Accidents will always defy and even mock the will of a collectivity, no matter how much or how definitively the social trust is insured and underwritten. Again, "Politics" bears this creed out forthrightly with its prescription for minimal government, lest the natural power of property be interfered with unnecessarily. The domain of control, in the case of the social individual, is attenuated when the inevitable accident upsets the human will to stabilize it.

Thus insurability is a destructive fiction, accidents sap the will, and any hope for real mastery dissolves. Indeed, the terms of mastery reverse. The insurance office, as an adjunct of a greater machine, actually increases the number of accidents by incorporating the world into the pseudoinsurable realm of Property, thereby exposing it and fooling both individual and collective wills into even thinking of the possibility for control.[13] Humans, it turns out, are enslaved not only to Property but to the wrong kind of writing, which literally arrogates the will of the individual and exposes her that much more systematically to the hand of careless fortune.[14]

This is not only the view of property, writing, and possible transcendence through poetic mediation that most critics and students have come to know as "Emersonian."[15] It is also a component of some of the most important nineteenth-century critiques of money and property and its concentrations of material power and representational delusion. And yet, as we will see, Emerson's thinking would come to reject that critique in response to episodes of loss and recovery. In realizing that his life, too, was unavoidably underwritten by its own representational uncertainties—in the idiosyncrasies of private fate and public expression—Emerson moved, along with American society, to embrace the insurance office as both necessary fact and symbol.

I want to turn now to two biographical moments: first, the loss of his son; and, later, the burning of his house. These episodes, along with the texts that respond to them, demonstrate how the negation of "Self-Reliance" was, over time, abandoned in favor of the socially (if not publicly) redemptive poetics of underwriting.

Waking to Remember Him

On January 27, 1842, Emerson lost his first son and namesake, Waldo. In an extraordinary series of letters to family members and friends, beginning on January 28, 1842, and stretching into mid-February, he reported his grief. It would seem that this loss would not build character—or, to paraphrase a key section of a grandiloquent letter to Harrison Otis Blake in 1839, "the purging off of these accidents" would *not* bode "enlargement."[16] Rather, it caused increased exposure ("enlargement") of a different kind, one made fecund and visible by the paradox of loss as it was filtered through the struggle to represent that loss.

While Emerson had encountered painful loss in the years before—his first wife, Ellen; his brothers—the death of Waldo hit him harder and seemed to point up the problems with his triumphant early vision of representation. The letters may then be understood as the beginning of Emerson's critical reevaluation of the poetics of accidental loss. It is a reevaluation that will lead him back to the foundational underwriting poetics of Franklin, formulated by Franklin's steadier engagement with loss over a century earlier.

In the letters, Emerson displays a distressed personal connection to language abstractly construed; he makes manifest how hard it is to rethink written expression in pained practice when writing has become nothing less than an emblem for absolute loss and negation. On January 28, Emerson began to write a series of four letters communicating the loss of Waldo. He wrote to his aunt, Mary Moody Emerson, in terms that evoke a subconscious fantasy of perfection and innocence: "I slept in his neighborhood & woke to remember him"; "My darling . . . has fled out of my arms like a dream" (Joel Myerson, ed., *The*

Selected Letters of Ralph Waldo Emerson, 262. To Margaret Fuller he wrote: "My little boy must die also. All his wonderful beauty could not save him" (263). And to Elizabeth Palmer Peabody he wrote, ". . . with him has departed all that is glad & festal & almost all that is social even . . . " (263). But all these utterances seem merely a prelude to an extraordinary description of this intellectual and emotional wound. That description, in his outward correspondence, was achieved by a particular kind of linguistic negation.

I want to pay specific attention to Emerson's letter to his friend Caroline Sturgis, written on or around February 23, 1842. In it, Emerson comes closest to measuring the depth of his sadness:

I am stripped of all generosity of nature: He was my ornament, I had need of no other, and from the greatest patrician I am become plebeian at a blow. He as much as any, perhaps he more than any of my little company of friends . . . gave a license to my habitual fancy of magnifying each particular in my modest round of experiences to stand for a general & mundane fact, for I cannot tell you what pleasing depths of gentleness & courtesy & friendship I found for myself in little private passages between that boy & me [266].

Emerson's loss is figured not only delicately, in terms of his lost son's friendship, but also quite boldly, as an intellectual privation. Without Waldo, his penchant for reading the exterior world as a compendium of symbols was no longer valid or fulfilling, as it had been before Waldo's death. Somehow, Waldo's presence within the Emerson home made the world outside easier to read and then represent.[17]

The loss of the boy meant a crisis of apprehending the world through texts, where Waldo comes to mean the difference between memory and presence, between the invisible and the embodied, between what is inside and what is outside. In his futile attempt to reconstitute an adored image and a palpable vitality that were already fading, he casts about for a saving representation. Later in the same letter, he challenges Sturgis to recreate a verbal picture of the boy (266):

O yes, if you have pictures of this Child also in your memory, in your head, do not fail, I entreat you, to draw them all for me on paper. But you will not have,—I sadly believe;—the Real refuses to be represented when it is taken to heart, and a copy is heartily wanted. I who have words & descriptions for everything which moderately interests me, have no line, no memorandum, in these dark weeks to set down, wherewith I might keep my little strong Beauty freshly before me. And because I should be overglad that you could draw for me now, I may know you will not be able?

There are two counterunderwriting moments in this passage. The first comes with the curious pun on "heart" in the sentence "the Real refuses to be represented when it is taken to heart, and a copy is heartily wanted." Representation in the face of loss is now a tricky question of competing wills: the Real stubbornly refuses to be copied when it is the object of a bereft father's will. The heart in this case seems to be the pivotal—indeed, self-contradictory—medium: it locks the Real into its refusing stance and yet generates the need to release its copies. Whatever the heart might be, it is not always benevolent in the event of loss. Even more frightening for the world of loss Emerson was now questioning, the heart—the seat of intuitive intellection—has no simple artery to representation or the Real.

The second oddity lies in the difficulty of sustaining the interrogative quality of the last sentence. Just how is it a question? How might Sturgis be expected to respond? The question mark at the end of his assertion of negation seems to wrench the reader, along with Emerson, into the vain hope of breaching that loss—of finding a way across the gap between Waldo before and Waldo after, between efficacious language and unkind muteness. The illogical question mark not only expresses his absolute vexation with representation as it relates to losing Waldo, it also extends that vexation to his correspondent, sharing his inability to underwrite appropriately.

The loss of Waldo demonstrated to Emerson the "beauty" essential to his "accidental" poetics. This series of letters seems to have been productive precisely because it constitutes such an abject admission of failure.[18] His struggle to wrestle words commensurate to the greatness of his loss was never satisfactorily won; and yet he began an important process of adapting his representational poetics as a result of it.

↩

This self-conscious faltering in the act of corresponding the loss outside himself stands in fascinating contrast to the unselfconscious volubility he gives the loss in his own journal. The entry for January 30, 1842, is florid in its detail of the life of Waldo, his language and narration easy in their evocation of the boy as a memory. Emerson swings lyrically from poetic fragments in paratactic sequence ("decorated for me the morning star, & the evening cloud, how much more all the particulars of daily economy"[19]) to narrative ("He dictated a letter to his cousin Willie on Monday night to thank him for the Magic Lantern which he had sent him, and said I wish you would tell Cousin Willie that I have so many presents that I do not need that he should send me any more unless he wishes to very much"; William H. Gilman and J. E. Parsons, eds., *The Journals and Miscellaneous Notebooks of Ralph Waldo Emerson: 1841–1843*, vol. 8, 164) and finally to dialogue (166):

Mamma, may I have this bell which I have been making, to stand by the side of my bed.
Yes it may stand there.
But Mamma I am afraid it will alarm you. It may sound in the middle of the night

and it will be heard over the whole town, it will be louder than ten thousand hawks it
will be heard across the water, and in all the countries. It will be heard all over the world.
It will sound like some great glass thing which falls down & breaks all to pieces.
Waldo asked If the strings of the harp open when he touches them?

So ends his entry for January 30. According to Gilman and Parsons, Emerson
left two pages entirely blank following the entry. Gilman and Parsons, along
with Gay Wilson Allen, have speculated that Emerson intended at some later
date to fill those pages with remembrances.[20] But, given the nuanced representational relationships that Emerson was forging with the things and people attributable to an individual in the world, we might expect such deliberate era-
sures or absences. Rather than a fund set against future thoughts, perhaps those
blank pages are his best testament to the ineffability that came with the loss;
rather than question loss verbally, he made space for it as a way of signifying it.

Almost nowhere else in the journals do we find Emerson directly questioning whether the Real might be represented, or even be permanently out of
reach, as he does in his correspondence.[21] The closest he comes is in the first entry, written in a new notebook that he began a week after the death of Waldo,
dated February 4, 1842:

I have read that Sheridan made a good deal of *experimental writing* with a view to take
what might fall, if any wit should transpire in all the waste pages. I in my dark hours may
scratch the page if perchance any hour of recent life may project a hand from the dark-
ness & inscribe a record. Twice today it has seemed to me that Truth is our only armor
in all passages of life & death. Wit is cheap & anger is cheap, but nothing is gained by
them. But if you cannot argue or explain your self to the other party, cleave to the truth
against me, against thee, and you gain a station from which you can never be dislodged.
The other party will forget the words that you spoke, but the part which you took pleads
for you forever [199; emphasis in original].

But even here, in this note of pessimism, we sense that a change has been
wrought. The comparisons with the great critique of the effects of modernity in
"Self-Reliance" are irresistible: his notebooks do not impair his memory so
much as refuse it until the accidents (the "fall") of meaning "inscribe a record";
his libraries do not overload his wit so much as provide the opportunity for
reconciliation or, even better, a chance at correspondence which tells everything
("The other party will forget the words that you spoke, but the part which you
took pleads for you forever") in the act of speech. These private modes are revised by the accident of loss into a hotly pursued *private* domain where "wit" is
no longer socially useful or even privately attractive. Representational poetics
are a subject for correspondence, for exposed verbal extensions beyond the self.
Emerson, at a moment of great pessimism, asks for an underwriting, accidental
or intentional. This faith in language is an improvement; for, writing to Sturgis
several days earlier, he asks for help that he knows can never come.

The Accident of Symbols

Emerson's view of the significance of accidents would continue to evolve out of crisis in the next year or so. Indeed, he soon begins to return from the agony of deconstructive negation, literally refinding things with words. The representational implications of accidental loss—so movingly expressed in the letters consequent to Waldo's death—are also wrestled with in "The Poet" (1844).[22] This reconstructed poet—in contrast to the deconstructing poet of "Self-Reliance," who was in constant antagonism with commerce and property—seems at home in a world where accidents serve to define and make precious everything that may be apprehended symbolically. Indeed, to understand accidents is to understand the concept of the symbol itself:

> We are symbols and inhabit symbols; workmen, work, and tools, words and things, birth and death, all are emblems but we sympathize with the symbols, and being infatuated with the economical uses of things, we do not know that they are thoughts. The poet, by an ulterior intellectual perception, gives them a power which makes their old use forgotten, and puts eyes and a tongue into every dumb and inanimate object. *He perceives the independence of the thought on the symbol, the stability of the thought, the accidency and fugacity of the symbol* [*Essays and Lectures*, 456; emphasis added].

Emerson describes how the poet masters all sciences, since it is the poet who understands "all the facts of animal economy," the range and distribution of events that make organic life motile and seminal as well as inherently finite and prone to loss. Echoing the theory of writing he had laid out in "Self-Reliance," Emerson speaks of the incidental property of symbolic language: "This expression or naming is not art, but a second nature, grown out of the first, as a leaf out of a tree. What we call nature is a certain self-regulated motion or change . . ." (*Essays and Lectures*, 457) Here, then, the self can be said to be successfully regulating chance (in the form of its necessary ally, "change").

But this is where the similarity with "Self-Reliance" ends. There is, after a period of negation and sad indulgence in the poetics of the void, hope for words that indemnify the world and stabilize it through the process of change and becoming. And yet such confidence could not be realized without that reckoning with the void. Note that Emerson is no longer afraid of using the word "insure," reflecting his newfound faith in the possibility of absorbing accidents and absence, and then moving on. As the products of Nature, we may participate in the beautiful fact that "Nature, through all her kingdoms, *insures* herself" (*Essays and Lectures*, 457). And, even more elaborately, " . . . let us, with new hope, observe how nature, by worthier impulses, has *ensured the poet's fidelity to his office of announcement and affirming, namely by the beauty of things, which becomes a new and higher beauty when expressed*" (452; emphasis added). Nature is the ally of the poet, since she is the incidental and accidental property of the poet's art: "So when the soul of the poet has come to ripeness of thought, she detaches and sends away from it its poems or songs,—a fearless, sleepless, deathless progeny, which is not exposed to the accidents of the weary kingdom of time . . . " (457–58).

The accidents here are not the accidents of "Self-Reliance." They are, for all intents and purposes, outside the grammar of writing, an intimation of the sublime, since the poet now is a more expansively figured artist, encompassing once contrary modes of regulating the self. The poet, as an agent of a naturalized regime of representation that is relevant to both nature and commerce, may now free us *within* the insurance office: "He unlocks our chains and admits us to a new scene" (463).[23] That adaptation to and acceptance of the acquisition and accidental loss of things, as well as the notion that financial sums might be fairly placed upon human existence—nothing less, in short, than the logic of capitalist modernity itself—would continue to develop into explicit emotional and intellectual consolation.

In "Experience," Emerson addresses the loss of Waldo, now two years later. It is Emerson's great prose answer to the loss, and to the notion of the accident and its effect on the idea of inwardly directed expressive individualism that we saw in "Self-Reliance." Sharon Cameron has written persuasively that "Experience" has its own logic derived from the elegy. Cameron notes the disjunctive or dissociative shift Emerson takes in disavowing the depth of grief he thinks he ought to feel, in marveling that he has learned nothing from the loss. She makes the incisive point that Emerson's emotional quandary is tied to his recognition that representation itself needed to be rethought in the act of grieving:

Grief—"which like all the rest, plays about the surface, and never introduces me into reality"—withholds contact with a reality that does not equivocate with experience, because unlike death, to which Emerson compares it, grief does not end experience. What is being redefined, then, is the idea about our relation to experience—about whether that relation is one of surface or depth.[24]

We see this attempt to focus on both foreground (the event of Waldo's death) as well as background (the social and emotional relationships that Waldo made "real") played out in numerous places in "Experience." The following passage has become particularly famous:

Grief too will make us idealists. In the death of my son, now more than two years ago, I seem to have lost a beautiful estate,—no more. I cannot get it nearer to me. If tomorrow I should be informed of the bankruptcy of my principal debtors, the loss of my property would be a great inconvenience to me, perhaps, for many years; but it would leave me as it found me,—neither better nor worse. So is it with calamity: it does not touch me: something which I fancied was a part of me, *which could not be torn away without tearing me, nor enlarged without enriching me*, falls off from me, and leaves no scar. It was caducous [*Essays and Lectures*, 473, emphasis added].

Emerson's metaphor is familiar: the human agent of "Self-Reliance," as an entity either to be enlarged and fortified or shrunken and depleted, is now impervious to negative modification. No longer is a distinction made between kinds of property; rather, property is an accident, a part of experience. Property and the "ideal" exist apart, and they correspond through writing. The outward is as immune to harm as the inward; again, writing and property are forms of beauty itself, since they are linked by the symbolic power of accidency. They are both "caducous."

And then there is the concluding section, in which Emerson has completely recovered from the abject misery and impotence we saw in the letters to Sturgis:

I take this evanescence and lubricity of all objects, which lets them slip through our fingers then when we clutch hardest, to be the most unhandsome part of our condition. Nature does not like to be observed, and likes that we should be her fools and playmates. We may have the sphere for our cricket-ball, but not a berry for our philosophy. Direct strokes she never gave us power to make; all our blows glance, all our hits are accidents [*Essays and Lectures*, 473].

Fitting that Emerson seizes on the metaphor of a game as he makes his way through a maze of descriptions for loss and chance.[25] Cricket is not to be taken lightly but rather to be fit into a philosophy that requires discipline. While we may be "fools" and "playmates," we have it within our "sphere" to understand the "evanescence and lubricity" of our place in Nature. Once we have that understanding, we have it within our power to make rules and create devices to cope with chance. *Losing* no longer has to result in *loss*. One can suppose that the insurance office is where the new rules and practices of losing might be enacted.

ↄ

But when the game is over, what then? Where do the things of this world go when their chances and risks are finally eliminated? Emerson writes in Journal J, on January 30, that "I ought to call upon the winds to describe my boy, my fast receding boy" (Gilman and Parsons, eds., *Journals*, vol. 8, 165). In doing so, he suggests the trope of the "South-wind" as a restorative force in his great poetic expression of the loss of Waldo, "Threnody" (1846). Emerson shows the despair we've come to know elsewhere in his writing: "But over the dead he [the South-wind] has no power, / The lost, the lost, he cannot restore . . . (117).[26] The repetitive invocation of finality in the phrase "the lost" emphasizes what he cannot summon as material fact. And, again, Waldo was a feature of his home, his possession, his environment, whose passing has rendered incoherent his tenancy in every detail: "I see my empty house," and contrasts this with the restorative powers of a tree, as if he, too, might be able to regenerate his "limb": "I see my trees repair their boughs . . . / Far and wide she cannot find him; / My hopes pursue, they cannot bind him" (117). Desire and will are impotent in the wake of chance destruction: "Nature, who *lost*, cannot remake him; / Fate let him *fall*, Fate can't retake him . . . " (117). Loss and accidents are complicit in their mutual impotence after the fact (117): "I had the right, few days ago, / Thy steps to watch, thy place to know: / How have I forfeited the right?"

The discourse of property rights—a mocking deployment—cannot explain this loss. The "eloquent child" seems to have left the father with no rights, not even to listen. This legal trope is compounded always by perceptual denial, an inability to find Waldo with his senses: "Now Love and Pride, alas! In vain, / Up and down their glances strain" (119). And then, later, the natural world expresses a denial of social vision (the ostrich's forgetfulness and the loss of one element of a vital system "loss of larger in the less"):

> . . . the feet
> Of the most beautiful and sweet
> Of human youth had left the hill
> And garden,—they were bound and still,
> There's not a sparrow or a wren,
> There's not a blade of autumn grain,
> Which the four seasons do not tend
> And tides of life and increase lend;
> And every chick of every bird,
> And weed and rock-moss is preferred.
> O ostrich-like forgetfulness!
> O loss of larger in the less! [119–20]

This privatized pain is experienced against the backdrop of all that the ostrich chooses not to view—to wit, the social:

> Some went and came about the dead;
> And some in books of solace read;
> Some to their friends the tidings say;
> Some went to write, some went to pray;
> One tarried here, there hurried one;
> But their heart abode with none.
> Covetous death bereaved us all,
> To aggrandize one funeral.
> The eager fate which carried thee
> Took the largest part of me:
> For this losing is true dying;
> This is lordly man's down-lying,
> This his slow but sure reclining,
> Star by star his world resigning [121].

The refusing heart of the Sturgis letter is made to speak:

> The deep Heart answered, 'Weepest thou? . . .
> [. . .]
> 'T is not within the force of fate
> the fate-conjoined to separate.
> But thou, my votary, weepest thou?
> I gave thee sight—where is it now?
> I taught thy heart beyond the reach
> Of ritual, bible, or of speech;
> Wrote in thy mind's transparent table,
> As far as the incommunicable;
> Taught thee each private sign to raise
> Lit by the supersolar blaze.
> Past utterance, and past belief,
> And past the blasphemy of grief,
> The mysteries of Nature's heart;
> And though no Muse can these impart,
> Throb thine with Nature's throbbing breast,
> And all is clear from east to west.
> I came to thee as to a friend . . . [122].

He's starting to get answers:

> Life is life which generates,
> And many-seeming life is one,—
> Wilt thou transfix and make it none?
> Its onward force too starkly pent
> In figure, bone and lineament?
> Nor see the genius of the whole
> Ascendant in the private soul,
> Beckon it when to go and come,
> Self-announced its hour of doom? [123]

And the culmination comes as a relief, wherein loss is reincorporated and we look ahead to the idea that grief makes us all idealists, but of a sort that views the ideal as a place with objective contingencies. Things are lost and pursued there. Heaven is

> Built of furtherance and pursuing,
> Not of spent deeds, but of doing.
> Silent rushes the swift Lord
> Through ruined systems still restored,
> Broadsowing, bleak and void to bless,
> Plants with worlds the wilderness;
> Waters with tears of ancient sorrow
> Apples of Eden ripe to-morrow

House and tenant go to ground
Lost in God, in Godhead found [124].

Heaven is thus a place where the mind seeks after permanence, a sacred spatial and temporal mode of dynamic, actively lyrical, being. And redemption within that place may be found in the act of releasing. But note the conceptual difference here, which makes his elegy more than just a commendation of the departed soul to God: release is possible only when one is secure in the idea that there is an underwritten tether to the realm of material acquisition and possession. And Heaven, as an imaginative refuge, is a site that *enables* representation, in spite of the possibility of loss. Salvation in material fact is a function of an idealist heaven. And while salvation is heaven-directed, it envisions a world that can still be lived in—really inhabited and cared for, without fear of sudden loss.

Fate

Consolation soon converted to affirmation and a peculiarly hearty articulation of social policy; the change found its best enunciation in 1860's *The Conduct of Life*. Speaking in the Darwinian voice of social survivalism that was beginning its emergence into corporate discourses of the mid-nineteenth century, Emerson writes in the book's opening chapter, "Fate":

Nature is no sentimentalist,—does not cosset or pamper us. We must see that the world is rough and surly, and will not mind drowning a man or a woman; but swallows our ship like a grain of dust. The cold, inconsiderate of persons, tingles your blood, benumbs your feet, freezes a man like an apple. The diseases, the elements, fortune, gravity, lightning, respect no persons. The way of Providence is a little rude.[27]

The essay "Fate" and the rest of *The Conduct of Life* expand on this analytic antisentimentalism. Emerson is keen throughout to show the idea of accidents yielding fortunate distinctions in organic experience—how it makes some people smarter "musically" or others more talented in "story-telling" (9). Emerson regards much of human experience, from personal morality to politics, as due to accidents in physiological development. It is "power and circumstance" above all which govern, and to understand that is now to accept the range of underwriting techniques and knowledge that serves such masters. He hails "Statistics" as the science that might be most reliable in leading us to a recognition of our all-important "limitations":

We cannot trifle with this reality, this cropping-out in our planted gardens of the core of the world. No picture of life can have any veracity that does not admit the odious facts. A man's power is hooped in by a necessity, which, by many experiments, he touches on every side, until he learns its arc [16].

It is here that Emerson returns to the question of a *social* will, as opposed to the self-reliant monism he began his career with: How might the writing mind maximize its choices in a world that is intent on limiting all its chances, its unrealized potentials? Now Emerson writes, "To hazard the contradiction,—freedom is necessary." By this he means to say that freedom is possible only after we accept the fate of accidency and inquire actively into the role that chance (or limits) may play in the way we conduct ourselves; "His sound relation to these facts is to use and command, not to cringe to them" (p. 19). It is somewhat ironic that Emerson builds his tract to the very heights of sentiment, managing to conclude floridly about the serene neutrality of his equanimity:

Let us build altars to the Beautiful Necessity, which secures that all is made of one piece. . . . Let us build to the Beautiful Necessity, which makes man brave in believing that he cannot shun a danger that is appointed, nor incur one that is not; to the Necessity which rudely or softly educates him to the perception that there are no contingencies; that Law rules throughout existence, a Law which is not intelligent but intelligence—not personal, nor impersonal,—it disdains words and passes understanding [42].

Despite its appearance, he has not, through the offices of representation-as-Power (in short, statistics), deconstructed language back into inefficacy or muteness. He has merely admitted how it is that "the Law," the Beautiful Necessariness of his own loss, could easily elude him for so long. Some thing, the law of power, has returned to him after all these years. The place in which he now stood was the solid foundation of underwriting. With language now real and "transcendent," it would seem he could dwell contentedly in the social ramifications of uncertainty.

House Goes to Ground

Such comfort was tested by another instance of "beautiful necessity." Emerson's journal entry for July 24, 1872, reads simply: "House burned."[28] Such terseness stands in contrast to the volubility of his journal entry on the loss of Waldo (part of this is no doubt due to the physical exhaustion of a night spent fighting the fire in the rain). Also striking, when compared with the death of Waldo, is the amount of written expression by those other than Emerson on the fact and meaning of the loss. Public writing on the event was considerably more copious. According to the *Boston Daily Advertiser* for July 25, 1872:

A few hours after daybreak yesterday morning the people of the usually quiet town of Concord were startled by . . . a large conflagration . . . which subsequently proved to be the burning of the residence of Ralph Waldo Emerson. The fire was first observed by persons passing by . . . the library and all the furniture of the house [was] saved [by firemen and citizens]. The house was almost totally destroyed, except the walls of the lower floor.... In the attic were a number of books and valuable manuscripts belonging to the late William Emerson of New York some of which were badly damaged and others destroyed. It is supposed that the fire originated in a defective flue, that it caught on Tuesday morning and has been smouldering ever since. The value of the house was estimated at $5000, and was insured for $2500.[29]

When placed within the context of the relentlessly private, closely held written exposure of his previous major loss—the Real refusing to be represented when the human core, the heart, is involved—a series of ironies emerge. It is ironic that it was the townspeople of Concord who, passing by the library, first alerted the fire company and other "citizens" to the blaze. And it is no less ironic that Emerson was drastically underinsured for the property.[30] But the crowning irony of this accident came when Emerson saw it necessary to store his remaining books in the "Court-House which," he wrote to James Elliot Cabot two days after the fire, "now belongs to the Insurance Company, & has room to spare" (Myerson, ed., *The Selected Letters of Ralph Waldo Emerson*, 444) .

John McAleer, in his biography *Ralph Waldo Emerson: Days of Encounter*, describes the fire and its aftermath as the scene of a loving community of friends and neighbors coming to Emerson's rescue.[31] Young boys rushed into the smoke to retrieve almost all of his papers and books. Even the underinsured condition of the property proved not disastrous, as Judge Hoar initiated a charitable series of donations that was designed to preserve Emerson's dignity and help rebuild. James Russell Lowell, Caroline Sturgis Tappan, and Thomas Gold Appleton are but a few of the notables who wrote large checks to remunerate him for the loss of his house. As Emerson wrote to Hoar: "Names of dear and noble friends; names also of high respect with me, but on which I had no known claims; names, too, that carried me back many years, as they were of friends of friends of mine more than of me, and thus I seemed to be drawing on the virtues of the departed."[32] And he would write to LeBaron Russell a month after the fire: "My misfortunes, as I have lived so far in this world, have been so few that I have never needed to ask direct aid of the host of good men and women who have cheered my life, though many a gift has come to me. This late calamity, however rude and devastating, soon began to look more wonderful in its salvages than its ruins" (Myerson, ed., *The Selected Letters of Ralph Waldo Emerson*, 446).

Two weeks prior to the fire, Emerson wrote in a journal that "We would all be public men if we could afford it. I am wholly private: such is the poverty of my constitution" (Joel Porte, ed., *Emerson in his Journals*, 567). This confession seems to send the irony and lessons of the burning into the category of metaphysical reversal; the great public lecturer of the 1830's and 1840's now finds himself "wholly private," whereupon he learns once again that no man, if he writes and reads, is ever "wholly private." Death, fires, and insurance assure us of that. After the fire, Emerson is finally a man who accepts the poverty of individualism and sees the need for the underwritten public as a constituting foundation of the private writer. While it may be erroneous to claim he abandoned the two sorts of property associated with the freewriting, self-reliant individual of 1839–1841, we may fairly claim a kind of enlargement, for both better and worse, in his thinking. This new ground became for Emerson a site of receptivity to the underwritten world that so eagerly pursued the stabilization, if not elimination, of the balance between possession and loss.

Beauty Unannounced

Emerson ends his first series of essays contemplating the nature of beauty as it relates to the normative nightmare of modernity he decries in "Self-Reliance." A messianic future tense subtends the passage, pointing us toward some deferred fulfillment.[33] Beauty, he writes,

will come, as always, unannounced, and spring up between the feet of brave and earnest men. It is in vain that we look for genius to reiterate its miracles in the old arts; it is its instinct to find beauty and holiness in new and necessary facts, in the field and roadside, in the shop and mill. Proceeding from a religious heart it will raise to a divine use the railroad, the insurance office, the joint-stock company, our law, our primary assemblies, our commerce, the galvanic battery, the electric jar, the prism, and the chemist's retort, in which we seek now only an economical use. . . . When science is learned in love, and its powers are wielded by love, they will appear the supplements and continuations of the material creation.[34]

The mention predates (1841) the death of Waldo and the burning of his house, but it suggests that Emerson always had a strain of accommodation threaded within his thought; indeed, one is tempted to say that it could not have been otherwise, since Emerson's historical and cultural moment was relentless in its need to insure and underwrite the world. And to turn the deconstructive screw yet again, one might say that this axiom of accommodation suggested, early on, its radical rejection. The accidents that "fell" found the discourse already there, like a foundational frieze in his thinking, to be relieved and discerned by the course of the unforeseen.

This chastened yet assured discourse is evidence that Emerson was always of more than one mind when it came to the representational implications of everyday life and its epic worries. But the pragmatism of his recasting the "heart" of the Sturgis letter into the possibility for miraculous beauty is no less astonishing.[35] Accidents, and the bourgeois need to compensate the loss they entail, seem to mock and then enable the restless squaring of social moralism and individual fate he attempted throughout his work.[36] Uncertainty presents an emotionally and theoretically exacting test of symbolic validity for one of the preeminent philosophers of representation, and all this in an age that elevated probabilism to a category of knowledge.[37]

For Emerson, when accidents happen they feel like chance, writ specific and painful. But with time they lead to new kinds of knowledge, expression, and belief, all of which in turn lead to exchange and lasting value.[38] Emerson's evolution takes us from the definition of "accident" as "fall"—an effect of random necessity—to that of a property, a kind of grammar inherent to organic experience, "as in beauty." With that evolution, Franklin's narrative control found a home, too, in the postromantic disruptions of Emerson's nineteenth-century corporate individualism. Insurance and accidents became indispensable ways of describing modern conditions—"enslaving" and yet teaching what those bonds felt like, demonstrating through bifurcated private and public economies of value which emotional attachments were lasting. Through accidents, and fierce resistance to them even after the fact, he knew this world and not any other—a world specified by and attributable to the things that happen in it.

REFERENCE MATTER

Notes

Preface

1. Stevens was mulling the pros and cons of nationalized insurance schemes, such as social security, in the context of liberal democracies and fascist and communist states. For a discussion of the piece in Stevens's literature, see Joseph Harrington, "Wallace Stevens and the Poetics of National Insurance." See also Alan Filreis, *Wallace Stevens and the Actual World*.

2. For the definitive account of the evolution of this idea within liberal political theory, see C. B. Macpherson, *The Political Theory of Possessive Individualism: Hobbes to Locke*.

3. The British insurance industry grew along with—and assisted while profiting greatly from—the mercantilist expansion of British colonial holdings. See Raymond Flower and Michael Wynn Jones, *Lloyd's of London: An Illustrated History*, chap. 2.

4. This is, strictly speaking, not true. The insured is still losing, albeit a more manageable amount, in the form of a usually monetized premium, deductible, or coinsurance. Nonetheless, I think the force of the idea is worth taking note of—that insurance by and large promises a world with a vastly reduced risk of loss.

5. For a general history of the insurance and underwriting business, see Karl H. Van D'Elden, "The Development of the Insurance Concept and Insurance Law in the Middle Ages." Van D'Elden makes a strong case for the evolution of insurance underwriting as part of the developing notion of public welfare. The insurance industry has long been proud and prolific in telling the story of its evolution; see Prudential Insurance Company of America, *The Documentary History of Insurance: 1000 B.C.–1875 A.D.* A number of books on the history of Lloyd's of London contain excellent accounts of the evolution of insurance: see Hugh Cockerell, *Lloyd's of London: A Portrait*; see also Antony Brown, *Hazard Unlimited: The Story of Lloyd's of London*. Perhaps the two best scholarly sources for the history and theory of insurance are Oliver M. Westall, ed., *The Historian and the Business of Insurance*, and Geoffrey Clark, *Betting on Lives: The Culture of Life Insurance in England, 1695–1775*. A good documentary history is the six-volume *History of Insurance* edited by David Jenkins and Takau Yoneyama. Another source is Viviana A. Rotman

Zelizer, *Morals and Markets: The Development of Life Insurance in the United States*. Much of Zelizer's analysis is sociological and focuses on life insurance.

6. Spencer L. Kimball, "The Purpose of Insurance Regulation: A Preliminary Inquiry into the Theory of Insurance Law," 524.

7. There is no shortage of historical works on the intellectual and social history of property. Alan Ryan's *Property* is an excellent overview. On more historically specific notions of property and consumption, see Macpherson, *The Political Theory of Possessive Individualism*, and C. B. Macpherson, "The Meaning of Property." See also J. G. A. Pocock, *Virtue, Commerce, History: Essays on Political Thought and History*; Ann Bermingham and John Brewer, eds., *The Consumption of Culture, 1600–1800: Image, Object, Text*; John Brewer and Susan Staves, eds., *Early Modern Conceptions of Property*; John Brewer and Roy Porter, eds., *Consumption and the World of Goods*.

8. Robert H. Jerry II *Understanding Insurance Law*.

9. Barry Supple has written about insurance as a historical enterprise that, in its close affiliation with the emerging science of chance, exemplifies important epistemological innovations: "Insurance combines elements of gambling and of certainty—speculative hazard and the reduction or even elimination of chance by using the predictability of 'random' occurrences in large numbers of instances. Appealing above all to the desire for stability and predictability, the business of insurance has evolved through competition and the vigorous exploration of novelty, as well as by some of the most effective collusive devices in modern business history. The act of insurance is based on the mutual pooling of resources and hazards, but has flowered through proprietary profit-making as well as (occasionally) mutual organisations and even (over the last few decades) public provision"; see Barry Supple, "Insurance in British History."

Introduction

1. McCusker and Menard declare the insurance broker, of all the new agents springing up in "exchange alley's and public inns," "probably the most important [men of commerce] in the colonial period," since they were keys in the devolution of mercantilist practices in the colonies; see John J. McCusker and Russell R. Renard, *The Economy of British America, 1607–1789*, 347–48. Insurance underwriting often took place in coffee-houses like the famous London Coffee House of Philadelphia, which sat at Front and Market Streets, near Copson's office. For a wonderful description of the role of coffee-houses in colonial cities, see David Shields, *Civil Tongues and Polite Letters in British America*, chap. 3.

2. According to Ruwell's history of American insurance, the formation of colonial American insurance companies paralleled that of the British. Ruwell writes, "In the United States, marine underwriting began by private underwriting in a manner almost identical to that of Lloyd's"; see Mary Elizabeth Ruwell, *Eighteenth-Century Capitalism: The Formation of American Marine Insurance Companies*, 38. Perkins's superb history holds that American insurers eventually left British modes behind, abandoning private syndicate underwriting, such as Lloyd's, and pioneering mutuals and corporate structures almost exclusively; see Edwin J. Perkins, *American Public Finance and Financial Services, 1700–1815*, 292.

3. The term "underwriting," as I explain below, has several other financially derived

meanings (bond underwriting, stock underwriting, and so forth). In this book I want to restrict myself in general to its insurance connections. When referring to underwriting in the context of business, I will be using it in the insurance sense of the word. I hope my deployment within this book of its figurative connotations will be self-explanatory.

4. See Perkins, *American Public Finance and Financial Services*, 294. He makes this point especially forcefully with regard to fire insurance.

5. For a discussion of the phrase as it relates to economic theory and development, see Julian Hoppit, "Political Arithmetic in Eighteenth-Century England."

6. Quoted in William H. Fowler, "Marine Insurance in Boston: The Early Years of the Boston Marine Insurance Company, 1799–1807," 156. See also C. Mitchell Bradford, *A Premium on Progress: An Outline History of the American Marine Insurance Market, 1820–1970*.

7. See McCusker and Menard, *The Economy of British America*, for the best and most forceful rendition of this thesis. Michael Kammen, *Empire and Interest: The American Colonies and the Politics of Mercantilism*, also provides a lucid explanation of the dynamics of colonial American mercantilism.

8. It seems that the occupation of merchant, or agent of London exporters, was useful to one interested in launching an underwriting house. According to Doerflinger, the rising merchant class aspired to the same things underwriters required: "contacts, capital, or experience"; see Thomas M. Doerflinger, *A Vigorous Spirit of Enterprise: Merchants and Economic Development in Revolutionary Philadelphia*, 29. Doerflinger notes that John Kidd was also a merchant who did business with the London firm Neate and Neave.

9. For interesting statistics about the rise of underwriting solicitations see Perkins, *American Public Finance and Financial Services*, 290.

10. Ibid., 294.

11. Ibid., 297. Perkins's discussion of the evolution of fire insurance is detailed and fascinating.

12. Ibid., 290. Perkins points out that during the 1760's the practice of reinsurance became widespread, indicating a sophisticated understanding of risk and the stores of capital necessary to underwrite other underwriters.

13. Fowler, "Marine Insurance in Boston," 158, provides an excellent account of the scarcity of viable underwriters in Boston. One can assume a similar situation in Philadelphia during the same period.

14. On this point, see ibid., 164. With reference to the development of New York City's financial markets and the underestimated power of insurance companies, see Margaret G. Myers, *The New York Money Market*, 41: "By 1860 the total capital of insurance companies of all kinds doing business in New York state was about 75 millions, a sum slightly above the capital of the banks in New York City at that time."

15. For full descriptions of this legitimizing, see Geoffrey Clark, *Betting on Lives: The Culture of Life Insurance in England, 1695–1775*.

16. See Perkins, *American Public Finance and Financial Services*, 301.

17. The collection by Martha Woodmansee and Mark Osteen, eds., *The New Economic Criticism: Studies at the Intersection of Literature and Economics*, signals a possible opening up of the field into many areas of literary study. Goux and Heinzelman have

also made important contributions; see Jean-Joseph Goux, *The Coiners of Language*, and Kurt Heinzelman, *The Economics of the Imagination*.

18. On the evolution of currency and monetary symbology, see Marc Shell, *Art and Money*; Marc Shell, *Money, Language, and Thought: Literary and Philosophical Economies from the Medieval to the Modern Era*; and Marc Shell, *The Economy of Literature*. I should note that Shell only goes so far in discussing important distinctions in the meaning and method of varieties of colonial money. Paper money was government-issued scrip, which stood in for metal specie—metonymically, as it were—and relied for its value on a strictly representational association with metal made by the authority of the government. Meanwhile, bank notes, used most often as a kind of personal check drawn on a third-party entity, were the other major form of colonial and early national currency. They both constitute the variety of fiduciary money I discuss here: paper currency, which promised a redemption at a future date, and which used the value constituted therein as a source of value. I thank Jennifer Jordan Baker for helping me to sort out these concepts. For a good summary, see Robert Garson, "Counting Money: The U.S. Dollar and American Nationhood, 1781–1820." For a more detailed exposition, see Perkins, *American Public Finance and Financial Services*, 42–55. For a discussion of the role of currency finance in the management of public debt during the Revolution, see E. James Ferguson, "Currency Finance: An Interpretation of Colonial Monetary Practices." For discussions of the relationship between paper money and the politics of national independence, wherein the intricacies of the colonists' call for and comfort with paper money was a major spur to revolutionary action, see Joseph Albert Ernst, "The Currency Act Repeal Movement: A Study of Imperial Politics and Revolutionary Crisis, 1764–1767," and Jack P. Greene, "The Currency Act of 1764 in Imperial-Colonial Relations, 1764–1776." It should also be noted that the roots of the insurance business share with the evolution of paper money an interest in securing money or loans with collateral, whether human bodies or land; see Clark, *Betting on Lives: The Culture of Life Insurance in England, 1695–1775*; Ruwell, *Eighteenth-Century Capitalism*, 10–11; Ferguson, "Currency Finance." For a more recent, specifically colonial resource, see the online archive of the Leslie Brock Center for the Study of Colonial Currency at http://etext.lib.virginia.edu/users/brock.

19. It must be acknowledged that oral contracts of insurance are legally valid, strictly speaking. But in practice the written contract carries far more legal certainty. One suspects that this has little to do with any presupposed notion of the clarity and fixity of written expression, but rather with the unreliability of corroboration and disinterested witnessing.

20. In their introduction, "Taking Account of the New Economic Criticism," Woodmansee and Osteen discuss the important distinction between homologous and analogous forms, first posited by F. Rossi-Landi in his *Linguistics and Economics* (1975). My discussion may be said to reflect (with all due caveats pointed out by Woodmansee and Osteen) the homological relationship between insurance underwriting and key tropic modes (after Shell) of American literature.

21. For a discussion of the idea of conservation of property as it relates to the emergence of the bourgeois public sphere, see Jurgen Habermas, *The Structural Transformation of the Public Sphere*, 56. According to Habermas, Locke's foundational principle of

"preservation of property" is essential to "self-interpretation derived from the categories of the public sphere in the world of letters; the interests of the owners of private property could converge with that of the freedom of the individual in general" (56).

22. It is of course possible to imagine situations, not uncommon ones, where property that has a material reality (a house) is also ascribed a negative value (it is condemned or has a lien against it). The underwriting process then warrants conditions under which the property may be transformed into a positive monetary value (destruction of one property, rebuilding, and then sale or habitation of the new house). In any case, the idea of conservation is invoked as a reclamation of value which has been lost in the past. Indeed, one might view such a case as a historical underwriting, whereas most underwriting concerns itself with future values.

23. Certainly, it may be argued that Rotman's argument remains in force, but he ignores the role of insurance as a form of a capital market itself.

24. This conservative principle is also the operative function behind corporate theory, which essentially guarantees the immortality of a personlike organization founded on property and monetary assets.

25. For a good summary of the American history of property law regarding real estate and deeds, see Lawrence M. Friedman, *A History of American Law*, 234–45.

26. This is of course dependent upon one's independence in the labor market, whether one is free or slave, indentured or not. I take up this aspect of underwriting in chap. 2.

27. The study of the rise of finance capital and its relationship to the novel has been especially vigorous in British eighteenth-century studies. See James Thompson, *Models of Value: Eighteenth-Century Political Economy and the Novel*; Colin Nicholson, *Writing and the Rise of Finance: Capital Satires of the Early Eighteenth Century*; Samuel L. Macey, *Money and the Novel: Mercenary Motivation in Defoe and His Immediate Successors*. For accounts not exclusively limited to the eighteenth century, see John Vernon, *Money and Fiction: Literary Realism in the Nineteenth and Early Twentieth Centuries*; Anthony Purdy, ed., *Literature and Money*.

28. The pioneering work that discusses the wider cultural significance of the corporate model is of course Alan Trachtenberg, *The Incorporation of America: Culture and Society in the Gilded Age*.

29. See Michel Foucault, *"Society Must Be Defended": Lectures at the Collège de France, 1975–76*, 242–43.

30. Perkins observes that after the Constitution was adopted, insurance companies became part of the proliferation of incorporation that marked the period. Prices were kept low to encourage widespread public participation; see Perkins, *American Public Finance and Financial Services*, 291. Fowler is instructive as well: "Boston's experience in the postwar world was mirrored in other American ports, particularly Philadelphia. Philadelphians had underwritten their commerce in much the same way as Bostonians, that is, at first as individuals and then, through an evolution, in more formal associations. . . . [T]he example of Philadelphia was not lost on Boston. Incorporation offered numerous advantages for merchants and underwriters alike, including access to greater capital as well as a fair degree of permanence and stability"; see Fowler, "Marine Insurance in Boston," 159.

31. For a recent exploration of this phenomenon in the context of Revolutionary

politics, see T. H. Breen, *The Marketplace of Revolution: How Consumer Politics Shaped American Independence.*

32. See Larzer Ziff, *Writing in the New Nation: Prose, Print, and Politics in the Early United States*, xi.

33. None of these insurable entities, especially human lives, were accepted uncontroversially; see Clark, *Betting on Lives*, 77–114.

34. Ibid., 85–88.

35. "The creation of the insurance companies was a further development of the business corporation and the capital market of Britain. They were joint stock 'monied' enterprises whose promotion was related to the opportunities of speculation implied in the development of the Stock Exchange"; see Ruwell, *Eighteenth-Century Capitalism*, 34. Many of the earliest marine and fire insurance enterprises were mutuals, dependent for capital on the policyholders themselves. This, of course, changed in the early national period. Perkins, incidentally, seems to dispute Ruwell's assertion that the British led the way to corporate insurance, holding that they remained wedded to private syndicates; see Perkins, *American Public Finance and Financial Services*, 292.

36. Perkins, *American Public Finance and Financial Services*, 9.

37. See Banks McDowell, *The Crisis in Insurance Regulation*, 1–17.

38. See Jerry, *Understanding Insurance Law*, 51. This fact means that the insurance industry is regulated in a fairly extraordinary way, at the state level, a practice that was eventually codified by the McCarran-Ferguson Act. Jerry points out that this restrictive ethos goes back to the 1794 charter granted to the Insurance Company of North America, which "prohibited the company from engaging in other businesses, required that the deposits be placed in the Bank of Pennsylvania, limited the company's investment in real estate, and specified minimum amounts of liquid assets to be kept in reserve to pay losses" (54). In a different context, Latin America is learning this lesson before we are.

39. See Tamara Plakins Thornton, *Handwriting in America: A Cultural History*, esp. chap. 1, "The Lost World of Colonial Handwriting." Thornton says Boston offers the best example of this use of handwriting for mercantile practices.

40. See Hawthorne Daniel, *The Hartford of Hartford: An Insurance Company's Part in a Century and a Half of American History.*

41. For different and sometimes complementary descriptions of public and private spheres through manuscript and print writing, see Michael Warner, *The Letters of the Republic: Publication and the Public Sphere in Eighteenth-Century America,* and Shields, *Civil Tongues and Polite Letters in British America.*

42. By way of interesting contrast, Michael Warner points out that the writing and then the printing of the Constitution were buttressed by the argument that the general unanimous nature of the document was precisely what made it republican: written documents were inherently "tyrannical"; see Warner, *The Letters of the Republic*, 91–107.

43. Browne and Quinn make a similar claim for the particular relevance of deconstruction to critiquing economic rhetoric. Their view is, however, slightly different insofar as they hold that deconstruction allows us to analyze the unitary subject of economic logic; I am interested in using deconstruction primarily to question the structure of socializing risk through texts. I do, however, enact a version of their method in chap. 4. See M. Neil Browne and J. Kevin Quinn, "Dominant Economic Metaphors and the Postmodern Subversion of the Subject." In Jacques Derrida, *Given Time: Counterfeit Money,*

and especially in the essay "The Madness of Economic Reason," Mauss's gift theory and economic discourse are deconstructed.

44. See Browne and Quinn, "Dominant Economic Metaphors and the Postmodern Subversion of the Subject."

45. On this notion of unstable and inconsistent axiomatic systems as they relate to Gödel's theorems, see Woodmansee and Osteen, eds., *The New Economic Criticism*, 27.

46. Quoted in Guyora Binder and Robert Weisberg, *Literary Criticisms of Law*, 419.

47. See François Ewald, "Genetics, Insurance, and Risk," 23.

48. This echoes Derrida's famous example of the founding documents of the American republic, which call into existence that which premises their ability to speak at all; see Jacques Derrida, *Otobiographies*. It also underscores the abandonment of the theory of intrinsic materiality in property law effected by the dematerialization of the law and the "incarnation of the word" after the Civil War; see Stephen Best, *Fugitive's Properties*, esp. 37–41.

49. I follow Rice's shrewd observation that Dumont's thesis applies well to the American eighteenth century; see Louis Dumont, *From Mandeville to Marx: The Genesis and Triumph of Economic Ideology*.

50. See Ellen E. Schultz, "Companies Sue Union Retirees to Cut Promised Health Benefits."

51. Best, in *Fugitive's Properties*, makes this argument more fully than I could hope to here. His explication and genealogy of Blackstone's legal transformation of property, from a concept grounded by material claims to the famous "bundle of rights," is particularly relevant.

52. This is in keeping with the evolution of genres of fiction in the United States. As Cathy Davidson, Michael Gilmore, and Jay Grossman have pointed out, eighteenth-century novelists feared for the credibility of their fictions and were thus compelled to call their works "histories." One wonders whether the rise of fictions associated with legal and commercial texts contributed to making a cultural space for the fictions of literature. See Jay Grossman, *Reconstituting the American Renaissance*.

53. This follows Bataille, who held that "all meaningful social rituals—including and especially art and poetry—involve loss and sacrifice"; see Woodmansee and Osteen, eds., *The New Economic Criticism*, 29.

54. There is a robust body of pamphlet literature, written well into the second half of the eighteenth century, extolling the religious doctrine of assurance, a body of writing whose theological intentions overlap in interesting ways with the burgeoning materialist sense of the word.

55. Adam Smith, *The Wealth of Nations*, 108–9.

56. Jeremy Bentham, *An Introduction to the Principles of Morals and Legislation*, 14–15.

57. See Mary Poovey, *A History of the Modern Fact: Problems of Knowledge in the Sciences of Wealth and Society*, 38.

58. See Clark, *Betting On Lives*, 114. For the best account of the role of the science of probability in the cultural history of the West, see also Ian Hacking, *The Emergence of Probability: A Philosophical Study of Early Ideas About Probability, Induction, and Statistical Inference*. Interestingly, there is evidence for a shift in the eighteenth century in the standard language used in insurance policies. Sometime after the middle of the century,

contracts began to stop using God as the primary invocation of providence and luck and began to assert that such policies drew upon the drafters of the policies themselves for the fates of their properties. A 1913 pamphlet by Mrs. Cornelius Stevenson (perhaps better known as the pioneering archaeologist Sarah York Stevenson) puts it well. According to this pamphlet, "the earliest of John Saunders' policies [1749] . . . begins with the words: 'In the name of God, Amen.' . . . European merchants originally passed through the same mental processes as did our colonial ancestors with regard to the unrighteousness of securing themselves against disasters that, in their time, were regarded as the expressions of divine wrath. However this may be, only eight years after the writing of the earliest known policy issued upon this continent, this compromise preamble had already been abandoned [to] 'Whereas we,' etc."; see Sarah York Stevenson, "Insurance and Business Adventure in the Days of Shakespeare and in Those of William Penn," 266–67.

59. For the best explanation of the nuances of insurance contracts, see Edwin W. Patterson, *Essentials of Insurance Law: An Outline of Legal Doctrines in Their Relations to Insurance Practices.*

60. A recent slogan for ACE, a global insurance and reinsurance giant that is the descendant of the Insurance Company of North America (founded in 1792), seems to understand this aspect of insurance: "Protection. It's not the end. It's the beginning. Continue."

61. Three of the most influential explorations of this critique in American writing of the nineteenth century are Michael Gilmore, *American Romanticism and the Marketplace*; Walter Benn Michaels, *The Gold Standard and the Logic of Naturalism*; and Walter Benn Michaels and Donald Pease, eds., *The American Renaissance Reconsidered.*

62. This issue has received long-overdue attention in the past decade, with the discovery of marine insurance taken out on slave cargo in insurance company archives, most notably those of Aetna. California passed SB 2199 in 2000 to promote disclosure of contemporary insurance companies' involvement in the slave insurance profits. See "California Department of Insurance Slavery Era Insurance Registry Report to the California Legislature" (May 2002), 4-5.

63. See Perkins, *American Public Finance and Financial Services*, 302.

64. Lee applied for the insurance in 1859. A Lincoln policy from 1861 is in the Hartford's archives. Lee's house was behind Union lines during the war, which made it impossible for him to pay taxes on the property. The Union began to bury its dead on the grounds, which eventually became Arlington National Cemetery. His policy, presumably, became worthless. I am indebted to Tom Cutrer for bringing this anecdote to my attention.

65. See Tim Weiner, "Feeling Secure Is a Risky Business." For important analyses of the risks involved in the increasing systemization of modernity, see Paul Virilio in *Virilio Live: Selected Interviews*, and Charles Perrow, *Normal Accidents: Living with High-Risk Technologies.* I should point out that the writing of this book took place in the aftermath of the tragedy of September 11, 2001. The effect of this event on the assessment of risk and safety in everyday life is enormous. It must also be noted that part of the narrative of the bombings of the World Trade Center has been the mysterious trade in futures on reinsurance companies that underwrote the towers. Moreover, the attempt to compensate those lost in the destruction has been subject to problems that underwriting attempts to forestall—agree upon the payout amount before the event. Underwriting, for

all its power to secure and compensate, is still a textual event fraught with an unnerving vulnerability to manipulation, and, therefore—given the deconstructive premise that seems to be an apt analytic frame for thinking about this kind of textuality—to uncertainty.

66. See David Golumbia, "Hypercapital."

67. For a fascinating analysis of two postmodern novels' use of risk theory, see Ursula K. Heise, "Toxins, Drugs, and Global Systems: Risk and Narrative in the Contemporary Novel."

68. See François Ewald, "The Return of Descartes's Malicious Demon: An Outline of a Philosophy of Precaution."

Chapter 1

1. There is an excellent body of criticism and biography taking notice of Franklin's less celebrated pessimism, and even his "dark side." But these evaluations view Franklin's worldview as an outgrowth of his pessimism about the nature of humanity and virtue rather than the experience of humans in an inhospitable world. And none make explicit the connection between his economic ideologies and the notion of a fundamentally corrupt human agency. For these critics, pessimism and optimism hinge solely on the question of virtue in Franklin rather than on the nature of the society and universe he is responding to. As David Larson has pointed out, the critical field runs the gamut from declaring Franklin a Hobbesian pessimist (J. A. Leo Lemay) to describing him as an optimist in the mold of the Earl of Shaftesbury (A. O. Aldridge), but the truth about his view of human virtue was somewhere in the middle. See David M. Larson, "Franklin on the Nature of Man and the Possibility of Virtue"; Ronald A. Bosco, " 'He that best understands the world, least likes it': The Dark Side of Benjamin Franklin."

2. See Myra Jehlen, "Imitate Socrates and Jesus: The Making of a Good American," in *Readings at the Edge of Literature*. Jehlen's account of the paradoxical interiority of Franklin's self-generating prose is masterful. I follow many of her insights into Franklin's manipulation of virtue and representation in the service of commercial success.

3. See Michael Zuckerman, "Doing Good While Doing Well: Benevolence and Self-Interest in Franklin's *Autobiography*."

4. See H. W. Brands, *The First American: The Life and Times of Benjamin Franklin*.

5. I have relied for this account on the introduction to Max Farrand, *Benjamin Franklin's Memoirs: A Parallel Text Edition*, and on Larzer Ziff, *Writing in the New Nation: Prose, Print, and Politics in the Early United States*, for Ziff's recounting of later revisions. Farrand's text has been superseded by Leonard W. Labaree, ed., *The Papers of Benjamin Franklin: 1750–1753*, and Labaree's has been superseded by J. A. Leo Lemay and P. M. Zall, *The Autobiography of Benjamin Franklin: A Genetic Text*. Ziff records the byzantine fate of Franklin's authoritative *Autobiography* (120), and what I say here seems to square with subsequent authorities. For an incisive discussion of the poetics of death that structures the *Autobiography* without making it a document of interiorized anxiety, see Jennifer T. Kennedy, "Death Effects: Revisiting the Conceit of Franklin's *Memoir*." Kennedy reads a death scene that seems to have truly affected Franklin, but in a typically externalized and ironic way: "The end of Denham's life is the end of Franklin's merchant career, a professional expiration for Franklin at the same time that it is a personal loss. Instead of regretting death, Franklin comically regrets life: the need to face death a sec-

ond time coinciding with the need to find a new trade. This is the humorous inverse of the fantasy of the relived life—Franklin suffers from the disagreeable need to relive the 'Work' of death. By using the word 'Work' to describe the process of dying, Franklin creates a further connection between his employment dilemma and his experience of illness" (229).

6. Levin, among many others, places Franklin's view of the universe on the cusp between the Calvinist world and that of emergent capitalism; see David Levin, "The Autobiography of Benjamin Franklin: The Puritan Experimenter in Life and Art," 263: "Whether he was a Puritan or not . . . the young . . . of Franklin's time had to walk a perilous way in the world. And if . . . he was leaving his childhood community as well as the restraints and comforts of his childhood religious faith, . . . he faced those dangers with very little help from outside himself. He had precious little help in the experience of others, for often his experience was new for the entire society. . . . Franklin described plain economic fact as well as moral truth when he said, 'It is hard for an empty sack to stand upright.'" Larzer Ziff takes this sort of observation and pushes it further into an account of how trust and credit underwrite the new representative self: "It is notable that Franklin's advice aims at the securing of credit, the lifeblood of trade and, increasingly (as confidence), the lifeblood of community in a society governed by trade. A man is as good as the amount of trust he can command rather than the amount of property he possesses. . . . He coins his good reputation in the form of notes and if his reputation fails, then like counterfeit money his notes become valueless because unbacked"; see Ziff, *Writing in the New Nation*, 70.

7. It is interesting to note that Franklin, in attempting to finally answer Vaughan's plea for an autobiography, wrote on his return voyage not "the remaining notes of my life, which you [a friend] desire" but three of what Farrand calls his most extensive and useful essays, "one on navigation, another on smoky chimneys, and the third a description of his smoke-consuming stove"; see Farrand, *Benjamin Franklin's Memoirs*, xxii. One could view this as an unconscious substitution—his thoughts on improving the risks of shipping, and home heating/cooking standing in for the very life of Franklin.

8. Jennifer Jordan Baker, "Franklin's *Autobiography* and the Credibility of Personality," is a fine exception to this trend. Baker links Franklin's representative poetics with both his personal philosophy of money and the dominant early (mercantilist) and late (capitalist) eighteenth-century modes of thinking about financial circulation.

9. There are two lines of analysis worth invoking here for context. One is religious, in which Franklin is seeking to rebuke a local culture of orthodoxy, thereby striking a blow for a rising class of individualist merchants and republicans. The other involves a much broader swath of intellectual history and political theory; that is, the eighteenth century's emergent theories of Lockean property, culminating in the political economy of Adam Smith, offer a way of understanding the Franklin's concerns in the texts I have chosen to focus on. Thus the concern with anxiety may be read as apprehension with a Hobbesian world of social insecurity and with how we might construct political remedies for insecurity. My own method is to take note of that argument but not make it central. I'm concerned primarily with how loss is converted, in Franklin's mind, into a commercial theory with local effects.

10. The disquiet about loss may also have been spurred by the colonies-wide effect of the bursting of the South Sea bubble in 1720, which not only intensified the dearth of

currency but also placed great strain on mortgaged property; see Brands, *The First American*, 39.

11. For a history of the tontine, see Robert M. Jennings, Donald F. Swanson, and Andrew P. Trout, "Alexander Hamilton's Tontine Proposal."

12. Clark points out that such life insurance societies were popular in England because they served a similar "clubbing" function among creditors in need of an informal banking network when credit became tight. Franklin may have had this in mind, seeing also that he picked up the name "Friendly Society" from the well-known English Friendly Society of the late seventeenth and early eighteenth centuries. Interestingly, one aspect of friendly societies that Franklin neglects—perhaps in keeping with the strict public-spiritedness of his appeal—is the notion that such investments beat market interest rates; see Clark, *Betting on Lives*, 88–91.

13. Breitwieser notes that Franklin's first major nemesis was Cotton Mather. His brother's *New England Courant* was a vehicle for his satire of the Puritan worldview. Seen in this context, the insurance scheme seems an appropriate counter to the power of the will as it is delimited by Puritan notions of self-governance. See Mitchell Breitwieser, *Cotton Mather and Benjamin Franklin: The Price of Representative Personality*, 10–11.

14. Geoffrey Clark makes an important distinction between the self-governing nature of friendly societies and the more proprietary and legalistic nature of joint-stock companies (which most life insurance evolved into): "Life insurance societies typically were constituted as self-governing associations of policyholders rather than as proprietary companies, and they therefore possessed the characteristics of both businesses and clubs"; see Clark, *Betting on Lives*, 54. Franklin maintains this ethos well into his schemes for fire insurance and hospital funding. For an explanation of the legal differences between mutual and stock/corporate insurance companies, see Robert H. Jerry II, *Understanding Insurance Law*, 41.

15. Cotton Mather, *Pascentius: A very brief essay upon the methods of piety, wherein people in whom the difficulties of the times have caused anxieties, May have a comfortable assurance of being at all times comfortably provided for.*

16. Brands mentions *Bonifacius* and *Silentiarius* as precursors to Silence Dogood, but not *Pascentius*; see Brands, *The First American*, 26.

17. On the print war carried out in the pages of the *New England Courant* between the Franklins and Mather, see David Shields, *Civil Tongues and Polite Letters in British America*, 170–72.

18. See no. 46 (Addison), Monday, Apr. 23, 1711, in Gregory G. Smith, ed., *The Spectator*, vol. 1, 170–71.

19. See Shields, *Civil Tongues and Polite Letters in British America*, 265, on the various methods of publicity and their relation to eighteenth-century notions of authority in America, especially as this relates to Franklin's proliferating pseudonyms.

20. Rice's discussion of authorship and property is compatible with my thesis. Rice holds that authors, by the second half of the eighteenth century, had gained autonomy by "transforming printed texts from a practical means for assertive sociopolitical commentary into the more inert medium of property and commodity"; see Grantland Rice, *The Transformation of Authorship in America*, 4. To a degree, Rice's thesis on Franklin is also consistent with my emphases on print commodities and narrating the self. Rice's view of reification as an implicitly Franklinian topos would seem to be a different facet

of my analysis, where reification was part of the Franklinian need to evacuate the shadows of danger and assert the agency of the writing author.

21. Warner's discussion of Franklin's pseudonymity, what he calls his "absorption into generality," is helpful. Warner writes: "The games Franklin typically plays with his personae often take this form: a fantasmatic self-splitting or self-objectification that results in a concealed or absent agent behind a manipulated surface"; see Michael Warner, *The Letters of the Republic: Publication and the Public Sphere in Eighteenth-Century America*, 78. Warner claims at one point in his discussion of Franklin that Franklin was perceived as the model of civic virtue because he was supremely disinterested and therefore impartial in the exercise of rational choice (76–77). Warner goes on to imply that Franklin had a "stake" in such a perception. But he never does anatomize the stake as such. Warner (73–96) does not mention the Dogood paper I discuss here.

22. Brands, *The First American*, 74, makes the interesting point that Franklin is careful to say that printing the essay was an erratum, not the writing of it. Brands notes further that Franklin later took care to burn all the copies he had not already circulated to friends.

23. C. B. Macpherson, *The Political Theory of Possessive Individualism: Hobbes to Locke*, 32–33, quotes Hobbes's argument in chap. 6 of *Leviathan* for viewing humans as "self-moving machines," an idea that had resonance elsewhere in Franklin's thinking: "When in the mind of man, Appetites, and Aversions, Hopes, and Feares, concerning one and the same thing, arise alternatively; and divers good and evill consequences of the doing, or omitting the thing propounded, come successively into our thoughts; so that sometimes we have an Appetite to it; sometimes an Aversion from it; sometimes Hope to be able to do it; sometimes Despaire, or Feare to attempt it; the whole summe of Desires, Aversion, Hopes and Fears, continued till the thing be either done, or thought impossible, is that we call DELIBERATION."

24. Interestingly, Franklin had trouble taking his own advice. After playing—and losing to—the famous chess-playing robotic "Turk" of Wolfgang von Kempalen, Franklin did not record the loss in his diary. It could just be embarrassment on Franklin's part, but one is tempted to see this as a moment when he came face to face, as it were, with something particularly frightening—the end of human agency—and so found the experience inexpressible; see Jennifer Schuessler, "Hello, Dolly!," 29–31.

25. Brands, The First American, 155, notes that Franklin was in fact greatly affected by the death of Franky: "For Franky he made an exception [to his optimistic credo]. The grieving father allowed himself—or perhaps he simply could not help it—to wonder what the boy would have become. For the rest of his life the sight of other boys caused him to reflect on Franky."

26. Franklin's letter of May 9, 1753, to Peter Collinson is justly famous for its addressing issues of social obligation to the poor. While I think it is significant that its writing came in the midst of many of Franklin's public underwriting projects (fire insurance, the hospital, the college), I don't address it here. My sense is that it doesn't take us any further into the causes of improvidence, nor any further into its remedies other than a kind of benevolent "teach the poor to fish" advisement.

27. Franklin describes his raising a lottery for the defense of Philadelphia in the 1740's during Britain's ongoing conflict with Spain and, later, with France. The lottery

filled successfully, and the money was used to build a battery south of the city; see Lemay and Zall, *The Autobiography of Benjamin Franklin*, 110, 111–13.

28. See also Mary Elizabeth Ruwell, *Eighteenth-Century Capitalism: The Formation of American Marine Insurance Companies*, 20: "Another traditional way of investing money was in lotteries. . . . Although the chances of winning were slim, the successful lottery player did gain an easy fortune. Lotteries were occasionally viewed with suspicion as a form of gambling; in 1729, for example, they were outlawed in Philadelphia, but special legislation continued the practice. For the most part, they were considered a kind of voluntary tax for paving streets, erecting wharves, buildings and similar works, with a contingent profitable for such as held the lucky numbers. One hundred and fifty-eight lotteries were licensed before 1776, of which 132 benefited civic or state purposes. In 1773 a lottery was set up to encourage the grape growing industry. The Continental Congress established a lottery to finance the Revolution. In Pennsylvania, lotteries were used to pave streets, to bridge the Conestoga and other creeks, to build churches, to erect a lighthouse at Cape Henlopen and to found the school that was to become the University of Pennsylvania." See also Pauline Maier, "The Revolutionary Origins of the American Corporation," 51–84. Maier details the arguments surrounding the extraordinary rise in corporate entities during and after the Revolution, showing how the distinction between public and private corporations remained disputed into the nineteenth century.

29. Note the differentiation by Ruwell between an insurance company and a mere insurance broker (John Copson, 1721).

30. See Barry Supple, "Insurance in British History."

31. See François Ewald, "Insurance and Risk."

32. Much of this discussion centers on the fascinating practice whereby the earliest English and continental European life insurance policies were, in effect, bets placed on the longevity of persons (such as Popes) in whom the insurer had no "real interest"; see Clark, *Betting on Lives*, 17–27.

33. See P. G. M. Dickson, *The Financial Revolution*, 45: "By 1688 private and public finance both in England and abroad had therefore developed and improved and had already moved on to a longer-term basis. A contradictory trend was the addiction of contemporaries to gambling on a massive scale. It was an age of wagers on the lives of private and public men, the chances of war, and the occurrence of natural events, as well as the issue of a horse-race, the fall of dice, the turn of a card. The helps to explain the keen public interest in lotteries." See also Ian Hacking, *The Emergence of Probability: A Philosophical Study of Early Ideas About Probability, Induction, and Statistical Inference*, and Patricia Cline Cohen, *A Calculating People: The Spread of Numeracy in Early America*. One is also tempted to see connections with the evolution of municipal and commercial corporatism in eighteenth-century America; for an excellent discussion of the public/private aspects of this process, see Maier, "The Revolutionary Origins of the American Corporation," 51–84.

34. There was conflict, however over the funding of the hospital: "Some critics even alleged that many of the city's residents did not favor the scheme. To this Franklin replied that the citizens were so strong in support that they would subscribe L2000—an assertion opponents of the petition 'considered as a most extravagant supposition, and utterly impossible. On this,' wrote Franklin, 'I form'd my plan.' He obtained leave to

bring in a bill to incorporate the contributors and grant them a blank sum of money, making the grant conditional on the contributors raising an equal sum by voluntary effort. 'This condition carried the bill through; for the members who had oppos'd the Grant, and now conceiv'd they might have the credit of being charitable without the expence, agreed to its passage.' The bill passed unanimously February 7, and on May 11 . . . it became law"; see Labaree, ed., *The Papers of Benjamin Franklin: 1750–1753*, 109.

35. Ibid., 281.

36. Philadelphia Contributionship for the Insurance of Houses from Loss by Fire, *The Deed of Settlement of the Society for Insuring of Houses, In and Near Philadelphia*.

37. See Carole Shammas, "The Space Problem in Early United States Cities."

38. See Labaree, ed., *The Papers of Benjamin Franklin: 1750–1753*, 282–83.

39. As I have explained in the introduction (following the observation of Edwin Perkins), fire insurance demanded a patience and corporate optimism about the future that the relatively short-term marine insurance industry never required.

40. See Alwin E. Bulau, *Footprints of Assurance*.

41. In a discussion of the *Autobiography* as a narrative of representative repression relying upon Calvinist fathers for its models, Pieschel shrewdly shows how Franklin has been misread as a turn away from the poetics of his Calvinist predecessors: "It is Franklin's repeated reference to dangerous waters, metaphorical or literal, which contradicts Kenneth Dauber's assertion that the *Autobiography* is 'the foundation of a new literature forever free of the my the myth of a fall' . . . However benignly Franklin warns against wandering or straying, he *does* warn, implying that his paradise is not guaranteed to all"; see Bridget Smith Pieschel, "Franklin: The Young Man's Guide to Success." But it is important to remember that this surviving typology of danger and anxiety is part of the poetics of representation that befits an underwriting culture. Franklin is impossible without Mather. Indeed, Pieschell herself goes on to show how Franklin is keen to demonstrate the failures and heedlessness of his friends and acquaintances as examples of their falling below the line of his own narrative of improvement.

42. See Labaree, ed., *The Papers of Benjamin Franklin: 1750–1753*, 247.

43. Benjamin Franklin, *The Complete Poor Richard's Almanacks: 1733–1758*, vol. 2.

44. Clark shows that Puritans were not entirely against the use of drawing lots. Indeed, he quotes a sixteenth-century Puritan divine "admonish[ing] his countrymen that because 'the use of lot is a solemn act of religion, it may not be applied to sporting' "; see Clark, *Betting on Lives*, 35. According to Clark, the religious features of insurance were set out by English anti-Catholic propaganda and its concurrent national innovations in raising funds for state wars: "William's wars against the domineering anti-Christ (as the French king was described) heightened not only taxes but also religious expectations, and these combined with the heady commercial atmosphere of Defoe's projecting age to form a potent amalgam of national pride, religious mission, and economic experimentation. The nascent life insurance movement exemplified this commercial and Christian synthesis. The proposals issued by life insurance societies commonly cited the charitable, educational, and religious benefits that could result from taking out a life insurance policy, and though the noblest of those aspirations were seldom realized, it remains true that many of the managers and members of life insurance societies sincerely sought to square private profit with public improvement" (34).

45. On this point, see Joanne Cutting-Gray, "Franklin's *Autobiography*: Politics of the Public Self." She holds that Franklin proposes we " 'procure wealth,' but only in order to 'secure virtue" (35), and that freedom was the link between public spirit (virtue publicly effected) and private welfare. Her argument parallels mine in that she shows Franklin's mode of acquisitiveness and self-interest to be a species of public-mindedness that does not automatically reinscribe the values of the atomized individual back into the public sphere.

46. A similar argument is made in Heinz Otto Sibum, "The Bookkeeper of Nature: Benjamin Franklin's Electrical Research and the Development of Experimental Natural Philosophy in the Eighteenth Century."

47. See Breitwieser, *Cotton Mather and Benjamin Franklin*, 223.

48. See Jay Fliegelman, *Declaring Independence: Jefferson, Natural Language, and the Culture of Performance*.

49. Breitwieser goes on to say that the Lukácsian representative man "attempts to enhance thoughts, feelings, scruples, and drives that are consonant with human nature as he has diagnosed it, and to discourage or expunge all that seems discordant, including any attraction he may feel toward adversary definitions of human nature"; see Breitwieser, *Cotton Mather and Benjamin Franklin*, 3. As Breitwieser conceives it, his study is of the "aspirational" nature of Mather's and Franklin's self-constructions, which means, in essence, that he limits himself to conscious choices made by each man and so must in some sense take them at their word.

50. Pennsylvania Society for Promoting the Abolition of Slavery, *An Address to the Public from the Pennsylvania Society for Promoting the Abolition of Slavery, and the Relief of Free Negroes, Unlawfully Held in Bondage*.

Chapter 2

1. See Julian Mason, *The Poems of Phillis Wheatley*, 115. Subsequent references will be noted in the text. I should note that two excellent editions of Wheatley's work have appeared during the writing of this book; see Vincent Carretta, ed., *Phillis Wheatley: Complete Writings*; and Phillis Wheatley, The Collected Works of Phillis Wheatley, ed. John Shields.

2. See Betsy Erkkila, "Phillis Wheatley and the Black American Revolution," 231.

3. The insistent ethereality of Wheatley's elegies should be indexed to the story of her kidnapping, a "snatching" which finds its way into moments of deep irony in many of her best poems on sovereignty. For an excellent discussion of this, see Paula Bennett, "Phillis Wheatley's Vocation and the Paradox of the 'African Muse.' " Bennett shows that Wheatley was extremely subtle in her deployment of the verb "snatch." Bennett points out that Wheatley's allusion to Pope's famous line "snatch a grace beyond the reach of art" (from Pope's *Essay on Criticism*, 1.153) signals her obsessive reworking of the notion of appropriate and inappropriate thefts.

4. Lawrence M. Friedman, in *A History of American Law*, says the following of "consideration": "Another major principle of contract law was its insistence on a true bargain between parties. One party must have made an offer, which the other must have literally accepted. And offer and acceptance had to be glued together with a mysterious substance called *consideration*. Consideration was a term of many meanings; it signified,

among other things, the *quid pro quo,* the exchange element of the contract" (277). It should be clear that consideration is yet another almost ineffable notion that points us in the direction of nonmaterial trust and reciprocity.

5. See Vincent Carretta, *Unchained Voices,* for a definitive discussion of the appropriateness of the term "Afro-American" as opposed to "Afro-British."

6. See Robert Kendrick, "Other Questions: Phillis Wheatley and the Ethics of Interpretation." For a discussion of Wheatley's "public presence," see Walt Nott, "From 'Uncultivated Barbarian' to 'Poetical Genius': The Public Presence of Phillis Wheatley."

7. Terrence Collins, "Phillis Wheatley: The Dark Side of the Poetry."

8. See Hilene Flanzbaum, "Unprecedented Liberties: Re-reading Phillis Wheatley." For an interesting discussion of Flanzbaum's reading, and of Wheatley's manipulation of the poetic tradition in general, see Marsha Watson, "A Classic Case: Phillis Wheatley and Her Poetry."

9. I am borrowing the term "moral aesthetics" from Frank Shuffelton's nuanced and suggestive discussion of Wheatley in "Phillis Wheatley, the Aesthetic, and the Form of Life," in *Studies in Eighteenth-Century Culture,* Volume 26, Syndy M. Conger and Julie C. Hayes, eds. (Baltimore: The Johns Hopkins University Press).

10. To suggest this is not to imply that Wheatley's voice is inauthentic. On the contrary, I want to argue that what has kept recent critics so interested in her as a writer has been her ability to recede and come into focus, as if manipulating the terms of subjectivity behind the mask of the poetic performance, inviting critics to invent better frames and benevolent corrections. I am part of that critical tendency.

11. See Henry Louis Gates Jr., ed., "Writing, 'Race,' and the Difference it Makes."

12. It is worth noting that the word "advertisement," according to the *Oxford English Dictionary,* went from a primary meaning, in the fifteenth and sixteenth centuries, focused on the use of a notification in the changing of an individual's mind to a more familiar meaning which signifies the more forthrightly public, broadcasting nature of the advertising text.

13. The profiling of this roster of underwriters as overwhelmingly male contrasts in interesting ways with the observation made by John Shields, in the notes to the Schomburg Library edition of Wheatley's collected works, that Wheatley stands as the first literary figure to be promoted commercially and intellectually solely by women; Shields goes so far as to call her the "mother of American women writers" (quoted in Christopher Felker, " 'The Tongues of the learned are insufficient': Phillis Wheatley, Publishing Objectives, and Personal Liberty").

14. For a discussion of the form of Wheatley's elegies, see Mukhtar Ali Isani, "Phillis Wheatley and the Elegiac Mode." Frank Shuffelton, in "Phillis Wheatley, the Aesthetic, and the Form of Life," makes the point that her poetic models were probably less likely to be the elegiac odes of Pope than to be those of Milton and Edward Young (81). For a discussion of elegies in the colonial New England tradition, see Matthew P. Brown, " 'BOSTON/SOB NOT': Elegiac Performance in Early New England and Materialist Studies of the Book."

15. This slippage is made evident by revisions to subsequent editions of Wheatley's poetry. In the 1802 edition (printed for Thomas & Thomas by David Newhall, Walpole N.H.), the underwriting letter from her master is called an "advertisement." I thank the Library Company of Philadelphia for help in locating this volume.

16. On the relationships among copyright, authorship, and artistic originality, see Martha Woodmansee, *The Author, Art, and the Market: Rereading the History of Aesthetics*, and Mark Rose, *Authors and Owners: The Invention of Copyright*. See also Grantland S. Rice, *The Transformation of Authorship in America*.

17. For a thoughtful discussion of the evolution of the concept of genius in the eighteenth century and the concurrent evolution of copyright law, see Mark Rose, *Authors and Owners*, 6–8, 114–28. Wheatley obviously presents a problem both for new copyright law and for the concept of genius that it underwrote with a claim of perpetual right.

18. See Vincent Carretta, "Phillis Wheatley, the Mansfield Decision of 1771, and the Choice of Identity."

19. See Teresa Michaels, " 'That Sole and Despotic Dominion': Slaves, Wives, and Games in Blackstone's *Commentaries*."

20. See Mary Poovey, *A History of the Modern Fact: Problems of Knowledge in the Sciences of Wealth and Society*.

21. Boston's commercial environment during Wheatley's lifetime was volatile in many ways. According to David Hancock, in his essay in Conrad Edick Wright and Katheryn P. Veins, eds., *Entrepreneurs: The Boston Business Community, 1700–1850*, Boston was by 1750 the most populous city in the colonies. But by 1775 it was only the third most populous, after Philadelphia and New York. Boston was, it appears, an increasingly bad market for business of all sorts, experiencing "frequent short-term economic dislocations" (83) during the 1750's and 1760's. Hancock also points out Boston's lagging behind the financial endowments of rival cities: "The want of institutional endowments also kept Boston from competing effectively with much younger port towns. Unlike Philadelphia, for instance, Boston possessed no banks and few insurance houses. It enjoyed few regulations or organizations that controlled the conduct of trade. And its currency, fluctuating wildly, moved generally downwards" (83). Thus Wheatley's commercial Boston was one of crisis, an esteemed place in the colonial cultural and political scene, but seemingly rudderless in the way of commercial and financial resources and direction. Consequently, Wheatley wrote in and among people who saw themselves as part of an ever-decreasing business elite. Moreover, Wheatley's Boston was a city with a weak sense of its own financial capital. Underwriting of all sorts—from insurance to public financings—must have seemed an unnervingly precarious office. And yet things began to change in the 1770's for certain classes of wealth. John W. Tyler, in his essay, points to 1771 as an important year in the transformation of the Boston merchant community: "Merchants' assessments increased 346 percent from 1771 to 1790" (Wright and Veins, eds., *Entrepreneurs*, 104). Boston would go on to become America's busiest port city during the war. Accordingly, the merchant community began to expand greatly from 1771 onward. That this happened in spite of the departure of Loyalists to Halifax during March 1776 makes the renovating quality of the new decade almost all the more remarkable.

22. See Michaels, " 'That Sole and Despotic Dominion,' " 202.

23. This fact might offer insights into Susanna Wheatley's and the Countess of Huntingdon's dual patronage of Wheatley. The legal concept of wife, underwritten by common-law notions of property, is one that I do not pursue in this study at the length it might deserve.

24. See Eugene Genovese, *Roll, Jordan, Roll: The World the Slaves Made*.

25. It would seem that Wheatley's signature is, in a sense, more powerful than those of her underwriters. Perhaps because of this, she is the victim of one of the most famous counterunderwritings in American literature. Thomas Jefferson ("Query XIV," in *Notes on the State of Virginia*, 140) derided the possibility of an authentically powerful print artistry. He refers to her as "Phillis Whately" in spite of the authentication of her authorship by his peers. He takes special aim at an idea of imagination that is ruled by the methods of the faculty of understanding rather than by the visceral responsiveness of emotion: "Among blacks is misery enough, God knows, but no poetry. Love is the peculiar oestrum of the poet. Their love is ardent, but it kindles the senses only, not the imagination. Religion, indeed, has produced a Phyllis Whately; but it could not produce a poet. The compositions published under her name are below the dignity of criticism." That last sentence may be read either as a fascinating redundancy or as an even more interesting double distinction. Her name, along with her work, is below the dignity of criticism; or the compositions, taken aside from the fact of her name, her identity, are not worth comment. Either Jefferson is acutely aware that the means of "producing" "Phillis Wheatley" are bound up in the highly charged sphere of race and economics or he merely falls there of his own rhetorical weight. For Jefferson, such passive-aggressive slippages were typical of his own race-tormented fear of exposure before a public sphere dedicated to justice. Her peculiar talent represented the terror of property liberating itself, using the signifiers of proper authenticity to reassign value in accordance with what might be just. In his attempt to put her outside the dignity of criticism, Jefferson underwrote the very trope of textual fundamentalism. For Wheatley, the space beneath what is worthy, emblematized by her passion for proper burials, was worth imaginatively occupying.

26. An interesting perspective on this tangle of issues is offered by Foucault ("What Is an Author?"): "Our culture has metamorphosed this idea of narrative, or writing, as something designed to ward off death. Writing has become linked to sacrifice, even to the sacrifice of life . . . [H]e must assume the role of the dead man in the game of writing"; see Michel Foucault, *The Foucault Reader*.

27. See Frank Shuffelton, "Phillis Wheatley, the Aesthetic, and the Form of Life."

28. I am borrowing this notion of surrender as fundamental to commercial exchange from Georg Simmel, who has become an important reference for many recent economic critics; see Georg Simmel, *The Philosophy of Money*.

29. See Walter Benn Michaels, *The Gold Standard and the Logic of Naturalism: American Literature at the Turn of the Century*.

30. In *The Philosophy of Money*, Simmel explains that money is both a force for liberation and the hollowing out of what freedom has come to mean in the new economic psychology. Perhaps this accounts for some of the paradoxes of Wheatley's reinscribing, from the position of her own enslavement, what it means to own something.

Chapter 3

1. See Hawthorne Daniel, *The Hartford of Hartford: An Insurance Company's Part in a Century and a Half of American History*. One suspects that eighteenth-century New England towns were primed for commercial innovation, given their origins in entrepreneurship; see John Frederick Martin, *Profits in the Wilderness: Entrepreneurship and the Founding of New England Towns in the Seventeenth Century*.

2. On the importance of the British Constitution, and thus the primacy of contracts

in governance and social cohesion in Whig ideology, see Richard M. Rollins, *The Long Journey of Noah Webster*, 27. Rollins draws on Bernard Bailyn, *The Ideological Origins of the American Revolution*.

3. Noah Webster, "Remarks on the Manners, Government, and Debt of the United States," in *A Collection of Essays and Fugitiv Writings on Moral, Historical, Political and Literary Subjects*, 82. Subsequent references will be noted in the text.

4. See David Simpson, *The Politics of American English*, 56–58, for a discussion of Webster's attempt to use language as a means of distinguishing America's attempt to declassify itself socioeconomically. Simpson intriguingly invokes Webster as part of a counter-Derridean move in behalf of written egalitarianism.

5. Richard M. Rollins, ed., *The Autobiographies of Noah Webster: From the Letters and Essays, Memoir, and Diary*, 171–72. Subsequent references will be noted in the text.

6. On the subject of Webster's philosophical affiliations and the idea of order over uncertainty, see V. P. Bynack, "Noah Webster's Linguistic Thought and the Idea of an American National Culture."

7. Unger notes that Webster was pressured by Ezra Stiles to change the name of what had been *The American Instructor* to *A Grammatical Institute* and was never completely satisfied with the change. He never changed the title back, however. See Harlow Giles Unger, *Noah Webster: The Life and Times of an American Patriot*, 56.

8. Noah Webster, *An American Dictionary of the English Language*.

9. For a similar argument about national order and linguistic propriety, see Christopher Looby, "Phonetics and Politics: Franklin's Alphabet as a Political Design." Looby makes the point (7) that Webster and Franklin had a lot in common regarding their mutual belief in national and linguistic order.

10. See John S. Morgan, *Noah Webster*, 53.

11. Noah Webster, *A Compendious Dictionary of the English Language: A Facsimile of the First (1806) Edition*.

12. I am indebted here to Best's discussion of Hannah Arendt's notion of contractual closure and narrativity; see Stephen F. Best, *Fugitive's Properties*, 133–36.

13. For the best account of the relationship between the vocation of law and literary pursuits, see Robert A. Ferguson, *Law and Letters in American Culture*. Webster, a Yale-trained lawyer, gets little attention from Ferguson.

14. Simmel observes that one of the fundamental properties of money is its grammatical usefulness as a networking tool. Simmel quotes Spinoza's observation that money is "the compendium of all things" and conceptualizes it as "the unconditional terminus a quo to everything, as well as the unconditional terminus ad quem from everything"; quoted in Gianfranco Poggi, *Money and the Modern Mind: Georg Simmel's Philosophy of Money*.

15. For a thorough discussion of the role of money in the process of national consolidation, see Robert Garson, "Counting Money: The U.S. Dollar and American Nationhood, 1781–1820."

16. See Unger, *Noah Webster*, 254.

17. His Patriot articles, which came on the heels of the Bank series in the *New England Courant*, went even further in calling for "the establishment of a publicly funded society for promoting arts, sciences, husbandry, and domestic manufactures"; see ibid., 172.

18. Noah Webster, "Letter to the Secretary of the Treasury, on the Commerce and

Currency of the United States," 36. Webster's view anticipated the dominant view of contract that would take hold in the nineteenth century, wherein the final contract document became the repository of all interpretable designs. Lawrence M. Friedman, in *A History of American Law*, 276–77, points out that American contract law seized on the idea of the "document itself" in its exclusion of "parole-evidence" (that is, all conversation and writing occurring prior to the final contract text).

19. Webster's view anticipated the dominant view of contract that would take hold in the nineteenth century, in which the final contract document became the repository of all interpretable designs. Friedman points out that American contract law seized on the idea of the "document itself" in its exclusion of "parole-evidence" (that is, all conversation and writing occurring prior to the final contract text); see Lawrence M. Friedman, *A History of American Law*, 276–77.

20. See Bynack, "Noah Webster's Linguistic Thought and the Idea of an American National Culture," 104–5.

21. Unger makes it clear that Webster was expert in the marketing of his work, understanding the selling of his work to be coextensive with the health and wealth of the country. There is, for instance, the correspondence between Webster and Benjamin Franklin, from whom Webster sought an endorsement. Webster makes plain his belief in the power of authority over what he revealingly terms "our" language, which I take him to mean here as a newly uniform, orthographically logical version of American English shared by him and Franklin: "I [Webster] am happy that a plan of reforming our Alphabet is so well received by a gentleman who thoroughly understands the subject; and am more and more convinced from the present sentiments of the Americans that a judicious attempt to introduce it needs but the support of a few eminent characters to be carried into effect"; quoted in Unger, *Noah Webster*, 114.

22. Farnsworth and Young put it well for the purposes of my discussion: "Contract is the principal mechanism for allocating and distributing financial risks. This is the object of guarantee and insurance contracts, in particular. If agreements could not be defined with some degree of precision, as a skilled drafter can do, the costs of uncertainty would stifle many an enterprise, and the affliction of insecurity would be uncontrolled"; see E. Allan Farnsworth and William F. Young, *Contracts: Cases and Materials*, vii.

23. See Mary Elizabeth Ruwell, *Eighteenth-Century Capitalism: The Formation of American Marine Insurance Companies*; William H. Fowler, "Marine Insurance in Boston: The Early Years of the Boston Marine Insurance Company, 1799–1807."

24. See Emily Ellsworth Ford Skeel, ed., *Notes on the Life of Noah Webster*, 84.

25. Perhaps it is no small coincidence that one of the signal cases in what Presser and Zainaldin call the "rise of the 'classical theory' of contracts" in America was a 1796 case involving a dispute over whether a bill of exchange could be settled in French paper money ("assignats") or specie ("French crowns"). Webster's concern was apparently one that found expression in the case of *Searight* v. *Calbraith* (21 Fed.Cas. 927), which spoke to the establishing of intent and the reconciling of differences of language and money through contracts and legal interpretation; see Stephen B. Presser and Jamil S. Zainaldin, *Law and Jurisprudence in American History*, 272–75.

26. For a fascinating account of Hazard's life and his advocacy of the idea of public records, see Fred Shelley, "Ebenezer Hazard: America's First Historical Editor." According to Marquis James, Hazard had been appointed surveyor of post offices during the

Revolution and later was postmaster general, from 1782 until 1789; see James, *Biography of a Business, 1792–1942: Insurance Company of North America*, 12.

27. It is interesting to note that the case that established the statutory primacy of copyright law, *Wheaton* v. *Peters* (1834), also involved the compilation of state papers in the form of court documents.

28. Noah Webster, *Miscellaneous Papers, on Political and Commercial Subjects*.

29. See Martha Woodmansee, *The Author, Art, and the Market: Rereading the History of Aesthetics*, 42. On this point, see also Mark Rose, "The Author in Court: *Pope v. Curll* (1741)."

30. I borrow this useful dichotomy from the discussion of copyright in Grantland Rice, *The Transformation of Authorship in America*, esp. chap. 4. For an important elaboration of this dichotomy, see Meredith McGill, *American Literature and the Culture of Reprinting*, esp. chap. 1, in which she argues convincingly that American copyright law was more ambivalent than that of the British in according authorial property rights.

31. Leaffer points out the differences between two civil law traditions: that in which the social is preeminent in the impetus behind copyright, and that in which the author has primary entitlement; see Marshall A. Leaffer, *Understanding Copyright Law*.

32. See Howard B. Abrams, Sheldon W. Halperin, and David E. Shipley, eds., *Copyright Cases and Materials*, 1.

33. Quoted in the introduction to Martha Woodmansee and Peter Jaszi, eds., *The Construction of Authorship: Textual Appropriation in Law and Literature*.

34. I am aware that my discussion of Webster primarily in terms of authorial property runs counter to an argument that I find powerful and persuasive: McGill's contention that nineteenth-century copyright emerged from a legal and economic dialectic between an economic culture premised on the sanctity of authorial property and an audience-based, republican culture of reprinting; see Meredith McGill, *American Literature and the Culture of Reprinting*. Webster's case may be emblematic of certain aspects of McGill's thesis, particularly in Webster's belief in the intrinsically public nature of commodified lexicons and grammars that might earn him a profit. But in his war with illicit reprinting he seems to default to a kind of hyperprivatized self-interest that strikes me as deeply author-centered. One wonders to what extent the culture of reprinting and the culture of underwriting were involved in similar dialectics.

35. On the reasons why Webster was particularly motivated to pursue copyright protection, see John S. Morgan, *Noah Webster*, 49: "During Webster's lifetime, the book had many regional printers because slow transportation made it impractical for a single firm to service more than a limited area. This complicated publishing immensely and made extensive pirating relatively easy. . . . A printer or a group of them sometimes underwrote a book, but usually the author in early America had to finance the publication himself. Occasionally, a fortunate author would find a patron or a group of patrons, called subscribers, to finance him. Webster tried all these methods during his career, but he usually ended by financing the publication himself."

36. See Benjamin Kaplan, *An Unhurried View of Copyright*, 27.

37. Mansfield, in *Mill* v. *Race* (1758), wrote that authorial copyright was "equally detached from the manuscript, or any other physical existence whatsoever"; quoted in Mark Rose, *Authors and Owners: The Invention of Copyright*, 129.

38. See Unger, *Noah Webster*, 322.

39. Ibid., 60.

40. On the influence of Rousseau on Webster's thinking about social obligations and the General Will, see Rollins, ed., *The Autobiographies of Noah Webster*, 28.

41. See Harry R. Warfel, ed., *Letters of Noah Webster*, 417.

Chapter 4

1. Michaels points out that 1850 marked the beginning of "one of the peak periods in American land speculation"; see Walter Benn Michaels, "Romance and Real Estate," in Walter Benn Michaels and Donald E. Pease, eds., *The American Renaissance Reconsidered*, 158. Melville's critique of property in "The Lightning-Rod Man" is also an appraisal of such speculation—where speculation is a socializing of the tenuous rhetoric of sales and ownership that, in turn, ceaselessly seeks further underwriting.

2. See Nan Goodman, *Shifting the Blame: Literature, Law, and the Theory of Accidents in Nineteenth-Century America*, 3–8.

3. Melville bought his first property with a loan from his father-in-law, Judge Lemuel Shaw, on September 14, 1850. The acquisition required moving his family from Manhattan to Pittsfield, Massachusetts. Much of the 1850's saw his property being constantly revaluated. See Jay Leyda, *The Melville Log: A Documentary Life of Herman Melville, 1819–1891*, 358–494.

4. See Simon Schaffer, "Natural Philosophy and Public Spectacle in the Eighteenth Century"; see also Heinz Otto Sibum, "The Bookkeeper of Nature: Benjamin Franklin's Electrical Research and the Development of Experimental Natural Philosophy in the Eighteenth Century."

5. Benjamin Franklin is one of the major subtexts underwriting "The Lightning-Rod Man." "The Lightning-Rod Man" and *Israel Potter* were probably composed within the same time period, and both saw publication in *Putnam's Monthly* in the summer of 1854; see Leyda, *The Melville Log*, 490–91. According to Walter E. Bezanson's historical note to the Northwestern University Press/Newberry Library edition of *Israel Potter*, Melville "read widely in Benjamin Franklin's collected writings" (quoted in Merton Sealts, *Melville's Reading*, 91) during the writing of the novel. The connection between Franklin's invention and Melville is discussed in Allen Moore Emery, "Melville on Science: 'The Lightning-Rod Man.'"

6. See Judith Slater, "The Domestic Adventurer in Melville's Tales."

7. That Melville was an assiduous and attentive reader of Schopenhauer, especially *Studies in Pessimissm* and *World as Will and Idea*, should not be too surprising; see Walker Cowen, *Melville's Marginalia*.

8. Several scholars point to Cotton Mather's *Magnalia Christi Americana* as one of the primary sources for the story. See Mary K. Bercaw, *Melville's Sources*; Jay Leyda, introduction to *The Complete Stories of Herman Melville*, quoted in Richard Harter Fogle, *Melville's Shorter Tales*, 56; and Sealts, *Melville's Reading*. Verdier points to Milton's *Paradise Regained* as another source; see Douglas Verdier, "Who Is the Lightning-Rod Man?"

9. Marvin Fisher, "'The Lightning-Rod Man': Melville's Testament of Rejection," analyzes this peculiarly paradoxical brand of optimism.

10. I first came across this suggestive quotation in conjunction with Melville in Michael Paul Rogin, *Subversive Genealogy: The Politics and Art of Herman Melville*, 17.

11. "The Lightning-Rod Man" has generated a fairly vigorous critical conversation; for a summary of the criticism, see Darryl Hattenhauer, "The Confident Man: The Narrator of Melville's 'The Lightning-Rod Man.'" Baldwin attempts to place the story in the discourses of commerce but leaves it vastly undertheorized; see Marc D. Baldwin, "Herman Melville's 'The Lightning-Rod Man': Discourse of the Deal."

12. Melville's other short stories—"Cock-A-Doodle-Doo," "I and My Chimney," "Bartleby the Scrivener"—are almost uniform in their obsession with the possibility for immunity to both deprivation and acquisitiveness. This homogeneity has not been analyzed.

13. Melville had read Pascal as early as the mid-1840's; see Bercaw, *Melville's Sources*.

14. This schematic is eclectically derived. Of course, play has been theorized from a variety of perspectives. From the perspective of psychoanalysis, see, for instance, Sigmund Freud, "Beyond the Pleasure Principle" and "The Artist and Daydreaming," in *Beyond the Pleasure Principle*. From the perspective of cultural anthropology, consider Geertzian "socializing." From the perspective of deconstruction, Derrida writes that "play includes the work of meaning or the meaning of work, and includes them not in terms of knowledge, but in terms of inscription: meaning is a function of play, is inscribed in a certain place in the configuration of meaningless play"; see Jacques Derrida, "From Restricted to General Economy," 260. Each theorization, recirculated through the terms of property and sales, yields an account of meaning that is similarly unstable and language-based. For studies on the cultural and literary significance of play in the American nineteenth century, see Ann Vincent Fabian, *Card Sharps, Dream Books, and Bucket Shops: Gambling in Nineteenth-Century America*; Bill Brown, *The Material Unconscious: American Amusement, Stephen Crane, and the Economies of Play*.

15. See Ian Hacking, *The Emergence of Probability*, 11–18. Hacking's discussion of the dualistic nature of probability—its simultaneous focus on the eventuality of chance and on the "epistemological" assessment of first propositions (chance as against credibility, as Hacking puts it)—is immensely helpful for thinking through this quandary. I want to suggest that Melville is aware of both aspects of chance and safety, and that they command difficult responses on the part of the interested property owner.

16. There is a bit of irony in this situation, since Melville was an inveterate destroyer by fire of his personal papers and letters; see Leyda, *The Melville Log*, xiii–xiv.

17. On the durability of paper and print through time, see Elizabeth L. Eisenstein, *The Printing Press as an Agent of Change: Communications and Cultural Transformations in Early Modern Europe*, 116, where she discusses Jefferson's recommendation to print and disseminate publicly as a way to avoid so-called inevitable accidents.

18. See Hershel Parker, *Herman Melville: A Biography, 1851–1891*, 188.

19. See Sheila Post-Lauria, *Correspondent Colorings: Melville in the Marketplace*, where Post-Lauria makes the salient point that *Putnam's* was more socially and politically critical than *Harper's*. Indeed, she points out that *Harper's* was the venue for most of Melville's short fictional works that are commonly read as "personal allegories" of "going under." But such an understanding once again places "The Lightning-Rod Man" in a tellingly anomalous position in the canon of his short fiction.

20. This situation parallels the fate of paper money in the great debate of the day, premised on the concept of nothing and the worry about loss of value. Texts were lost, but the plates to duplicate them were preserved. Materiality, as a result, has taken on the

cast of the immaterial. For more on this, see Marc Shell, *Money, Language, and Thought: Literary and Philosophical Economies from the Medieval to the Modern Era.*

21. See Herman Melville, *The Piazza Tales and Other Prose Pieces: 1839–1860*, 118. Subsequent references will be noted in the text.

22. The name "Jupiter" has obvious significance: the Roman sky-god who brings lightning and light to the earth. But he is also noted for making the places he inflicts lightning upon *his property*. Moreover, Jupiter was the god concerned with contractual behavior, integrity, and right-dealing. In this light, the irony of the naming is both richer and more telling in its relation to property as a theme.

23. This may be read as a parody of Poe, who himself was parodying the operatic style of sensationalism—and who, of course, was locked onto the comic possibilities of the terrors of gothic housing (*The Fall of the House of Usher*, *The Cask of Amontillado*, *Murders in the Rue Morgue*, and so forth).

24. I take my conceptual lead here from the neo-Kantian historian Huizinga, who makes a powerful case for the interdependence of the rational and the ludic in the imagination of historical narrativity; see Johan Huizinga, *Homo Ludens: A Study of the Play Element in Human Culture.*

25. On the story as it exemplifies scientism and Puritanism, see Thomas Werge, "Melville's Satanic Salesman: Scientism and Puritanism in 'The Lightning-Rod Man.'"

26. See Lorenz Kruger, "The Slow Rise of Probabilism: Philosophical Arguments in the Nineteenth Century." Kruger's analysis provides a historical foundation for thinking about the methods of statistical probabilism as they relate to the epistemology of Kant and LaPlace. In short, he gives us a place to look historically for the explanation of causality as a function of chance and determinism.

27. Quoted in Mitchell Breitwieser, *Cotton Mather and Benjamin Franklin: The Price of Representative Personality*, 210.

28. Brian Rotman, *Signifying Nothing*, follows the deft analysis of this controversy that is offered in Shell, *Money, Language, and Thought.*

29. Interestingly, I am not the first to make the connection between Melville's fiction and the idea of nothingness as a motivating and structuring trope. Melville's fascination with nothingness is cited in the introduction to Shell, *Money, Language, and Thought.* And, as Shell points out, Charles Feidelson led the way in *Symbolism and American Literature*, where Feidelson eloquently discusses Melville's nihilistic fascination— in *Pierre*, among other places in his fiction—with the "empty x."

30. This may also be understood as an instance of Melville's inquiry into the idealization of the relations between natural (Ricardoan) surplus and social (economic) surplus. For a discussion of the relationships among Marx and Derrida, Marxism and deconstruction, and this specific issue, see Michael Ryan, *Marxism and Deconstruction: A Critical Articulation*, 54.

31. On the question of the asymmetry between truth and falsehood, and of how logic is tied to the claims of the accidental and the universal, see the fascinating essay by John Vignaux Smyth, "A Glance at SunSet: Numerical Fundaments in Frege, Wittgenstein, Shakespeare, Beckett."

32. An irony should be recognized. The notes to "The Lightning-Rod Man" in the Northwestern University Press/Newberry Library edition of Melville's *The Piazza Tales*

and Other Prose Pieces observe that it "was the one Melville tale regularly in print and available to the public throughout the remainder of his lifetime" (600).

33. For an excellent assessment of the historical background of "Bartleby the Scrivener," see Barbara Foley, "From Wall Street to Astor Place: Historicizing Melville's 'Bartleby.'"

34. Quirk makes the same claim, adding *Redburn* and Stubb from *Moby-Dick* as precursors; see Tom Quirk, *Melville's Confidence-Man: From Knave to Knight*, 12.

35. Herman Melville, *The Confidence-Man: His Masquerade*.

36. See Lawrence M. Friedman, *A History of American Law*, 440–45.

Chapter 5

1. Ralph Waldo Emerson, *Ralph Waldo Emerson: Essays and Lectures*, 279–80. Subsequent references will be noted in the text.

2. For an excellent discussion of the philosophical genealogies of "Self-Reliance," see George Kateb, *Emerson and Self-Reliance*.

3. On the relationship among accidents, literature, and the development of tort law in the nineteenth century, see Nan Goodman, *Shifting the Blame: Literature, Law, and the Theory of Accidents in Nineteenth-Century America*.

4. My thesis is part of a trend of interpreting Emerson's work as an attempt to accommodate the world rather than transcend it, a trend that goes back to Stephen Whicher, *Freedom and Fate: An Inner Life of Ralph Waldo Emerson* and that finds one of its best recent iterations in David M. Robinson, *Emerson and the Conduct of Life: Pragmatism and Ethical Purpose in the Later Work*. The argument of Michael T. Gilmore, *American Romanticism and the Marketplace*, is emblematic, locating an embrace of the market and commodity in Emerson's later work, such as "Wealth" (1851–52; 1860) and finding the great critiques of capital in the early work, such as "The Transcendentalist" (1841). For a summary and somewhat radical twist on this trend, see Michael Lopez, *Emerson and Power: Creative Antagonism in the Nineteenth Century*. My point in this chapter is not so much to extend the critical trend as to link its evolution with an important and underexamined discourse of capital that was gaining social dominance during Emerson's lifetime.

5. Packer places the crucial moment for Emerson's evaluation of the poetics of business in the spring 1837 stock market crash and its subsequent depression: "But the financial catastrophe did more than arouse prophetic glee at the failure of the sinful world. It revealed to Emerson something essential about the nature of the mind's relation to reality, about its secret hungers, its periodic crises of self-distrust, its immense capacity for symbolization. . . . [H]e gradually came to understand that their [tycoons'] aims were not so far from his own as they might appear to an objective observer; tycoons were poets who chose to write their epics in cash"; see B. L. Packer, *Emerson's Fall*, 96, esp. the chapter titled "Portable Property." Porte holds that while 1837 was undoubtedly pivotal, Emerson remained financially secure throughout its subsequent crisis: "By 1844, when he published his second series of *Essays*, Emerson could serenely announce to a nation just beginning to emerge from hard times that 'money . . . in its effects and laws' is 'as beautiful as roses' [and that] 'Property keeps the accounts of the world, as is always moral.' . . . Such sentiments, admittedly, are very far from representing the best of

Emerson, but they *are* his sentiments and suggest how his own relative financial ease could affect his notions"; see Joel Porte, *Representative Man: Ralph Waldo Emerson in His Time*, 251.

6. I regret that I do not pursue more fully here the implications of such a statement made within the context of the provocative discourses of race and slavery. The discourse of accidents in Emerson, which often works under the guise of fate and change, finds emphatic and bizarre iteration within the discourse of race toward the end of his life, in *The Conduct of Life* (1860). Anita Hay Patterson, *From Emerson to King: Democracy, Race, and the Politics of Protest*, has described Emerson's "dialectical" relationship to owner- ship; her argument is suggestive for an understanding of Emerson's ambivalence in con- fronting community, individualism, and the "power" of property. Jay Grossman, *Recon- stituting the American Renaissance: Emerson, Whitman, and the Politics of Representation*, is also a good source for thinking through the question of slavery in terms of competing poetics of representation.

7. Emerson's polemical view of property stands in stark contrast both to Lockean "natural rights" foundations of property law (misguided as to the effects of good for- tune) and to the mostly utilitarian legal notions of property current in the first half of the nineteenth century (the inorganic notion of things that accrue to the self). For a good source on the history of American property law, see Jesse Dukeminier and James E. Krier, *Property*.

8. A response evident in any number of like-minded writers of the period, especially Henry David Thoreau.

9. For a discussion of the deconstructive concept of natural and unnatural writing as they relate to property, see Michael Ryan, *Marxism and Deconstruction: A Critical Ar- ticulation*, 56–57.

10. Patterson, *From Emerson to King*, 216, makes the same observation.

11. As a trope, the "ground" of property is, as we see further on in this essay, funda- mental to Emerson's idea of loss. Emerson would write shortly after the death of Waldo, on January 30, 1842, that "the landscape was dishonored by this loss"; see Joel Porte, ed., *Emerson in his Journals*, 266.

12. Marx employs the grounding and breathing tropes in his own rather parallel dis- cussion of the self's creation of the objective world in both natural(ist) and alienating modes: "Whenever real, corporeal *man,* man with his feet firmly on the solid ground, man exhaling and inhaling all the forces of nature, establishes his real, objective essen- tial powers as alien objects by his externalization, it is not the act of positing which is the subject in this process: it is the subjectivity of objective essential powers, whose action, therefore, must also be something objective"; see Karl Marx, *Economic and Philosophic Manuscripts of 1844*, 115. Recall as well the famous passage in which Locke prescribes the arrogating power of the human will to make property its own, to increase its natural share: "Though the Earth, and all inferior Creatures common to all Men, yet every Man has a Property in his own Person. This no Body has any Right to but himself. The Labour of his Body, and the Work of his Hands, we may say, are properly his. Whatsover then he removes out of the State that Nature hath provided, and left it in, he hath mixed his Labour with, and joyned to it something that is his own, and thereby makes it his Property"; see John Locke, *Two Treatises of Government*, 305–6.

13. Emerson wrote to Harrison Gray Otis Blake on August 1, 1839, about the clergy's

proper relation to society—whose ideal he refers to as a "selfreliance"—in many of the terms I have been talking about: "Man seems to me the one fact: the forms of the church & of society—the framework which he creates & casts aside day by day. The whole of duty seems to consist in purging off these accidents & obeying the aboriginal truth. I dare not say these things lightly—, I feel the shame of saying them at all.—The simplicity of Duty accuses our distracted & unholy lives. But I wish to say—at least, let our theory not be slavish; let us hope infinitely: & accustom ourselves to the reflection that the true Fall of man is the disesteem of man; the true Redemption self trust; the growth of character is only the enlargement of this . . ."; see Joel Myerson, ed., *The Selected Letters of Ralph Waldo Emerson*, 196. Emerson seems to want to limit the bounds of potential "enlargement" to the growth of character which comes with constant critical attention to the "forms" of social and religious life that threaten to stand in for who we are as in-dependent, non-"accidental," un-Fallen selves.

14. For a relevant discussion of Emerson's relationship to emerging capital and fi-nancial formations, especially the concept of the trust as an expression of the invisible eyeball and the erasable self, see Howard Horwitz, "The Standard Oil Trust as Emerson-ian Hero"; see also Howard Horwitz, *By the Law of Nature: Form and Value in Nine-teenth-Century America*. Horwitz looks especially to subsequent Emersonian articula-tions of the economy of transcendentalism. Citing the agentless self as the source logic of the trust, Horwitz provides an important argument about the business and social im-plications of certain kinds of relationships between property and self.

15. And, for that matter, Thoreauvian; witness the echo of Emerson's antirepresen-tative poetics in the following passage from "Civil Disobedience": "The American has dwindled into an Odd Fellow—one who may be known by the development of his or-gan of gregariousness, and a manifest lack of intellect and cheerful self-reliance; whose first and chief concern, on coming into the world, is to see that the almshouses are in good repair; and, before yet he has lawfully donned the virile garb, to collect a fund to the support of the widows and orphans that may be; who, in short, ventures to live only by the aid of the Mutual Insurance company, which has promised to bury him decently."

16. See Myerson, ed., *The Selected Letters of Ralph Waldo Emerson*, 196. Subsequent citations will be noted in the text.

17. Porte argues that Emerson's notion of compensation, articulated in his first vol-ume of essays, was difficult to maintain in the face of the loss of Waldo. "Experience" is, for Porte, the place where Emerson addresses the idea of the "uncalculated and uncalcu-lable" as it plays out in life; see Porte, ed., *Emerson in His Journals*, 273–75.

18. Patterson notes that Emerson had thought about property in terms of domestic loss when he wrote, in "Nature": "To a man laboring under a calamity, the heat of his own fire hath sadness in it." But it is clear that the nature of this somewhat unemotional assessment is qualitatively different from what he would experience after the death of Waldo, six years later; see Patterson, *From Emerson to King*, 37.

19. William H Gilman and J. E. Parsons, eds., *The Journals and Miscellaneous Note-books of Ralph Waldo Emerson: 1841–1843*, 163. Subsequent citations will be noted in the text.

20. See Gay Wilson Allen, *Waldo Emerson: A Biography*, 396.

21. Emerson put away the journal he had been using at the time of Waldo's death; see Allen, *Waldo Emerson*, 396.

22. Emerson wrote to Margaret Fuller on January 30, 1844, just prior to the publication of "The Poet": "When last Saturday night Lidian said, 'It is two years today— ' I only heard the bellstroke again. I have had no experiences no progress to put me into better intelligence with my calamity than when it was new." And yet Emerson evinces a much less radical negation with respect to writing his loss, and he seems to see the possibility of conceiving an idea of compensation: "   I read lately . . . of Ben Johnson's narrative . . . of the death of his son who died of the plague in London. Ben Johnson was at the time in the country, & saw the Boy in a vision, 'of a manly shape, & of that growth he thinks he shall be at the resurrection.' That same preternatural maturity did my beautiful statue assume the day after death, & so often comes to me to tax the world with frivolity"; see Myerson, ed., *The Selected Letters of Ralph Waldo Emerson*, 298.

23. Here, too, there is no longer talk of the "disease of the will," as in "Self-Reliance"; rather, the will can proceed under the correctly regulated and representative auspices of the poet.

24. See Sharon Cameron, "Representing Grief: Emerson's 'Experience,' " 19. This series of mourning essays and poems written after the death of Waldo has also been discussed, in terms similar to my own, by Jay Grossman, *Reconstituting the American Renaissance: Emerson, Whitman, and the Politics of Representation*.

25. Emerson had written to Margaret Fuller a year previous to the publication of "Experience" (June 7, 1843) in terms and in a tone which would be echoed in the essay: "I love life—never little,—and now, I think, more and more, entertained and puzzled though I be by this lubricity of it, and inaccessibleness of its pith and heart. The variety of our vital game delights me"; see Myerson, ed., *The Selected Letters of Ralph Waldo Emerson*, 221.

26. See Ralph Waldo Emerson, *Collected Poems and Translations*. Subsequent references will be noted in the text.

27. Ralph Waldo Emerson, "Fate," 4. Subsequent references will be noted in the text.

28. Porte, ed., *Emerson in His Journals*, 567.

29. Quoted in Myerson, ed., *The Selected Letters of Ralph Waldo Emerson*, 444.

30. See John McAleer, *Ralph Waldo Emerson: Days of Encounter*, 612.

31. Ibid., chap. 73, "Bush Ablaze."

32. Quoted in ibid., 615.

33. I thank Ramsey Eric Ramsey for suggesting this reading.

34. Ralph Waldo Emerson, "Art," in *Ralph Waldo Emerson: Essays and Lectures*, 440.

35. *The Conduct of Life* is perhaps his crassest expression of this later-life embrace of materialism and capitalist accumulation; see esp. chaps. 1 and 3, "Fate" and "Wealth." I save an analysis of this work for a longer version of the present essay.

36. His brand of liberalism, so well described recently by Christopher Newfield in *The Emerson Effect: Individualism and Submission in America*, can also be read through the problematic of underwriting. Liberalism's attempt to square equality with liberty is thwarted again and again in Emerson, while the terms with which it is contested are precisely the terms he uses to hash out the meaning of underwriting the Self. Newfield, working from Emerson's later essay "Quotation and Originality" (1859), offers an analysis of Emerson's linguistic evolution that is compatible with mine: "Emerson's return from a communism of linguistic agency to a market notion of private possession not

only reflects his actual society but also links his utopian idealism to the individualism that makes it so valuable" (164; see also 34, 180).

37. See Ian Hacking, *The Emergence of Probability: A Philosophical Study of Early Ideas About Probability, Induction, and Statistical Inference*, 11–18,

38. Simmel places the core of money's meaning in its ability to network and make explicit social substitutions (representations) rather than in an intrinsic property or worth of the object so designated: "But only money, by its very essence, gives this development its utmost expression; it is nothing but the pure form of exchangeability, it embodies that aspect or function which makes things economic, and which is not all there is to things, but *is* all there is to money itself"; see Georg Simmel, *The Philosophy of Money*, 130.

Works Cited

Abraham, Kenneth S. *Distributing Risk: Insurance, Legal Theory, and Public Policy*. New Haven, Conn.: Yale University Press, 1986.

Abrams, Howard B., Sheldon W. Halperin, and David E. Shipley, eds. *Copyright Cases and Materials*. St. Paul, Minn.: West, 1992.

Allen, Gay Wilson. *Waldo Emerson: A Biography*. New York: Viking Press, 1981.

Armitage, Joan. *Virilio Live: Selected Interviews*. Thousand Oaks, California: Sage Publications, 2001.

Baida, Peter. *Poor Richard's Legacy: American Business Values from Benjamin Franklin to Donald Trump*. New York: William Morrow, 1990.

Bailyn, Bernard. *The Ideological Origins of the American Revolution*. Cambridge, Mass.: Harvard University Press, 1967.

Baker, Jennifer Jordan. "Franklin's *Autobiography* and the Credibility of Personality." *Early American Literature* 35.3 (2000): 274–93.

Baldwin, Marc D. "Herman Melville's 'The Lightning-Rod Man': Discourse of the Deal." *Journal of the Short Story in English* 21 (1993): 9–18.

Bennett, Paula. "Phillis Wheatley's Vocation and the Paradox of the 'African Muse.'" *PMLA* 113.1 (1998): 64–77.

Bentham, Jeremy. *An Introduction to the Principles of Morals and Legislation*. South Kitchener, Ontario: Batoche Books, 2000.

Bercaw, Mary K. *Melville's Sources*. Evanston, Ill.: Northwestern University Press, 1987.

Bermingham, Ann, and John Brewer, eds. *The Consumption of Culture, 1600–1800: Image, Object, Text*. New York: Routledge, 1995.

Best, Stephen F. *Fugitive's Properties*. Chicago: University of Chicago Press, 2003.

Binder, Guyora, and Robert Weisberg. *Literary Criticisms of Law*. Princeton, N.J.: Princeton University Press, 2000.

Bosco, Ronald A. "'He that best understands the world, least likes it': The Dark Side of Benjamin Franklin." *Pennsylvania Magazine of History and Biography* 111.4 (1987): 525–54.

Bradford, C. Mitchell. *A Premium on Progress: An Outline History of the American Marine Insurance Market, 1820–1970*. New York: Newcomen Society, 1970.

Brands, H. W. *The First American: The Life and Times of Benjamin Franklin*. New York: Doubleday, 2000.

Breen, T. H. *The Marketplace of Revolution: How Consumer Politics Shaped American Independence*. New York: Oxford University Press, 2004.

Breitwieser, Mitchell. *Cotton Mather and Benjamin Franklin: The Price of Representative Personality*. Cambridge, England: Cambridge University Press, 1984.

Brewer, John, and Roy Porter, eds. *Consumption and the World of Goods*. New York: Routledge, 1993.

———, and Susan Staves, eds. *Early Modern Conceptions of Property*. New York: Routledge, 1995.

Brown, Antony. *Hazard Unlimited: The Story of Lloyd's of London*. London: Peter Davies, 1973.

Brown, Bill. *The Material Unconscious: American Amusement, Stephen Crane, and the Economies of Play*. Cambridge, Mass.: Harvard University Press, 1996.

Brown, Matthew P. "'BOSTON/SOB NOT': Elegiac Performance in Early New England and Materialist Studies of the Book." *American Quarterly* 50.2 (1998): 306–39.

Browne, M. Neil, and J. Kevin Quinn. "Dominant Economic Metaphors and the Postmodern Subversion of the Subject." In Martha Woodmansee and Mark Osteen, eds., *The New Economic Criticism: Studies at the Intersection of Literature and Economics*. New York: Routledge, 1999.

Bulau, Alwin E. *Footprints of Assurance*. New York: MacMillan, 1953.

Bynack, V. P. "Noah Webster's Linguistic Thought and the Idea of an American National Culture." *Journal of the History of Ideas* 45.1 (1984): 99–114.

"California Department of Insurance Slavery Era Insurance Registry Report to the California Legislature" (May 2002).

Cameron, Sharon. "Representing Grief: Emerson's 'Experience.'" *Representations* 15 (1986): 15–41.

Carretta, Vincent, ed. *Phillis Wheatley: Complete Writings*. New York: Penguin Books, 2001.

———. "Phillis Wheatley, the Mansfield Decision of 1771, and the Choice of Identity." In Kaus H. Schmidt and Fritz Fleischmann, eds., *Early America Re-Explored: New Readings in Colonial, Early National, and Antebellum Culture*. New York: Peter Lang, 2000.

———. *Unchained Voices: An Anthology of Black Authors in the English-Speaking World of the Eighteenth Century*. Lexington: University of Kentucky, 1996.

Carlson, David Gray, Drucilla Cornell, and Mechel Rosenfeld, eds. *Deconstruction and the Possibility of Justice*. New York: Routledge, 1992.

Clark, Geoffrey. *Betting on Lives: The Culture of Life Insurance in England, 1695–1775*. Manchester, England: Manchester University Press, 1999.

Cockerell, Hugh. *Lloyd's of London: A Portrait*. Homewood, Ill.: Dow Jones–Irwin, 1984.

Cohen, Patricia Cline. *A Calculating People: The Spread of Numeracy in Early America*. Chicago: University of Chicago Press, 1982.

Collins, Terrence. "Phillis Wheatley: The Dark Side of the Poetry." In William H. Robinson, ed., *Critical Essays on Phillis Wheatley*. Boston: G. K. Hall, 1982.

Cowen, Walker. *Melville's Marginalia*. 2 vols. New York: Garland, 1987.

Crane, Verner W., ed. *Benjamin Franklin's Letter to the Press, 1758–1775*. Chapel Hill: University of North Carolina Press, 1950.

Cutting-Gray, Joanne. "Franklin's *Autobiography*: Politics of the Public Self." *Prospects* 14 (1989): 31–43.

Daniel, Hawthorne. *The Hartford of Hartford: An Insurance Company's Part in a Century and a Half of American History*. New York: Random House, 1960.

Davidson, Cathy N. *Revolution and the Word: The Rise of the Novel in America*. New York: Oxford University Press, 1986.

Derrida, Jacques. "Force of Law: The 'Mystical Foundation of Authority.'" In David Gray Carlson, Drucilla Cornell, and Mechel Rosenfeld, eds., *Deconstruction and the Possibility of Justice*. New York: Routledge, 1992.

———. "From Restricted to General Economy." In *Writing and Difference*. Trans. Alan Bass. Chicago: University of Chicago Press, 1978.

———. *The Ear of the Other: Otobiography, Transference, Translation*. Ed. Christie V. McDonald. Trans. Peggy Kamuf. New York: Schocken Books, 1985.

———. *Given Time: Counterfeit Money*. Trans. Peggy Kamuf. Chicago: University of Chicago Press, 1992.

———. *Otobiographies*. Paris: Galilee, 1984.

———. "There Is No *One* Narcissism (Autobiophotographies)." In Elisabeth Weber, ed., *Points: Interviews, 1974–1994*. Stanford, Calif.: Stanford University Press.

Dickson, P. G. M. *The Financial Revolution: A Study of the Development of Public Credit, 1688–1756*. London: Macmillan, 1967.

———. *The Sun Insurance Office, 1710–1960*. London: Oxford University Press, 1960.

Doerflinger, Thomas M. *A Vigorous Spirit of Enterprise: Merchants and Economic Development in Revolutionary Philadelphia*. Chapel Hill: Institute of Early American History and Culture/University of North Carolina Press,1986.

Dukeminier, Jesse, and James E. Krier. *Property*. 3d ed. Boston: Little, Brown, 1993.

Dumont, Louis. *From Mandeville to Marx: The Genesis and Triumph of Economic Ideology*. Chicago: University of Chicago Press, 1977.

Eisenstein, Elizabeth L. *The Printing Press as an Agent of Change: Communications and Cultural Transformations in Early Modern Europe*. Vol. 1. Cambridge, England: Cambridge University Press, 1979.

Emerson, Ralph Waldo. *Collected Poems and Translations*. Ed. Harold Bloom and Paul Kane. New York: Library of America, 1994.

———. "Fate." In *The Conduct of Life*. Boston: Ticknor and Fields, 1860.

———. *Ralph Waldo Emerson: Essays and Lectures*. Ed. Joel Porte. New York: Library of America, 1983.

Emery, Allan Moore. "Melville on Science: 'The Lightning-Rod Man.'" *The New England Quarterly* 56.4 (1983): 555–68.

Erkkila, Betsy. "Phillis Wheatley and the Black American Revolution." In Frank Shuffelton, ed., *A Mixed Race: Ethnicity in Early America*. New York: Oxford University Press, 1993.

Ernst, Joseph Albert. "The Currency Act Repeal Movement: A Study of Imperial Politics and Revolutionary Crisis, 1764–1767." *William and Mary Quarterly* 25.2 (1968): 177–211.

Ewald, François. "Insurance and Risk." In G. Burchell, C. Gordon, and P. Miller, eds., *The Foucault Effect: Studies in Governmentality*. Chicago: University of Chicago Press, 1991.

———. "Genetics, Insurance, and Risk." In François Ewald, Tony McGleenan, and Urban Wiesling, eds., *Genetics and Insurance*. Oxford: Bios, 1999.

———. "The Return of Descartes's Malicious Demon: An Outline of a Philosophy of Precaution." In Tom Baker and Jonathan Simon, eds., *Embracing Risk: The Changing Culture of Insurance and Responsibility*. Chicago: University of Chicago Press, 2003.

Fabian, Ann Vincent. *Card Sharps, Dream Books, and Bucket Shops: Gambling in Nineteenth-Century America*. Ithaca, N.Y.: Cornell University Press, 1990.

Farnsworth, E. Allen, and William F. Young. *Contracts: Cases and Materials*. 5th ed. Westbury, Conn.: The Foundation Press, 1995.

Farrand, Max. *Benjamin Franklin's Memoirs: A Parallel Text Edition*. Berkeley: University of California Press, 1949.

Feidelson, Charles. *Symbolism and American Literature*. Chicago: University of Chicago Press, 1953.

Felker, Christopher. " 'The Tongues of the learned are insufficient': Phillis Wheatley, Publishing Objectives, and Personal Liberty." In Phillip Cohen, ed., *Texts and Textuality: Textual Instability, Theory, and Interpretation*. New York: Garland, 1997.

Ferguson, E. James. "Currency Finance: An Interpretation of Colonial Monetary Practices." *William and Mary Quarterly* 10.2 (1953): 153–80.

Ferguson, Robert A. *Law and Letters in American Culture*. Cambridge, Mass.: Harvard University Press, 1984.

Filreis, Alan. *Wallace Stevens and the Actual World*. Princeton, N.J.: Princeton University Press, 1991.

Fisher, Marvin. " 'The Lightning-Rod Man': Melville's Testament of Rejection." *Studies in Short Fiction* 19.7 (1970): 433–38.

Flanzbaum, Hilene. "Unprecedented Liberties: Re-reading Phillis Wheatley." *MELUS* 18.3 (1993): 71–81.

Fliegelman, Jay. *Declaring Independence: Jefferson, Natural Language, and the Culture of Performance*. Stanford, Calif.: Stanford University Press, 1993.

Flower, Raymond, and Michael Wynn Jones, eds. *Lloyd's of London: An Illustrated History*. London: Lloyd's of London Press Ltd., 1974.

Fogle, Richard Harter. *Melville's Shorter Tales*. Norman: University of Oklahoma Press, 1960.

Foley, Barbara. "From Wall Street to Astor Place: Historicizing Melville's 'Bartleby.' " *American Literature* 72.1 (2000): 87–116.

Ford, Elizabeth Ellsworth Fowler, ed. *Notes on the Life of Noah Webster*. Vol. 2. New York: Burt Franklin, 1971.

Foucault, Michel.. *The Foucault Reader*. Ed. Paul Rabinow. New York: Pantheon, 1984.

———. *"Society Must Be Defended": Lectures at the Collège de France, 1975–76*. Ed. Mauro Bertani and Alessandro Fontana. Trans. David Macey. New York: Picador, 2003.

Fowler, William H. "Marine Insurance in Boston: The Early Years of the Boston Marine Insurance Company, 1799–1807." In Conrad Edick Wright and Katheryn P. Viens, eds., *Entrepreneurs: The Boston Business Community, 1700–1850*. Boston: Massachusetts Historical Society, 1997.

Franklin, Benjamin. *An Address to the Public from the Pennsylvania Society for Promoting the Abolition of Slavery, and the Relief of Free Negroes, Unlawfully Held in Bondage.* Philadelphia: Francis Bailey, 1789.

————. *The Complete Poor Richard's Almanacks: 1733–1758.* 2 vols. Barre, Mass.: Imprint Society, 1970.

————. *The Papers of Benjamin Franklin.* Ed. Leonard W. Labaree. Vol. 4. New Haven: Yale University Press, 1961.

Freud, Sigmund. *Beyond the Pleasure Principle.* Trans. James Strachey. New York: Liveright, 1950.

Friedman, Lawrence M. *A History of American Law.* 2d ed. New York: Simon & Schuster, 1985.

Garson, Robert. "Counting Money: The U.S. Dollar and American Nationhood, 1781–1820." *Journal of American Studies* 35 (2001): 21–46.

Gates, Henry Louis Jr. "Writing, 'Race,' and the Difference it Makes." In Henry Louis Gates Jr., ed., *"Race," Writing, and Difference.* Chicago: University of Chicago Press, 1986.

Geertz, Clifford. *The Interpretation of Cultures: Selected Essays.* New York: Basic Books, 1973.

Genovese, Eugene. *Roll, Jordan, Roll: The World the Slaves Made.* New York: Pantheon, 1974.

Gilman, William H., and J. E. Parsons, eds. *The Journals and Miscellaneous Notebooks of Ralph Waldo Emerson: 1841–1843.* Vol. 8. Cambridge: Belknap Press of Harvard University Press, 1970.

Gilmore, Michael T. *American Romanticism and the Marketplace.* Chicago: University of Chicago Press, 1985.

Golumbia, David. "Hypercapital." *Postmodern Culture* 7.1 (1996). http://muse.jhu.edu/journals/postmodern_culture/v007/7.1golumbia.html

Goodman, Nan. *Shifting the Blame: Literature, Law, and the Theory of Accidents in Nineteenth-Century America.* Princeton, N.J.: Princeton University Press, 1998.

Goux, Jean-Joseph. *The Coiners of Language.* Trans. Jennifer Curtiss Gage. Norman: University of Oklahoma Press, 1994.

Greene, Jack P. "The Currency Act of 1764 in Imperial-Colonial Relations, 1764–1776." *William and Mary Quarterly* 18.4 (1961): 485–518.

Grossman, Jay. *Reconstituting the American Renaissance: Emerson, Whitman, and the Politics of Representation.* Durham, N.C.: Duke University Press, 2003.

Habermas, Jurgen. *The Structural Transformation of the Public Sphere.* Trans. Thomas Burger and Frederick Lawrence. Cambridge, Mass.: M.I.T. Press, 1989.

Hacking, Ian. *The Emergence of Probability: A Philosophical Study of Early Ideas About Probability, Induction, and Statistical Inference.* Cambridge, England: Cambridge University Press, 1975.

Harrington, Joseph. "Wallace Stevens and the Poetics of National Insurance." *American Literature* 67.1 (1995): 95–114.

Hattenhauer, Darryl. "The Confident Man: The Narrator of Melville's 'The Lightning-Rod Man.'" *CLA* 33.2 (1989): 189–202.

Heinzelman, Kurt. *The Economics of the Imagination.* Amherst: University of Massachusetts Press, 1980.

Heise, Ursula K. "Toxins, Drugs, and Global Systems: Risk and Narrative in the Contemporary Novel." *American Literature* 74.4 (2002): 747–78.

Hoppit, Julian. "Political Arithmetic in Eighteenth-Century England." *The Economic History Review* 49.3 (1996): 516–40.

Horwitz, Howard. *By the Law of Nature: Form and Value in Nineteenth-Century America.* New York: Oxford University Press, 1991.

———. "The Standard Oil Trust as Emersonian Hero." *Raritan* 6.4 (1987): 97–119.

Huizinga, Johan. *Homo Ludens: A Study of the Play Element in Human Culture.* Boston: Beacon Press, 1955.

Hume, David. "Of Money." *Political Discourses.* Edinburgh: Printed by R. Fleming for A. Kincaid and A. Donaldson, 1752.

Isani, Mukhtar Ali. "Phillis Wheatley and the Elegiac Mode." In William H. Robinson, ed., *Critical Essays on Phillis Wheatley.* Boston: G. K. Hall, 1982.

James, Marquis. *Biography of a Business, 1792–1942: Insurance Company of North America.* New York: Bobbs-Merrill, 1942.

Jefferson, Thomas. *Notes on the State of Virginia.* Ed. William Peden. New York: Norton, 1972.

Jehlen, Myra. *Readings at the Edge of Literature.* Chicago: University of Chicago Press, 2002.

Jenkins, David, and Takau Yoneyama, eds. *History of Insurance.* 6 vols. London: Pickering and Chatto, 2000.

Jennings, Robert M., Donald F. Swanson, and Andrew P. Trout. "Alexander Hamilton's Tontine Proposal." *William and Mary Quarterly* 45.1 (1988): 107–15.

Jerry II, Robert H. *Understanding Insurance Law.* 2d ed. New York: Matthew Bender, 1996.

Kammen, Michael. *Empire and Interest: The American Colonies and the Politics of Mercantilism.* Philadelphia: J. B. Lippincott, 1970.

Kant, Immanuel. *Critique of Pure Reason.* Trans. Norman Kemp Smith. New York: St. Martin's Press, 1965.

Kaplan, Benjamin. *An Unhurried View of Copyright.* New York: Columbia University Press, 1967.

Kateb, George. *Emerson and Self-Reliance.* Thousand Oaks, Calif.: Sage, 1995.

Kavanagh, Thomas. *Enlightenment and the Shadows of Chance: The Novel and the Culture of Gambling in Eighteenth-Century France.* Baltimore: Johns Hopkins University Press, 1993.

Kendrick, Robert. "Other Questions: Phillis Wheatley and the Ethics of Interpretation." *Cultural Critique* 38 (1997–1998): 39–64.

Kennedy, Jennifer T. "Death Effects: Revisiting the Conceit of Franklin's *Memoir.*" *Early American Literature* 36.2 (2001): 201–34.

Kimball, Spencer L. "The Purpose of Insurance Regulation: A Preliminary Inquiry into the Theory of Insurance Law." *Minnesota Law Review* 45 (1961): 471–524.

Konvits, Milton, and Stephen Whicher, eds. *Emerson: A Collection of Critical Essays.* Englewood Cliffs, N.J.: Prentice Hall, 1962.

Kruger, Lorenz. "The Slow Rise of Probabilism: Philosophical Arguments in the Nineteenth Century." In Lorenz Kruger, Lorraine J. Daston, and Michael Heidelberger, eds., *The Probabilistic Revolution*, vol. 1: *Ideas in History*. Cambridge, Mass.: M.I.T. Press, 1987.

Larson, David M. "Franklin on the Nature of Man and the Possibility of Virtue." *Early American Literature* 10.2 (1975): 111–20.

Leaffer, Marshall A. *Understanding Copyright Law*. New York: Matthew Bender, 1999.

Lemay, J. A. Leo, ed. *Reappraising Benjamin Franklin: A Bicentennial Perspective*. Newark: University of Delaware Press, 1993.

———, and P. M. Zall, eds. *The Autobiography of Benjamin Franklin: A Genetic Text*. Knoxville: University of Tennessee Press, 1981.

Levin, David. "The Autobiography of Benjamin Franklin: The Puritan Experimenter in Life and Art." *Yale Review* 53.2 (1963): 258–75.

Leyda, Jay. *The Melville Log: A Documentary Life of Herman Melville, 1819–1891*. Vol. 1. New York: Harcourt, Brace, 1951.

Locke, John. *Two Treatises of Government*. Ed. Peter Laslett. London: Cambridge University Press, 1967.

Lockridge, Kenneth A. *Literacy in Colonial New England*. New York: Norton, 1974.

Looby, Christopher. "Phonetics and Politics: Franklin's Alphabet as a Political Design." *Eighteenth-Century Studies* 18.1 (1984): 1–34.

———. *Voicing America: Language, Literary Form, and the Origins of the United States*. Chicago: University of Chicago Press, 1996.

Lopez, Michael. *Emerson and Power: Creative Antagonism in the Nineteenth Century*. DeKalb: Northern Illinois University Press, 1996.

Lowery, John, and Phillip Rawlings. *Insurance Law: Principles and Doctrines*. Oxford: Hart Publishing, 1999.

Macey, Samuel L. *Money and the Novel: Mercenary Motivation in Defoe and His Immediate Successors*. Vancouver, British Columbia: Sono Nis Press, 1983.

Macpherson, C. B. "The Meaning of Property." In *Property: Mainstream and Critical Positions*. Toronto: University of Toronto Press, 1978.

———. *The Political Theory of Possessive Individualism: Hobbes to Locke*. New York: Oxford University Press, 1962.

Maier, Pauline. "The Revolutionary Origins of the American Corporation." *William and Mary Quarterly* 50.1 (1993): 51–84.

Mason, Julian. *The Poems of Phillis Wheatley*. Chapel Hill: University of North Carolina Press, 1989.

Mather, Cotton. *Magnalia Christi Americana: Or, The Ecclesiastical History of New England*. New York: Russell and Russell, 1967.

———. *Pascentius: A very brief essay upon the methods of piety, wherein people in whom the difficulties of the times have caused anxieties, May have a comfortable assurance of being at all times comfortably provided for*. Boston: Printed by B. Green, 1714.

Martin, John Frederick. *Profits in the Wilderness: Entrepreneurship and the Founding of New England Towns in the Seventeenth Century*. Chapel Hill: Institute of Early American History and Culture/University of North Carolina Press, 1991.

Marx, Karl. *Economic and Philosophic Manuscripts of 1844*. Ed. Dirk J. Struik. Trans. Martin Milligan. New York: International Publishers, 1964.

———. *Grundrisse: Foundations of the Critique of Political Economy*. Trans. Martin Nicolaus. New York: Vintage Books, 1973.

McAleer, John. *Ralph Waldo Emerson: Days of Encounter*. Boston: Little Brown, 1984.

McCusker, John J., and Russell R. Menard. *The Economy of British America, 1607–1789*. Chapel Hill: University of North Carolina Press, 1985.

McDowell, Banks. *The Crisis in Insurance Regulation*. Westport, Conn.: Quorum Books, 1994.

McGill, Meredith. *American Literature and the Culture of Reprinting*. Philadelphia: University of Pennsylvania Press, 2003.

Melville, Herman. *The Confidence-Man: His Masquerade*. New York: Oxford University Press, 1989.

———. *The Piazza Tales and Other Prose Pieces: 1839–1860*. Ed. Harrison Hayford, Alma A. MacDougall, and G. Thomas Tanselle. Evanston, Ill.: Northwestern University Press/Newberry Library, 1987.

Michaels, Teresa. " 'That Sole and Despotic Dominion': Slaves, Wives, and Games in Blackstone's *Commentaries.*" *Eighteenth-Century Studies* 27.2 (1993–1994): 195–216.

Michaels, Walter Benn. *The Gold Standard and the Logic of Naturalism: American Literature at the Turn of the Century*. Berkeley: University of California Press, 1987.

———, and Donald Pease, eds. *The American Renaissance Reconsidered*. Baltimore: Johns Hopkins University Press, 1985.

Morgan, John S. *Noah Webster*. New York: Mason/Charter, 1975.

Myers, Margaret G. *The New York Money Market*. Vol. 1. New York: Columbia University Press, 1931.

Myerson, Joel, ed. *The Selected Letters of Ralph Waldo Emerson*. New York: Columbia University Press, 1997.

"Destructive Fire, The Establishment of Harper & Brothers in Ruins." *The New York Daily Times*, Dec. 12, 1853.

Newfield, Christopher. *The Emerson Effect: Individualism and Submission in America*. Chicago: University of Chicago Press, 1996.

Nicholson, Colin. *Writing and the Rise of Finance: Capital Satires of the Early Eighteenth Century*. Cambridge, England: Cambridge University Press, 1994.

Nott, Walt. "From 'Uncultivated Barbarian' to 'Poetical Genius': The Public Presence of Phillis Wheatley." *MELUS* 18.3 (1993): 21–32.

Olson, Alison Gilbert. *Making the Empire Work: London and American Interest Groups, 1690–1790*. Cambridge, Mass.: Harvard University Press, 1992.

Packer, B. L. *Emerson's Fall*. New York: Continuum, 1982.

Parker, Hershel. *Herman Melville: A Biography, 1851–1891*. 2 vols. Baltimore: Johns Hopkins University Press, 2002.

Patterson, Anita Hay. *From Emerson to King: Democracy, Race, and the Politics of Protest*. New York: Oxford University Press, 1997.

Patterson, Edwin W. *Essentials of Insurance Law: An Outline of Legal Doctrines in Their Relations to Insurance Practices*. New York: McGraw-Hill, 1957.

Perkins, Edwin J. *American Public Finance and Financial Services, 1700–1815*. Columbus: Ohio State University Press, 1994.

Perrow, Charles. *Normal Accidents: Living with High-Risk Technologies*. New York: Basic Books, 1984.

Philadelphia Contributionship for the Insurance of Houses from Loss by Fire. *The Deed of Settlement of the Society for Insuring of Houses, In and Near Philadelphia*. Philadelphia: Printed by Benjamin Franklin and David Hall, 1751.

Pieschel, Bridget Smith. "Franklin: The Young Man's Guide to Success." *Mount Olive Review* 3 (1989): 33–44.

Pocock, J. G. A. *Virtue, Commerce, History: Essays on Political Thought and History, Chiefly in the Eighteenth Century*. New York: Cambridge University Press, 1985.

Poggi, Gianfranco. *Money and the Modern Mind: George Simmel's Philosophy of Money*. Berkeley: University of California Press, 1993.

Poovey, Mary. *A History of the Modern Fact: Problems of Knowledge in the Sciences of Wealth and Society*. Chicago: University of Chicago Press, 1998.

Porte, Joel, ed. *Emerson in His Journals*. Cambridge, Mass.: Belknap Press of Harvard University Press, 1982.

———. *Representative Man: Ralph Waldo Emerson in His Time*. New York: Oxford University Press, 1979.

Post-Lauria, Sheila. *Correspondent Colorings: Melville in the Marketplace*. Amherst: University of Massachusetts Press, 1996.

Presser, Stephen B., and Jamil S. Zainaldin. *Law and Jurisprudence in American History: Cases and Materials*. 3d ed. St. Paul, Minn.: West, 1995.

Prudential Insurance Company of America. *The Documentary History of Insurance: 1000 B.C.–1875 A.D.* Newark, N.J.: Prudential Press, 1915.

Purdy, Anthony, ed. *Literature and Money*. Atlanta: Rodopi, 1993.

Quirk, Tom. *Melville's Confidence-Man: From Knave to Knight*. Columbia: University of Missouri Press, 1982.

Rice, Grantland S. *The Transformation of Authorship in America*. Chicago: University of Chicago Press, 1997.

Robinson, David M. *Emerson and the Conduct of Life: Pragmatism and Ethical Purpose in the Later Work*. Cambridge, England: Cambridge University Press, 1993.

Robinson, William H., ed. *Critical Essays on Phillis Wheatley*. Boston: G. K. Hall, 1982.

Rogin, Michael Paul. *Subversive Genealogy: The Politics and Art of Herman Melville*. New York: Knopf, 1983.

Rollins, Richard M., ed. *The Autobiographies of Noah Webster: From the Letters and Essays, Memoir, and Diary*. Columbia: University of South Carolina Press, 1989.

———. *The Long Journey of Noah Webster*. Philadelphia: University of Pennsylvania Press, 1980.

Rose, Mark. "The Author in Court: *Pope* v. *Curll* (1741)." In Martha Woodmansee and Peter Jaszi, eds., *The Construction of Authorship: Textual Appropriation in Law and Literature*. Durham, N.C.: Duke University Press, 1994.

———. *Authors and Owners: The Invention of Copyright*. Cambridge, Mass.: Harvard University Press, 1993.

Rotman, Brian. *Signifying Nothing: The Semiotics of Zero*. London: Macmillan, 1987.

Ruwell, Mary Elizabeth. *Eighteenth-Century Capitalism: The Formation of American Marine Insurance Companies*. New York: Garland, 1993.

Ryan, Alan. *Property*. Berkshire, England: Open University Press, 1987.

Ryan, Michael. *Marxism and Deconstruction: A Critical Articulation*. Baltimore: Johns Hopkins University Press, 1982.

Schaffer, Simon. "Natural Philosophy and Public Spectacle in the Eighteenth Century." *History of Science* 21 (1983): 5.

Schopenhauer, Arthur. *Studies In Pessimism: A Series of Essays.* 9th ed. Trans. Thomas Bailey Saunders. London: G. Allen, 1913.

———. *The World as Will and Idea.* Vol. 2. New York: Scribner's, 1948.

Schuessler, Jennifer. "Hello, Dolly!" *The New York Review of Books.* 50.2 (2003): 29–31.

Schultz, Ellen E. "Companies Sue Union Retirees to Cut Promised Health Benefits." *The Wall Street Journal,* Nov. 10, 2004.

Sealts, Merton. *Melville's Reading.* Columbia: University of South Carolina Press, 1988.

Shammas, Carole. "The Space Problem in Early United States Cities." *William and Mary Quarterly* 57.3 (2000): 505–42.

Shell, Marc. *Art and Money.* Chicago: University of Chicago Press, 1995.

———. *The Economy of Literature.* Baltimore: Johns Hopkins University Press, 1978.

———. *Money, Language, and Thought: Literary and Philosophical Economies from the Medieval to the Modern Era.* Berkeley: University of California Press, 1982.

Shelley, Fred. "Ebenezer Hazard: America's First Historical Editor." *William and Mary Quarterly* 12.1 (1955): 44-73.

Shields, David. *Civil Tongues and Polite Letters in British America.* Chapel Hill: University of North Carolina Press, 1997.

Shuffelton, Frank. "Phillis Wheatley, the Aesthetic, and the Form of Life." In Syndy M. Conger and Julie C. Hayes, eds., *Studies in Eighteenth-Century Culture.* Vol. 26. Baltimore: Johns Hopkins University Press, 1995.

Sibum, Heinz Otto. "The Bookkeeper of Nature: Benjamin Franklin's Electrical Research and the Development of Experimental Natural Philosophy in the Eighteenth Century." In J. A. Leo Lemay, ed., *Reappraising Benjamin Franklin: A Bicentennial Perspective.* Newark: University of Delaware Press, 1993.

Simmel, Georg. *The Philosophy of Money.* Trans. Tom Bottomore and David Frisby. London: Routledge, 1999.

Simpson, David. *The Politics of American English, 1776–1850.* New York: Oxford University Press, 1986.

Slater, Judith. "The Domestic Adventurer in Melville's Tales." *American Literature* 37 (1965): 267–79.

Smith, Adam. *The Theory of Moral Sentiments.* London: Printed for A. Millar; and A. Kincaid and J. Bell, in Edinburgh, 1761.

———. *The Wealth of Nations.* New York: Modern Library, 1937.

Smith, Gregory G., ed. *The Spectator,* vol. 1. New York: Dutton, 1921.

Smyth, John Vignaux. "A Glance at SunSet: Numerical Fundaments in Frege, Wittgenstein, Shakespeare, Beckett." In Barbara Herrnstein Smith and Arkady Plotnitsky, eds., *Mathematics, Science, and Postclassical Theory.* Durham, N.C.: Duke University Press, 1997.

Stevenson, Sarah York. "Insurance and Business Adventure in the Days of Shakespeare and in Those of William Penn." *The Proceedings of the Numismatic and Antiquarian Society of Philadelphia.* Philadelphia: Library Company of Philadelphia, 1913.

Straus, Ralph. *Lloyd's: A Historical Sketch.* London: Hutchinson and Company, 1937.

Supple, Barry. "Insurance in British History." In Oliver M. Westall, ed., *The Historian and the Business of Insurance.* Manchester, England: Manchester University Press, 1984.

Thompson, James. *Models of Value: Eighteenth-Century Political Economy and the Novel.* Durham, N.C.: Duke University Press, 1996.

Thornton, Tamara Plakins. *Handwriting in America: A Cultural History.* New Haven, Conn.: Yale University Press, 1996.

Trachtenberg, Alan. *The Incorporation of America: Culture and Society in the Gilded Age.* New York: Hill and Wang, 1982.

Unger, Harlow Giles. *Noah Webster: The Life and Times of an American Patriot.* New York: Wiley, 1998.

Van D'Elden, Karl H. "The Development of the Insurance Concept and Insurance Law in the Middle Ages." In Harold J. Johnson, ed., *The Medieval Tradition of Natural Law.* Kalamazoo: Medieval Institute Publications, Western Michigan University, 1987.

Verdier, Douglas. "Who Is the Lightning-Rod Man?" *Studies in Short Fiction* 18:3 (1981): 273–79.

Vernon, John. *Money and Fiction: Literary Realism in the Nineteenth and Early Twentieth Centuries.* Ithaca, N.Y.: Cornell University Press, 1984.

Warfel, Harry R., ed. *Letters of Noah Webster.* New York: Library Publishers, 1953.

Warner, Michael. *The Letters of the Republic: Publication and the Public Sphere in Eighteenth-Century America.* Cambridge, Mass.: Harvard University Press, 1990.

Watson, Marsha. "A Classic Case: Phillis Wheatley and Her Poetry." *Early American Literature* 31.2 (1996): 103–32.

Webster, Noah. *An American Dictionary of the English Language.* New York: S. Converse, 1828.

———. *A Collection of Essays and Fugitiv Writings on Moral, Historical, Political and Literary Subjects.* Boston, 1790 (no publisher listed).

———. *A Collection of Papers on Political, Literary, and Moral Subjects.* New York: Burt Franklin, 1968.

———. *A Compendious Dictionary of the English Language: A Facsimile of the First (1806) Edition.* New York: Crown Publishers, 1970.

———. "Letter to the Secretary of the Treasury, on the Commerce and Currency of the United States." *Early American Imprints*, no. 49978. New York: C. S. Van Winkle, 1819.

———. *Miscellaneous Papers, on Political and Commercial Subjects.* New York: Burt Franklin, Research and Source Works Series, #145.

Weiner, Tim. "Feeling Secure Is a Risky Business." *New York Times*, Sept. 6, 1998.

Werge, Thomas. "Melville's Satanic Salesman: Scientism and Puritanism in 'The Lightning-Rod Man.'" *Christianity and Literature* 21.4 (1972): 6–12.

Westall, Oliver M., ed. *The Historian and the Business of Insurance.* Manchester, England: Manchester University Press, 1984.

Wheatley, Phillis. *The Collected Works of Phillis Wheatley.* Ed. John Shields. New York: Oxford University Press, 1988.

Whicher, Stephen. *Freedom and Fate: An Inner Life of Ralph Waldo Emerson.* Philadelphia: University of Pennsylvania Press, 1953.

Wilcox, Kirstin. "The Body into Print: Marketing Phillis Wheatley." *American Literature* 71.1 (1999): 1–29.

Wood, Gordon S. *The Radicalism of the American Revolution.* New York: Knopf, 1992.

Woodmansee, Martha. *The Author, Art, and the Market: Rereading the History of Aesthetics.* New York: Columbia University Press, 1994.

————, and Peter Jaszi, eds. *The Construction of Authorship: Textual Appropriation in Law and Literature.* Durham, N.C.: Duke University Press, 1994.

————, and Mark Osteen, eds. *The New Economic Criticism: Studies at the Intersection of Literature and Economics.* New York: Routledge, 1999.

Wright, Conrad Edick, and Katheryn P. Veins, eds. *Entrepreneurs: The Boston Business Community, 1700–1850.* Boston: Massachusetts Historical Society, 1997.

Zelizer, Viviana A. Rotman. *Morals and Markets: The Development of Life Insurance in the United States.* New York: Columbia University Press, 1979.

Ziff, Larzer. *Writing in the New Nation: Prose, Print, and Politics in the Early United States.* New Haven, Conn.: Yale University Press, 1991.

Zuckerman, Michael. "Doing Good While Doing Well: Benevolence and Self-Interest in Franklin's *Autobiography*." In J. A. Leo Lemay, ed., *Reappraising Benjamin Franklin: A Bicentennial Perspective.* Newark: University of Delaware Press, 1993.

Index

In this index an "f" after a number indicates a separate reference on the next page, and an "ff" indicates separate references on the next two pages. A continuous discussion over two or more pages is indicated by a span of page numbers, e.g., "57–59." *Passim* is used for a cluster of references in close but not consecutive sequence.

abolitionism (abolition movement), xvi, 31
accidental loss: Emerson on, 120, 124, 128–29
accidents, 32, 101ff, 107, 116–22 *passim*; Emerson on, 115, 123, 133, 136–37, 166n6; Franklin on, 36, 44, 60; Melville on, 98–99
accounting, 6, 10, 28–29, 39, 64, 86, 101
agency (human), 43, 49, 61, 149n31, 151–52n20, 153n24
American English: creation of, 82–84; ownership of, 83
American Revolution, the, 94, 144n18, 153n28, 160n26
anxiety, xiv, xvi, 46, 56, 58; Franklin and, 35; Franklin on, 55; Mather on, 41
authenticity, 9–12 *passim*, 17, 23, 55, 68f, 158n25; of signatures, 16; of Wheatley, xvi, 70–78 *passim*
authorship, xv, xvii, 24, 71, 92, 151n20

Beekman family, 4
Bentham, Jeremy, 16, 27
biopolitics, 9

bookkeeping, 12, 29, 64, 90; double-entry, 28–29, 64, 74; and rhetoric, 28ff
Breitwieser, Mitchell, 59–60, 109, 151n13, 155nn47, 49, 164n27

Cameron, Sharon, 129, 168n24
capitalism, xiv, xviii, 24f, 32, 43, 99, 101, 108
chance, 36, 38, 49f, 101–2, 119, 142n9, 163n15, 164n26; elimination of, 49; Emerson on, 121–22, 128–37 *passim*; Franklin and, 36ff, 61; Franklin on, 43–47, 57–58; in the modern era, 31–32; of loss, 26; Melville on, 101f, 106, 111; Wheatley and, 78
Civil War, 31, 147n48
Clark, Geoffrey, 29, 49f, 151n14, 154n44
coffeehouses, 4, 9, 142n1
comedy, in Melville's works, 100–2, 110–11
Constitution, the, 95, 145n30, 146n42
contract law, 15f, 93, 155–56n4, 159–60n18, 160n19
Copson, John, 1–3, 6
copyright (law), xvii, 92–94, 96, 157n17, 161n30; Webster's views on 93–94

corporations, 10, 153n28
creole English, 82

Dartmouth, Earl of, 69
debt, 8, 80, 84–90 passim, 96, 144n18
deconstruction, 14, 16, 23, 119, 123, 163n14
Derrida, Jacques, 14f, 29, 147n48, 163n14
dictionary: Webster's creation of, 83, 88, 93; underwriting force of, 119
Dogood, Silence (pseudonym for Benjamin Franklin), 38–44 passim, 67

education, 28, 51f, 81, 83, 91, 96, 154n44
electricity, 59
elegy, as a genre, 66, 70, 129, 133
Emerson, Ralph Waldo: on accidents, 115, 123, 133, 136–37, 166n6; death of son Waldo, 124–27, 129, 130–131, 167n18; "Experience," 120, 129, 168nn24, 25; "Fate," 120, 133; on chance, 121–22, 128–37 passim; on loss, 128–29; and pessimism, 128; "The Poet," 128, 168n22; "Poetry," 120; "Politics," 123; on risk, 130; and selfhood, 120; "Self-Reliance," 107, 115, 119–30 passim, 136, 168n23; "Threnody," 120, 130
Emerson, Waldo (son of Ralph Waldo), 124–31 passim, 167n18
Enlightenment, xii, 37, 61, 119
Erkkila, Betsy, 63
Ewald, Francois, 17, 32, 49, 147n47, 149n68, 153n31
exposure, 9, 30, 32, 40, 68, 122f, 135, 158n25; to loss, 90; to risk, 71, 80

Harper & Brothers fire, 102

firemarks, 54–55
Fliegelman, Jay, 61, 155n48
Foucault, Michel, 9–10, 13, 145n29, 158n26
Fowler, William H., 4f, 88, 143, 145n30, 160n23
Franklin, Benjamin, 99; on accidents, 36, 44, 60; and anxiety, 35, 55; The Autobiography, 35–37, 48, 55, 114; and chance, 36ff, 43–47, 57–58, 61; "A

Dissertation on Liberty and Necessity," 44–46; fundraising by, 51, 56; and lightning, 109; and money, 37–38; "The Morals of Chess," 46–49; optimism of, xvi, 36f, 44, 46, 60, 100, 149n1; pessimism of, 44–48 passim, 149n1; Poor Richard's Almanack, 56–59; reaction to son's death, 48; and rhetoric, 48, 52; on risk, 150n7; on safety, 49–57 passim; and selfhood, 59; worldview, 149n1
Friendly Society, The, 5, 40, 42
fundraising, by Franklin, 51, 56

gambling, 6, 49, 57, 149n9, 153nn28, 33
Gates, Henry Louis Jr., 68f
Grace: Calvinist conception of, 40; Wheatley on, 64–65

Hacking, Ian, 101, 147n58, 153n33, 163n15, 169n37
Hamilton, Alexander, 5, 89
handwriting, 11–12
Hartford Accident and Indemnity Company, xii
Hazard, Ebenezer, 52, 91f, 160n26
homeowner, 106–14 passim
Human Genome Project, 32
humanism, xviii, 62, 74; and Melville, xvii, 111
Hume, David, 86, 101
Huntingdon, Countess of, 69, 157n23

individualism, xviii, 22, 36, 38, 119f, 129, 136f, 166n6
insurance, xviii; disability, 80; fire, xv, 4–5; life, 6, 31, 91; marine, 3f, 30, 49, 91, 142n2; similarity to lotteries, 49–50; Stevens on insurance, 11; widow, xv, 49, 167n15
insurance contract, 8, 14–17, 23, 29f, 73, 88, 97, 115, 160n22
insurance law, xiii, 14, 115
insurance office, 1, 115, 119–24 passim, 129f
insurance underwriting, xii–xvi, 2–10 passim, 14–17 passim, 23–32 passim,